D0791657

I've known rivers:
I've known rivers ancient as the world and older than the
  flow of blood in human veins.

My soul has grown deep like the rivers.

I bathed in the Euphrates when dawns were young.
I built my hut near the Congo and it lulled me to sleep.
I looked upon the Nile and raised pyramids above it.
I heard the singing of the Mississippi when Abe Lincoln
  went down to New Orleans, and I've seen its muddy
  bosom turn all golden in the sunset.

I've known rivers;
Ancient, dusky rivers.

My soul has grown deep like the rivers.

                    Langston Hughes

Deep
Like the Rivers

Education in the Slave

Quarter Community

⊰❙ 1831–1865 ❙⊱

—

THOMAS L. WEBBER

W · W · NORTON & COMPANY · INC ·

NEW YORK

To
my brother Jerome A. Pollard
and all my slave informants and their descendants
for helping to educate me

Langston Hughes, "The Negro Speaks of Rivers" (To W. E. B. DuBois), from
The Dream Keeper And Other Poems. Copyright 1926, 1932, by Alfred A. Knopf,
Inc. Reprinted with the permission of the publisher.

Library of Congress Cataloging in Publication Data

Webber, Thomas L.
  Deep like the rivers.

  Includes bibliographical references and index.
  1. Slavery in the United States—Southern
States—Condition of slaves. 2. Plantation
life—Southern States—History. I. Title.
E443.W4   1978   301.44′93′0975   78-3410

ISBN 0 393 05685 6
1 2 3 4 5 6 7 8 9 0

Contents

Contents

Preface

"My feelings," wrote James Pennington, a fugitive slave from Maryland in 1850, "are always outraged when I hear them speak of 'kind masters,'—'Christian masters,'—the mildest form of slavery,'—'well fed and clothed slaves,' as extenuations of slavery; I am satisfied they either mean to pervert the truth, or they do not know what they say. The being of slavery, its soul and body, lives and moves in the chattel principle; the cart-whip, starvation, and nakedness, are its inevitable consequences to a greater or less extent, warring with the dispositions of men."[1] Other slaves and ex-slaves had equal difficulty laying to rest their memories of slavery. At the age of ninety-nine Ben Brown, born on a large Virginia plantation in 1837, told his interviewer: "Some nights I dream about de ole slave times an' I hear dem cryin' an' prayin': 'Oh, mastah, pray! Oh, mastah mercy! when dey are being whipped, an' I wake up cryin'. I set here in dis room and can remember mos' all of de ole life, can see it as plain as day, de hard work, de plantation, de whippings, an' de misery."[2] At the time of the Civil War ex-slaves made clear their feelings about slavery in a song:

1. No more peck o' corn for me,
   No more, no more;
   No more peck o' corn for me,
   Many tousand go.

2. No more driver's lash for me.
3. No more pint o' salt for me.
4. No more hundred lash for me.
5. No more mistress' call for me.[3]

For Stephen McCray, who grew up on an Alabama plantation of over three hundred slaves, a story about a raccoon and a dog best illustrated how he felt about being a slave. "The coon said to the dog, 'Why is it you're so fat and I am so poor, and we is both animals?' The dog said: 'I lay around Master's house and let him kick me and he gives me a piece of bread right on.' Said the coon to the dog: 'Better then that I stay poor.' Them's my sentiment. I don't believe in 'buse."[4] Harriet Robinson, an ex-slave from Texas, put similar sentiments more simply: "Them was slavery days, dog days."[5]

This book is about those days, slavery days. More importantly, it is about James Pennington, Ben Brown, Stephen McCray, Harriet Robinson, and their fellow slaves. For in writing, speaking, and singing about their slave experience the creators of the slave writings and oral literature have left, in addition to their impressions of slavery as an institution, a wealth of clues about what slaves understood and felt about their world and how they acquired these understandings and feelings.* The piecing together of these clues, as well as those found in the white sources, reveals a striking picture of what slaves actually learned as opposed to what was intended by the training of their masters. The sources also reveal the mechanisms by which the members of the quarter community were able to sustain and transmit to their children their values and understandings despite a slave system which deliberately limited their self-expression and outlawed any formalized, slave-controlled, educational practices.†

Because of the critical difference between what whites taught and what slaves learned, the study uses a definition of education

---

* For a fuller description of the sources used, see the Appendix. All quotations contained herein are transcribed exactly as contained in the original. This includes the retention of errors in spelling and grammar as well as the often inadequate attempts of interviewers to reproduce black dialect on paper.

† The term "quarters" is used to refer to that geographical location on the ante-bellum plantation known variously as "the slave quarter," the "Negro settlement," "niggertown," "slave row," which contained the living quarters of the fieldhands and their families. The slave quarter community is defined as those slaves throughout the South who related to a slave quarter as the center of their social activities and relationships, who shared a common set of values and attitudes, were organized in a familiar social structure, and displayed an awareness of their uniqueness and separate identity as a group. In general, the forming of a quarter community necessitated a plantation population of between fifteen and twenty slaves. Assuming, conservatively, that quarter communities were es-

Preface

which clearly distinguishes between the effort to transmit learning and the process by which learning actually occurs. Education
is defined as the knowledge, attitudes, values, skills and sensibilities which an individual, or a group, consciously or uncon-
sciously, has internalized. It is the content of what is learned.
Teaching in this context becomes the deliberate effort, successful or not, to educate.[6]

This book is organized around three questions. First, what was
it that whites wanted their slaves to learn and what teaching
methods did they employ? Second, what did slaves actually
learn? Third, where and from whom did slaves learn what they
learned? Part I attempts to set the broader stage, to portray the
larger plantation environment within which the education of the
quarter community occurred. It describes primarily the ways in
which white plantation owners attempted to control what it was
that slaves thought and felt. Chapter 2 deals with the goals and
methods of white secular training; Chapter 3 with white religious training.

Part II focuses on what slaves of the quarter community
learned. Though differing greatly in personality and motiva-
tion, a large number of quarter slaves internalized a set of
similar, though not identical, broad themes which gave shape
and meaning to the way they understood their world and acted
in it. This section applies the cultural theme methodology of
Morris Opler to the black slave sources and organizes the education of slaves into nine basic themes: Communality, Antipathy
Towards Whites, True Christianity, Black Superiority, White
Power, Family, Spirit World, Learning To Read and Write, Freedom.

How, where, and from whom slaves learned the values and
understandings embodied in their community's themes is the
core of Part III. Specifically, this section analyzes the organiza-

tablished on most plantations with twenty or more slaves, and using the generally
accepted estimate that fifty percent of the entire slave population lived on such
plantations, then approximately forty to fifty percent of all slaves were members
of the quarter community at any time. (This takes into account the problematic
membership in the quarter community of those slaves on the larger plantations
who were artisans, semiskilled workers, and house servants.)

Preface

tion and educational significance of the family, peer group, clan-destine congregation, songs and stories, and quarter community as a whole. Socialization/enculturation theory is used to argue that the people of the quarter community are best understood as a society within a society, rather than as a group of individuals within a closed, totally controlled institution such as a prison or a concentration camp. The final chapter compares the slave quarter with the American Indian Reservation. The Navaho data complied by Clyde Kluckhohn and Dorthea Leighton and the research done on the Mandan-Hidatsa by Edward Bruner support and deepen the book's conclusions about the nature of education in the slave quarter community.

The educational questions and perspectives, anthropological methodology, and Indian Reservation comparison represent a unique approach to the study of slavery. Such an approach goes beyond those historiographical models which stress the ability of whites to mold and control slave values and behavior to reveal the success of slaves in actively creating, controlling, and perpet-uating their own education. Blacks under slavery were not the bearers of an inferior culture slowly enlightened and civilized by a superior culture (Ulrich Philips). Nor were slaves torn from their African culture and placed in a slave system where their only choice was to mimic white culture (Stanley Elkins) or to slowly assimilate into white culture following the lead of favored house servants and slave artisans (E. Franklin Frazier, Robert Fogel, and Stanley Engerman). Slaves did not live in a state of cultural chaos "in a twilight zone between two ways of life . . . unable to obtain from either many of the attributes which dis-tinguish man from beast" (Kenneth Stampp). The relationship between plantation blacks and whites was not so completely and reciprocally paternalistic that slaves were unable to "express the simplest human feelings without reference" to their masters (Eugene Genovese).[7]

By the time of the Civil War black persons in America had ac-tively fashioned a new culture from both the culture fountain of their African past and the crucible of their experiences under slavery in the South. Slave culture had at its heart a set of cul-tural themes, forms of artistic expression, a religion, a family pattern, and a community structure which set blacks apart from whites and enabled them to form and control a world of their own values and definitions. The architects of this culture were the fieldhand masses and their house and town allies. It was these black men and women from whose common experiences sprang the songs and stories of American slavery, who nurtured the rites and beliefs of their community and religious life, and who instilled in their children and other slaves the cultural themes of their community.

This book tells the story of that educational process. It does so, whenever possible, in the words of those black men and women who experienced slavery, following the wisdom of the ex-slave from Tennessee who advised: "If you want Negro history you will have to get it from somebody who wore the shoe, and by and by from one to the other you will get a book."[8]

Deep
Like the Rivers

1

The Setting: Growing Up
in the Quarter Community

Dese all my fader's children,
Dese all my fader's children,
Dese all my fader's children,
Outshine de sun.

Allen, *Slave Songs*

For the black children of the quarter community the world of their home plantation was, for all intents and purposes, the entire world of their personal experience. Within its confines they encountered nearly all the physical and material realities of their childhoods and acquired the knowledge, attitudes, values, and skills with which they learned to view the world and make sense of their relationship to it.*

The physical condition and appearance of the cabins and other buildings that comprised the slave quarters depended greatly on the wealth and inclination of the plantation owner. On plantations of moderate size, where there was only one quarters, the cabins would be built several hundred yards away from the "great house" of the owner's family, near a spring and a ready supply of fuel from the nearby woods.[1] Commonly slaves wanted their cabins out of sight and hearing of the great house. "When left to themselves," writes Julia Harn, the daughter of a Georgia planter, "they wanted their cabins in some secluded

---

*In some quarter communities, probably the exceptions, the older children would be allowed to visit neighboring plantations. See page 185. Older slaves and to some extent young house servants had greater intercourse with people and places off the home plantation.

place, down in the hollow, or amid the trees, with only a path to their abode."[2] On large plantations of more than seventy or eighty slaves, two sets of cabins were often built: an "upper quarter," nearer the more distant fields, and a "lower quarter," closer to the great house.

By the time of the last three decades of slavery the typical slave cabin consisted of one large room.[3] Most often they were constructed of wood logs daubed with mud and sticks "made perfectly tight with mortar, with hog or cow hair worked in to make it stick in the crevises."[4] An ex-slave interviewed by the Fisk project remembers that when the dirt between the logs in the cabin he lived in as a slave would fall off, "you could look out and see the snow falling. Sometimes you would get up out of your warm bed and the side towards the wall would be full of snow."[5] On the Georgia seacoast the houses were often built with tabby, "a plaster of burned oyster shell, lime, and sand applied to a wattle surface; the roof was shingled with cypress or pine, and there was a chimney. . . ."[6] Louis Hughes, who was born a Virginia slave in 1832, describes a fairly typical slave quarters:

> Each cabin was about fourteen feet square, containing but one room, and was covered with oak boards, three feet in length, split out of logs by hand. These boards were not nailed on, but held in their places by what were termed weight-poles laid across them at right angles. There were in each room two windows, a door and a large, rude fireplace. The door and window frames, or facings, were held in their places by wooden pins, nails being used only in putting doors together.[7]

On the large Louisiana plantation where Charley Williams grew up, "De quarters was a little piece from de big house, and dey run along both sides of de road dat go to de fields. All one-room log cabins, but dey was good and warm, and everyone had a little open shed at de side whar we sleep in de summer to keep cool."[8] The small cabin on a Virginia plantation in which Austen Steward lived as a child had an earthen floor, small openings in the walls for windows, a stick and mud chimney and "the whole was put together in the rudest possible manner."[9]

The Setting

Most slave cabins had holes in the walls with wooden shutters for windows, which had the disadvantage, according to Margaret Nillin of Texas, of letting "flies in durin' de summer an' col' in durin' de winter. But if you shuts dat window dat shut out de light."[10] In the Mississippi slave cabin where Austin Parnell was raised the problem was not so much letting in the light as keeping out the rain and snow.

> I laid in bed many a night and looked up through the cracks in the roof. Snow would come through there when it snowed and cover the bed covers. We thought you couldn't build a roof so that it would keep out rain and snow, but we were mistaken. Before you would make a fire in them days, you had to sweep out the snow so that it wouldn't melt up in the house and make a mess.[11]

Another problem with many of the cabins was that the mud-and-sticks-chimneys would catch fire. According to Richard Carruthers, who lived as a slave in Texas, the log cabins of the quarters "burned down oftentimes. The chimney would catch fire, 'cause it was made out of sticks and clay and moss. Many the time we would have to get up at midnight and push the chimney away from the house to keep the house from burnin' up."[12]

On some plantations, households with many children were permitted to add a second room to their cabins. "My mother had so many children she had to have two rooms," recollects a Fisk informant. "It had old-fashioned windows that you would shut, no glass at all. There was a fireplace in each room that would come out on the inside. We called that the hob, and we chillen would climb on it sometimes."[13] In other quarters, cabins with two rooms with a chimney built between them was the rule for everybody.[14] Rarely would a cabin have more than two rooms although the cabin where Alec Pope lived in Georgia "had two rooms on de fust flo' and a loft up 'bove whar de boys most gen'ally slep' and de gals slep' downstairs."[15] On the Georgia plantation where Georgia Baker grew up, "De long, log cabins what us lived in was called 'shotgun' houses 'cause dey had three rooms, one behind the other in a row lak de barrel of a shotgun. All de chillun slept in one end room and de grown folkses slept in de other end room. . . . Gals slept on one side of de room and boys on de other in de chillun's rooms."[16] Olmsted reported even larger slave houses made of boards on some of the Virginia plantations of the James River. In these, up to eight families occupied what Olmsted observed to be "ornamental" structures each having its own "distinct sleeping-room and lock-up closets."[17] By the account of Jacob Stroyer, who lived as a slave on the large Singleton plantation in South Carolina, in such multi-family dwellings anyone "accustomed to the way in which the slaves lived in their cabins could tell as soon as they entered whether they were friendly or not, for when they did not agree the fires of the two families did not meet on the hearth, but there was a vacancy between them, that was a sign of disagreement."[18]

The furnishings of the quarter cabins were generally very simple, consisting of homemade chairs, tables, and beds which could be cleaned easily and scoured with sand. In most cabins the beds were constructed in a corner "with one leg out and the two walls supporting the other sides."[19] Celeste Avery, an ex-slave interviewed in Georgia, remembers that "The beds were bottomed with rope which ran backward and forward from one rail to the other. On this framework was placed a mattress of wheat straw. Each spring the mattresses were emptied and re-filled with fresh wheat straw."[20] Sometimes instead of cords, boards were used for support and mattresses might be filled with cotton, moss, leaves, or occasionally, feathers.[21] Addie Vinson, whose parents were both fieldhands on the Georgia plantation of Peter Vinson, recalls how she "laked dem matt'esses 'cause when de chinches got too bad you could shake out dat straw and burn it, den scald de tick and fill it wid fresh straw, and rest in peace again."[22] During the day the trundle beds on which the children slept were pushed under the big bed. "You would get it out at night, and the children would sleep in it, and in the morning you would push it back under the big bed. They had one room, and had everything in the one room, and they did that to save space."[23]

Other cabin furnishings included shuck-bottomed chairs, a wooden table, and tallow candles or lamps made out of fat light-wood torches.[24] Often boxes were used for everything from bureaus and chairs to storing food.[25] Even the most sparsely fur-

The Setting

nished cabin contained a wooden bench, a broom made of straw or corn shucks, and various cooking utensils. Gourds which slaves grew of many sizes had, as Robert Shepherd, who lived as a slave on the Echols plantation in Oglethrope County, Georgia, informs us, equally as many purposes. "Us loved to drink out of gourds. Dere was lots of gourds raised every year. Some of 'em was so big dey was used to keep eggs in and for lots of things us uses baskets for now. Dem little gourds made fine dippers."[26] Most slaves also possessed at least one big wooden water bucket and perhaps an even larger wash barrel. The most prominent aspect of many cabins was the large fireplace.

> De fireplaces was a heap bigger dan dey has now, for all de cookin' was done in open fireplaces den. 'Taters and cornpone was roasted in de ashes and most of the other victuals was biled in de big old pots what swung on cranes over de coals. Dey had long-handled fryin' pans and heavy iron skillets wid big, thick, tight-fittin' lids, and ovens of all sizes to bake in. All of dem things was used right dar in de fireplace. Dere never was no better tastin' sompin t' eat dan dat cooked in dem old cook-things in open fireplaces.[27]

Many slaves did much of their cooking in a large three-legged black pot nicknamed "the spider."

In general, both the black people of the quarters and the white authorities took care to insure that the cabins were clean and sanitary. On his South Carolina plantation, ex-Governor James H. Hammond scheduled elaborate spring and fall house cleanings. "The houses were to be emptied and their contents sunned, the wall and floors were to be scrubbed, the mattresses to be emptied and stuffed with fresh hay or shucks, the yard swept and the ground under the house sprinkled with lime. Furthermore, every house was to be whitewashed inside and out once a year. . . ."[28] Basil Hall, a widely traveled Englishman who visited the United States in 1827 and 1828, observed that the cottages of the quarters were "uncommonly neat and comfortable, and might have shamed those of many countries I have seen."[29] Though there were many exceptions (as on the Butler Island plantation of Fanny Kemble's husband, where she described the cabins as "filthy and wretched in the extreme"[30]) as a general rule the self-interest of both slave and owner prescribed that most cabins be clean and of crude comfort.

Near to their cabins many quarter residents cultivated a garden truck patch.[31] From his study of slavery in Kentucky, Ivan McDougle concludes that in Kentucky "as in Virginia, the slave was permitted to have a little 'truck-patch' of half an acre or more, where he could raise any crop that he desired. In Kentucky these small plots of ground were nearly always filled with sweet potatoes, tobacco and watermelons."[32] On some plantations slaves were also allowed a chicken yard and sometimes even a pigsty.[33] According to Kate Stone, whose mother owned a cotton plantation in northeast Louisiana of over 150 slaves, "It was a very lazy 'cullud pusson' who did not raise chickens and have eggs."[34] Many slaves also owned their own dogs.[35]

Besides household cabins the quarters of the large plantations often contained a number of work houses—a tannery, wash house, smithy—a "children's house" or "nursery," a "sick house," and a bachelor quarters where unmarried males lived together.[36] Many contemporary descriptions of such quarters relate that they gave the appearance of a "thriving little village."[37] Ben Brown lived as a slave for more than twenty-five years on a large Virginia plantation where "De log cabins what we live in on both sides de path make it look like a town."[38] On some plantations the quarter cabins were arranged in a circle. Clayton Holbert recalls that he and the other slaves on a large plantation in Tennessee "usually had a house of their own for their families. They usually built their houses in a circle, so you didn't have to go out the door hardly to go to the house next to you."[39] Harriet McFarlin, who was the slave of Colonel Jesse Chaney in both Texas and Arkansas, gave this description of the slave quarters to her interviewer:

> Colonel Chaney had lots and lots of slaves, and all their houses were in a row, all one-room cabins. Everything happened in that one room—birth, death, and everything, but in them days niggers kept their houses clean and their door yards too. These houses where they lived was called "quarters." I used to love to walk down by that row of houses. It looked like a town, and late of an

evening as you'd go by the doors you could smell meat a-frying, coffee making and good things cooking.[40]

Not all quarters, to be sure, were this neat and orderly. On some plantations the slave cabins were put up without plan, whenever the need arose and no attempt was made to give them a neat appearance.

It was in a physical setting such as this, within their mother's cabin, that the children of the quarters were born. Attended at first by only an experienced slave midwife, it was not long before they became a part of the natural commotion and human interaction of a household which sheltered, fed, slept, and provided for many of the human needs and wants of any number of individual slaves. Although the census records show that an average of between five and six slaves occupied slave cabins, quarter children at birth often became part of a houschold circle that contained, besides their parents and siblings, grandparents, aunts, uncles, cousins, and adopted children whose parents had died or been sold, or who had themselves been sold. John Brown, who was born on a large Virginia plantation where his mother was a fieldhand, reports, for instance, that his household included his mother, her three "natural children" and her three stepchildren in one room, and his cousin and her children in a second room.[41]

Whatever the living arrangements of her cabin home, for the first few weeks the newborn slave child was the center of attention and concern. On most plantations the baby's mother was allowed from two weeks' to a month's "lying-in time" during which she was permitted to rest from her work in the fields and devote her time entirely to her new child. For the first seven days the child and her mother, on many plantations, were attended frequently by the midwife.[42] Depending on plantation rule and regulation, the child's father was allowed to visit his wife and child as soon as news of the arrival carried to the fields.

The day after delivery, if it was fairly clear that the baby was a healthy one, a stream of friends and relations would come to congratulate the mother, meet the new member, and issue judgment upon his health, beauty (or lack of it) and possible future.

Thus, for example, a child born with a caul, "a veil over his face," might be thought to be gifted with the ability to see haunts and spirits.[43] A child born with a long or a large head might be marked to become a wise man.[44]

In addition, the new baby might receive a visit from the overseer, the mistress of the great house, or from the master himself checking out his new property. Sometimes, though infrequently, the white slaveowner named new quarter babies. Most often slaves were named by their parents, usually after an immediate family member or a member of an enlarged blood-kin group.[45] The date of the quarter child's birth was marked by the seasons or some important event. "Children often ask their parents their age," writes Henry Watson, who was born a slave in Virginia in 1813. "The answer is, 'this planting corn time, you are six, eight, or ten,' just as it may happen to be. . . ."[46]

Thus, the first weeks of the child's life brought him in contact with many of the prominent plantation personalities, both white and black, and were, by and large, weeks of peaceful companionship with his mother during the day and playful interaction with other family members at night. Well wrapped in a blanket and kept warm in a cradle before the fire or in his mother's bed; well fed from his mother's milk; and well cared for by any number of family members whose own sleep and peace depended on his quiet contentment, his life was a continual round of eating, sleeping, and physical comforting.

After the month or so of lying-in time was over and her mother returned to full-time work in the fields, the new child was most often cared for during the day at the plantation nursery. At the nursery the children of the quarters were tended by one or two women too old to work in the fields who were assisted by the older brothers and sisters of the infants. If a child had no older siblings mature enough to care for her, one of her older cousins was often appointed to the job.[47] On some plantations the general supervision of the nursery would be placed in the hands of some younger woman who had displayed a talent or an interest in the job. Occasionally, if an infant had a grandmother whose work days had passed, she would be cared for at her grandparents' cabin.

The Setting

The actual nursery building (or "nurse house" or "chilluns' house") was an enlarged cabin that contained most often both a sleeping room and a room for playing and eating.[48] In the sleeping room, rows of cradles were arranged for the infants too young to crawl around on the floor or outside in the yard. Outside there was usually a fenced-in yard where the toddlers could crawl in safety. Often during the hot days of summer, the cradles would be placed outdoors in the shade. The number of children cared for at the nursery varied according to the size of the plantation's slave population. On the typical large plantation the proportion of nonworking children to the rest of the slave population seems to have varied around thirty-three percent.[49]

Whether he was being cared for at the nursery, at his grandparents' cabin, or in his own home by one of his older sisters or brothers, the child's mother would be released from work to come and suckle him two or three times during the work day. On most plantations the nursing schedule allowed a feeding in the morning before the mother left for the fields, another about ten, a third at lunch time around twelve, a fourth at three, and a fifth upon mother's return from the fields at dark.[50] Most quarter mothers suckled their children for at least a year and often longer. Amanda McCray, who grew up a slave on the large Florida plantation of Redding Parnell, recalls that "It was a common occurrence to see a child of two or three years still nursing at the mother's breast."[51]

On those occasions when work was being done in fields too far away from the quarters to permit quick travel between field and nursery, suckling babies would often be carried to the fields, where they would be left in the shade at the end of the row, secured in a hammock-like cradle between two trees, or wrapped securely upon their mother's backs.[52] Jeff Bailey, an ex-slave from Arkansas, recounts being told that as a baby he was carried to the fields where, while he was sleeping in the cotton basket, all the cotton would be placed in the basket around him.[53]

As the black child was weaned, her mother's milk was supplemented with cow's or goat's milk and "the liquor from boiled cabbage, and bread and milk together."[54] The older children who were still too young to work would be served lunch and sometimes breakfast at the nursery, or at the "cook house." The fare consisted chiefly of whatever was being prepared to be carried to the fieldhands.[55] A picture of meals at one quarter cook house is provided by William L. Dunwoody, who was born a slave in South Carolina in the year 1840:

> After the old folks among the slaves had had their breakfast, the cook would blow a horn. That would be about nine o'clock or eight. All the children that were big enough would come to the cook shack. Some of them would bring small children that had been weaned but couldn't look after themselves. The cook would serve them whatever the old folks had for breakfast. They ate out of the same kind of dishes as the old folks.
>
> Between ten and eleven o'clock, the cook would blow the horn again and the children would come in from play. There would be a large bowl and a large spoon for each group of larger children. There would be enough in each group to get around the bowl comfortably. One would take a spoonful of what was in the bowl and then pass the spoon to his neighbor. His neighbor would take a spoonful and then pass the spoon and so on until everyone would have a spoonful. Then they would begin again, and so on until the bowl was empty. If they did not have enough then, the cook would put some more in the bowl. Most of the time, bread and milk was in the bowl; sometimes mush and milk. There was a small spoon and a small bowl for the smaller children in the group which the big children would use for them and pass around just like they passed around the big spoon.
>
> About two or three o'clock, the cook would blow the horn again. Time the children all got in there and et, it would be four or five o'clock. The old mammy would cut up the greens real fine and cut up meat into little pieces and boil it with cornmeal dumplings. They'd call it the pepper pot. Then she'd put some of the pepper pot into the bowls and we'd eat it. And it was good.[56]

Lunsford Lane, who was the slave of William Helm in Prince County, Virginia, remembers how greedily he and his friends fell upon the pot-liquor and corn-meal balls that had been mixed together, poured into a large common tray, and served to them in the middle of the yard.[57] In the Georgia quarters where Malhalia Shores grew up on the plantation of Jim Jackson, the children did not eat out of a common tray. "We had our plates and cup and took it to the pot and they put some victuals in 'em, then we went and et where we pleased."[58] The younger children in many quarters ate with their hands. The older ones used clam, oyster, or mussel shells, spoons whittled from wood, grouds, or pewter spoons if they were provided with them.[59] Fanny Kemble noticed that many of the children, and older folks, often ate and talked "squatting down upon their hams."[60]

Besides their regular food fare, many children were given various ingredients to make them grow strong and healthy. The favorite elixer of the quarter community seems to have been different kinds of herbal teas, although garlic and asefetida were used commonly also. Charlie King and his brothers and sisters, who lived on the large plantation of John King in Merriwether County, Georgia, started every day with a swig of burnt whiskey.[61] Many children were also adorned with charms and greegrees to ward off diseases.[62]

The clothing of most quarter children was a single garment made of varying types of cloth which fitted like a long shirt reaching to the ankles. "Boys until they got up large enough to work wore little slips," relates a Fisk informant. "We called them shirts; they'd sew it up like a sack and cut a hole in the neck for your head to go through, and you wore that till you were ten or twelve years old. There was not much difference in the dress of girls and boys."[63] Robert Anderson's clothes during childhood, in Green County, Maryland, were typical of those worn by many slave children.

> The clothes that I wore did not amount to much, just a one piece dress or gown. In shape this was more like a gunny sack, with a hole cut out in the bottom for me to stick my head through, and the corners cut out for arm holes. We never wore underclothes, not even in the winter, and a boy was ten or twelve years old before he was given a pair of pants and a shirt to replace the sack garment. We never had more than one at a time, and when they had to be washed we went naked until they had dried. When the garment had been worn until it would no longer hold together, or hold a patch, it was discarded and cut up for carpet rags, and another garment handed out. When one child outgrew a gown it was handed down to someone smaller. The fit was immaterial, because there was no shape to these one piece garments, other

than that of a sack. Some times old sacks were used to make these garments for the smaller children. One of these garments was made to last a year, and sometimes longer.[64]

Perhaps the chief complaint made against these shirts by the slaves was that when first worn their coarseness scratched and irritated the skin. Charles Lucas, who was raised in Loudon County, Virginia, recalls being "kept mostly at the quarters until twelve or thirteen, wearing nothing in the summer but a coarse crocus shirt. Many a time have I taken it by the two ends, and pulled it round a post to break down the sticks."[65]

In the cold weather of winter some quarter children put on two of these gowns if two were to be had. Occasionally a child was lucky enough to own a yarn undershirt or some yarn drawers which buttoned down over the knees to ward off the cold.[66] Plantation authorities rarely handed out shoes for children. "On frosty mornin's when I went to de spring to fetch a bucket of water," recollects Will Sheets, "you could see my feet tracks in de frost all de way dar and back."[67] Hats for children were also an infrequently indulged luxury, though they were sometimes fashioned by a skillful friend or relative from bullrushes or the bark of trees.[68] In general, plantation owners left it to quarter parents to clothe those children too young to work. "Little children," as one former slave recalls somewhat bitterly, "wore what their parents put on them."[69] In most quarters the clothes were washed on Wednesdays or Saturdays. In Alabama where Mingo White spent much of his childhood, "Wash day was on Wednesday. My mammy would have to take de clothes about three-quarters of a mile to de branch where de washin' was to be done. She didn't have no washboard like dey have nowdays. She had a paddle what she beat de clothes with. Everybody knowed when wash day was 'cause dey could hear de paddle for about three or four mile. 'Pow-pow-pow,' dats how it sound."[70]

As the children of the quarters were weaned and began to crawl and toddle about, they spent much of their time playing with the other black children of the nursery. On many plantations the quarters contained a fenced-in yard where the children could play in safety.[71] Their activities depended greatly upon the energy and inclination of the older children or "nurses" watching them. At the nursery of a South Carolina rice plantation Olmsted observed "a number of girls, eight or ten years old . . . occupied in holding and tending the youngest infants. Those a little older—the crawlers—were in the pen, and those big enough to toddle were playing on the steps, or before the house. Some of these, with two or three bigger ones, were singing and dancing about a fire they had made on the ground. . . . I watched for half an hour, and in all that time not a baby of them began to cry; nor have I ever heard one, at two or three other plantation-nurseries which I have visited."[72]

Occasionally, a nursery teacher would organize an imaginative routine of games and activities for her children. Susan Eppes, whose father owned a large Florida plantation of over three hundred slaves, tells of one such woman, Aunt Dinah, who ran her nursery "like the kindergarten of today" and whose "inventive brain kept the children always busy." She told stories, demonstrated how animals could be made from potatoes, orange thorns, and a few feathers, and helped her pupils "set table" with mats made of the green leaves of the jonquil, cups and saucers of acorns, dishes of hickory hulls and any gay bit of china they could find; and had them bake mud pies in a broken stove. She also helped them dress up as flowers and taught them to make decorations with chains of china blossoms and long strings of chinquapins. She even encouraged them to catch "Mammy Doddles" and terrapins to be kept in the nursery as pets.[73]

In most nurseries, however, the children, especially the older ones, were left to their own devices. Their time was spent largely playing among themselves and roaming through the fields and woods of the plantation.[74]

Whatever their activities during the day, upon the return of the older folks from the fields, the children would return to their own cabins for their evening meal. Evening chores were begun while supper was being prepared; the younger children would gather fuel for the fire and bring in water from the well. In Sam Aleckson's quarters, as in many, there was a spring between the big house and the quarters from which the slaves got their drinking water. "Every afternoon a long line of children might have been seen with "piggins" on their heads, taking in the supply for the night."[75] An ex-slave of the Fisk survey recalls going "to the spring to get water, with a bucket on top of my head, and one in each hand."[76] At least one of the older girls usually helped with the cooking and the other children worked in the truck patch.

After dinner, which in the summer would often be cooked and eaten outside around a fire, other chores were completed. Children of both sexes helped with washing, sewing, repairing furniture, and working in the garden. Often children were called upon to help their mother with the spinning. Fannie Moore, an ex-slave from South Carolina, recalls helping her mother spin enough thread every night to make the four cuts required by the white folks.

> Why sometime I never go to bed. Have to hold de light for her to see by. She have to piece quilts for de white folks too. Why, dey is a scar on my arm yet where my brother let de pine drip on me. Rich pine was all de light we ever had. My brother was a-holdin' de pine so's I can help mammy tack the quilt and he go to sleep and let it drop.[77]

Henry Cheatam, who was born a slave in 1830 near West Point, Mississippi, relates how he and his brothers and sisters would take off their "one-piece suit made outen ausenberg" and wash it and sleep while it dried.[78] Often children themselves were washed at night in big wooden wash tubs. Randel Lee, who lived as a slave in South Carolina, remembers how after a bath he "would sit a few minutes with his feet held to the fire so they could dry," as his mother rubbed "grease under the soles of his feet to keep him from taking cold."[79] The children's hair was usually combed with the card that was used for spinning. "That wouldn't get the lice out, but it would make it feel better. They had to use larkspur to get 'em out; that would always get the lice out of your head."[80]

On pleasant evenings after the chores had been completed, the older children were often allowed by their parents to play outside or to visit the cabins of their friends.[81] Frank Gill remembers how the people of his Mississippi quarters put "a big light out in de backyard" so that the children could play together at night.[82] Often the children sat around listening as the entire community brought their benches and chairs outside and sat around telling stories and singing songs.[83] Occasionally, the older children, if they were considered mature enough to be trusted, were allowed to participate in the more clandestine nocturnal activities of the quarter community. Often the older male children, and sometimes the girls, accompanied their elders on moonlit hunting and fishing expeditions. As they gew older still, quarter children began attending their community's feasts of stolen food prepared deep in the woods, unsanctioned dances, voodoo ceremonies, and meetings of the clandestine congregation.[84]

Most especially, nights were times of quiet family pleasures. Separated from their children for the entire, long workday, quarter parents took advantage of the night to play with and talk to their children. Often children would lie in bed and listen to the old folks sing or tell stories as they worked or simply sat around the fire.[85] Jack Island, an ex-slave from Arkansas, tells of watching the women spinning: ". . . ah'd lie dar a while an' watch 'em spin den ah'd go tuh sleep ergin, and leave 'em spinnin'!"[86] Davenport remembers how he and his brothers and sisters used to gather nuts in the woods and steal potatoes so their family could eat them at night. "At night when de work was all done and de candles was out us'd set 'round de fire and eat cracked nuts and 'taters. Us picked out de nuts with horseshoe nails and baked de 'taters in ashes. Den Mammy would pour herself and her old man a cup o' wine."[87]

In most slave cabins, especially in cold weather, the fireplace was the center of family gatherings. Mary Reynolds, an ex-slave from Louisiana, relates how the slaves would "bring in two-three big logs and put them on the fire, and they'd last a week."[88] Olmsted described the not untypical scene he witnessed on a Mississippi plantation:

> During the evening, all the cabins were illuminated by great fires, and, looking into one of them, I saw a very picturesque family group; a man sat on the ground making a basket, a woman

lounged on a chest in the chimney corner smoking a pipe, and a boy and two girls sat in a bed which had been drawn up opposite to her, completing the fireside circle. They were talking and laughing cheerfully.[89]

Sometimes if it was very cold the entire household might sit around the fire the entire night. "De 'possum in his hollow, de squirrel in his nest, and de rabbit in his bed, is at home," observes Charles Davis of South Carolina. "So de nigger, in a tight house wid a big hot fire, in winter, is at home, too."[90]

On most nights those slaves who had beds slept in them and those that had no beds slept on straw in front of the fire. One white observer wrote that slaves invariably would sleep "with the head to the fire. They will wrap their blankets around the head and the shoulders, or creep, head foremost into a bag or sack. . . ."[91] In many quarter cabins the small baby's cradle was placed in front of the fire at night. In others, it was the custom for children from one to three years of age to sleep in the big bed with their parents or one of the other grown-ups.[92] Dosia Harris of Georgia recalls that though many children slept on the floor she slept in a bed with her grandma.[93] Often one big bed would be built for all the children, who would sleep in it "crosswise." "It was plum' full in cold weather."[94]

Sundays and holidays were also times when the children of the quarters could participate in, or observe, family and community activities or merely play with their friends and relatives. On many plantations the children were not required to attend either the Sabbath schools or the worship services organized by the plantation whites for their slaves. Charles Colcock Jones, a white Presbyterian minister, lamented that "Negro children do not enjoy the advantages of the preached gospel; for the custom is, where no effort is made to alter it, for the children to remain at home on the Sabbath."[95] On some plantations the children did attend the white organized church services with their parents and many children attended Sabbath schools established especially for them.

Besides church, the Sunday activities of most quarters involved singing and storytelling, various games and athletic contests, and visiting among friends and relatives. For children with fathers who lived on neighboring plantations Sundays were especially important as the one day father was most certain to be able to visit.

Holidays, especially Christmas, crop-lying-by-time, the Fourth of July, and Easter were also times of family and community interaction which provided special meaning and excitement for quarter children. It was during evenings, Sundays, and holidays that the children of the quarters became acquainted with the structure, the style, and the leading personalities of their quarter community. Through their common experiences they learned the ways in which their community operated, how it made common decisions, planned secretive events, provided for common physical and recreational needs, and generally organized itself to be as independent as possible from the whims of the white personalities and the strictures of plantation rule and regulation.

Looking back on their childhood experiences, many of the men and women of the slave narratives cite the period up to the time when they were forced to become an institutionalized part of the white man's work force as the happiest time in their lives under slavery. Indeed, it is not uncommon for one of the autobiographers to recall that he was six, eight, or even fourteen before he began to realize the ramifications of what it might mean to be a slave. Frederick Douglass was seven before he had his "first introduction to the realities of the slave system."[96] Sam Aleckson was seven or eight, and it took the sale of his mother and two sisters before it dawned on him that his condition was not as good as that of any boy in the county. "With kind parents, two sweet little sisters, and every boyish wish gratified, the improbability of my succession to the presidential chair never once occurred to me."[97] J. Vance Lewis writes of his childhood in Louisiana: "As a barefoot boy my stay upon the farm had been pleasant. I played among the wild flowers and wandered in high glee over hill and hollow, enchanted with the beauty of nature, and knew not that I was a slave and the son of a slave."[98] Lunsford Lane offers the following testimony:

> On the 30th of May, 1803, I was ushered into the world; but I did not begin to see the rising of its dark clouds, nor fancy how they

might be broken and dispersed until some time afterwards. My infancy was spent upon the floor, in a rough cradle, or sometimes in my mother's arms. My early boyhood in playing with other boys and girls, colored and white, in the yard, and occasionally doing such little matters of labor as one of so young years could. I knew no difference between myself and the white children; nor did they seem to know any in turn.[99]

This is not to suggest, however, that all, or even most, quarter children experienced idyllic childhoods. Besides the fights, cruel jokes, mishaps, and punishments experienced within the quarters itself, the reality of life within the larger context of the white-controlled slave population touched most children and clouded even the most carefree of childhoods. Although direct contact with whites was infrequent for the child born and raised in the quarters, it was sometimes marked by harsh interaction. A. J. Mitchell recalls that when his master, Jack Clifton of Arkansas, was displeased with any of the children, he would "make us younguns put our head 'tween his legs and put that strap on us."[100] Often the relationship between the children of the quarters and the children of the white household was less than the harmonious one described by Lane. On the Maryland plantation where James Pennington lived as a slave child the "tyranny" of his master's two sons "early embittered" his life. Not only were James and his older brother "required to recognize these young sirs as our masters, but they felt themselves to be such; and in consequence of this feeling, they sought to treat us with the same air of authority that their father did the older slaves."[101] Pennington also describes the tyranny and abuse of the overseers. "These men seem to look with an evil eye upon children. . . . They seem to take pleasure in torturing the children of slaves, long before they are old enough to be put at the hoe, and consequently under the whip."[102]

Some slaves experienced a sudden traumatic event which directly touched their childhoods. Douglass was taken from his beloved grandmother.[103] Charlotte Martin's brother was whipped to death for taking part in a series of secret religious ceremonies.[104] Josiah Henson saw his father appear one day with a bloody head and a lacerated back. "His right ear had been cut off close to his head, and he had received a hundred lashes on his back. He had beaten the overseer for a brutal assault on my mother, and this was his punishment."[105] William Wells Brown remembers watching his mother being whipped for tardiness in going to the fields and how "the cold chills ran over me, and I wept aloud."[106] Other children saw their friends divested of a finger for attempting to learn to read, escapees tortured, and grandparents put off the plantation and told by the white authorities to fend for themselves.

Despite these "darker clouds" which overcast the early childhood years, few slave children seem to have realized the full significance of their slave status until their slave training began in earnest. On many large plantations those children destined to become fieldhands were left to grow strong and healthy until between the ages of ten and fourteen.* H. C. Bruce asserts that the custom in Virginia was not to put young blacks to work in the field before they had reached age thirteen.[107] On the South Carolina plantation where Peter Clifton grew up the rule for the older slaves was : " 'Wake up de slaves at daylight, begin work when they can see, and quit work when they can't see.' But they was careful of de rule dat say: 'you mustn't work a child, under twelve years old, in de field.' "[108] Sally remarked that "It is policy to leave the slaves to grow and strengthen, unfatigued by labor, until they are old enough to be constantly occupied, as a colt is left unshackled, with free range of the pastures, until the 'breakin' time comes."[109]

Many planters did, however, begin the "breaking" process before the slave child was strong enough to do a full-hand's work. Most quarter children between the ages of six and ten were given miscellaneous chores around the plantation. They tended sheep, milked cows, gathered firewood, toted water, helped with the cooking, assisted at the nursery, swept the yard, ran errands, and generally did whatever little jobs were needed done from moment to moment. Henry Johnson, who was raised "all over the state of Virginia," recalls that "when I was a little bit of a fellow, I used to pack water to twenty-five and thirty men in

---

* The training of house servants began much earlier.

one field, den go back to de house and bring enough water for breakfast de next morning. When I got a little bigger, I had to take a little hoe and dig weeds out of de crop."[110] Tom Baker of Alabama also describes the work of a water boy:

> I was a water boy for fifty fiel' han's dat worked in de sun all day long, an' I hadda carry many a bucket from de spring. It was a long walk—one fiel' ober from where most of dem was workin'. De spring run down between some willow trees an' it was powerful cool down dere in de shade. I use to lie on de moss an' let my bare belly git cool an' put my face in de outlet of de spring an' let de water trickle over my haid. Jus' about de time I gits a little rest one of dem niggers would call: "Water Boy! Bring dat bucket!" Den I grab up de bucket an' run back out in de hot sun.[111]

On what appears to have been a minority of plantations, children were given jobs to keep them busy most of the time. Jacob Branch of Texas recounts that he and the other children of his quarters were put to work as soon as they could toddle. "First us gather firewood. Iffen it freezin' or not us have to go to toughen us up. When us get l'il bigger us tend de cattle and feed hosses and hogs. By time us good sprouts us pickin' cotton and pullin' cane. Us ain't never idle."[112] Booker T. Washington, who grew up in Franklin County, Virginia, asserts with a touch of sadness that there was no period in his life that was devoted to play.

> From the time that I can remember anything, almost every day of my life has been occupied in some kind of labor; though I think I would now be a more useful man if I had had time for sports. During the period that I spent in slavery I was not large enough to be of much service, still I was occupied most of the time in cleaning the yards, carrying water to the men in the fields, or going to the mill, to which I used to take the corn, once a week, to be ground.[113]

Usually between the ages of ten and fourteen young blacks were forced to begin actual field work, though at first they were assigned special tasks. On the Mississippi plantation where Louis Hughes worked as a slave, children between the ages of nine and twelve, and women still suckling infants, were given the job of gathering the first bales of cotton from the lower part of the stalk where it opened months before the rest was ready for picking.[114] On tobacco plantations one of the principal jobs of the younger children was to pick worms off the tobacco leaves.[115]

As they grew older and stronger, children of the fields would be given regular but smaller tasks. Olmsted observed that all fieldhands "are divided into four classes, according to their physical capacities. The children beginning as 'quarter-hands,' advancing to 'half-hands,' and then to 'three-quarter hands'; and finally, when mature, and abled-bodied, healthy and strong, to 'full-hands.' "[116] Henry Waldon, describing how he and his sister worked one row on a Mississippi plantation, explains that "The two of us made a hand."[117] On many plantations an older fieldhand was assigned to teach the children how to do field work. Clayton Holbert relates that on the plantation in Tennessee where he learned to work as a fieldhand, "They always had a man in the field to teach the small boys to work, and I was one of the boys."[118] Andrew Moss, who received his slave training in Georgia, remembers how he was taught to stack his hoe at the end of the day's work and to chop with a little hoe which had a handle about the length of his arm. "I've walked many a mile, when I was a little feller, up and down de rows, followin' de grown folks, and chopping with de hoe round de corners where de earth was soft so de little 'uns could hoe easy."[119] Mary Reynolds tells how she held the hoe very unsteadily when an old woman was first put in charge of teaching the children of her Louisiana plantation how to "scrape the fields." "That old woman would be frantic. She'd show me and then turn 'bout to show some other little nigger, and I'd have the young corn cut clean as the grass. She say, 'For the love of God, you better larn it right, or Solomon will beat the breath out you body.' Old Man Solomon was the nigger driver."[120]

By the time they had become full-fledged fieldhands, the young blacks of the quarters, whatever their individual childhood experiences, came face to face with the stark reality that the white world held them as slaves, and intended to use its power to make them behave like ones. "When I began to work," writes Lunsford Lane, "I discovered the difference between myself and my master's white children. They began to order me about, and were told to do so by my master and mistress. . . . Indeed all things now made me *feel,* what I had before known only in words, *that I was a slave.* Deep was this feeling, and it preyed upon my heart like a never dying worm."[121] Many young slaves, like Frederick Douglass, began "to inquire into the origin and nature of slavery. Why are some people slaves and others masters?"[122]

How individual slaves answered these questions depended greatly upon their own unique personalities and upon the nature of the experiences and personal interactions they had encountered in the plantation environment. In drawing their own personal conclusions, however, most slaves were not left entirely to their own devices. Both the white society and the quarter community had a great stake in their answers and had long since deliberately begun to attempt to influence the nature of the values, attitudes, and understandings with which slaves struggled—both to understand themselves and to make sense of the world in which they lived.

PART I

WHITE TEACHING

The character of the negro is . . . like the plastic clay which may be molded into agreeable or disagreeable figures according to the skill of the molder.

H., *The Farmer's Register*

Introduction

From the point of view of the slaveholder, the primary teaching task of the slave plantation was to train slaves to handle effectively all the jobs relating to the running of his plantation. Under slavery blacks received job training in everything from the technical skills of carpentry, masonry, horse handling, sugar refining, blacksmithing, gardening, shoemaking, weaving, and domestic service to the less technical skills of field labor. The notion that the plantation was an effective vocational or industrial school, in which most purely academic skills were dispensed with (except of course for white children), is a clearly defensible proposition.[1]

In the pursuit of this primary teaching goal, however, most slave owners were smart enough to recognize the wisdom of seeking a secondary goal. In order to run a plantation profitably, plantation authorities knew they needed a work force that not only possessed the needed skills but, in addition, were willing to use their skills productively. Although some slaveholders relied solely upon a strict system of reward and punishment, most large plantation owners taught their slaves a carefully constructed set of attitudes and understandings aimed at encouraging their willingness to work to the best of their abilities.

Furthermore, since the plantation was a social as well as an economic institution, most planters also desired their slaves to learn certain social skills. For pecuniary, security, and sometimes ethical reasons, plantation owners believed it was in their best interest to teach their slaves not only the sensibilities of plantation etiquette but the values, attitudes, and understandings of obedient and trustworthy servants. An examination of the methods and intended results of this nonvocational training is the primary focus of the following two chapters.

2

Secular Training

We have as far as possible closed every avenue by which light may enter their minds. If we could extinguish the capacity to see the light our work would be completed.

> Unknown delegate,
> Virginia House of
> Delegates

The ostensible teaching goal of the planter class with respect to its slave population was to have them internalize the knowledge, attitudes, values, skills and sensibilities of the "perfect servant." This model slave would be: conscious of his own innate inferiority as a member of "the Negroid race"; overflowing with awe, respect, and childlike affection for the planter and his family; cheerfully mindful of the formalities of plantation etiquette and of the rules and regulations regarding slave behavior; firmly convinced of the morality of slavery and of the happy for tuity of his own slavehood, and that of his fellow slaves, in a plantation setting that represented, for "his kind," the best of all possible worlds.[2] Although few planters held out much hope for the physical actualization of such a servant, those who verbalized their training strategies argued the advisability of organizing the plantation and training slaves as if the creation of such an ideal were possible.[3]

A primary operating principle of most plantations, especially after the Nat Turner revolt and as abolition fever rose in the North, was to keep its slaves as ignorant as possible about the world beyond the confines of the home plantation.[4] With regard to fieldhands in particular, many plantation authorities apparently believed that the more ignorant the black, the better the slave. The basic means of nurturing this ignorance was to close off any avenue of access to knowledge of the larger world. Most plantations were made as sufficient to the needs and desires of blacks (as understood by whites) as possible. Although a trusted and favored servant sometimes might be granted permission to go to town or to visit friends and relatives off the plantation, the typical fieldhand, especially in the later years before the Civil War, was rarely allowed to leave the plantation except for a specific purpose such as attending a supervised church service. Marriages within the home plantation were encouraged, if not required, and many slaveholders made an attempt to buy the spouses of their slaves. Kenneth Stampp, quoting from the *Southern Cultivator,* writes that planters did not like their men to marry off the plantation because they would be exposed " 'to temptations from meeting and associating with negroes . . . with various habits and views.' Women with husbands abroad brought to the home estate slaves accustomed to different treatment and thus created a rendezvous for a 'medley of characters.' It was better for a master to buy husbands or wives for his bondsmen when necessary. Otherwise, 'if they cannot be suited at home,' it should be a settled principle that 'they must live single.' "[5]

Musicians, exhorters, white ministers, and doctors were brought to the plantation rather than letting blacks travel off home grounds. Many of the larger plantation owners set up their own exchanges where blacks could sell or trade their eggs, chickens, garden produce, straw and wood artifacts, and fish and game without necessitating barter with anyone off the plantation.[6] Any form of intercourse with the free colored or poor white population was expressly forbidden. Olmsted reports that one Louisiana sugar planter bought up all the land of the poor whites because he felt that their presence "demoralized" his black population by making them wish to be free, making them feel superior to some whites, and giving them opportunity to secure "luxuries which he did not wish them to have. It was better that negroes never saw anyone off their own plantation; that they had no intercourse with other white men than their owner or overseer. . . ."[7] "Slaves," recalls Bill Sims, who had been a slave himself in Missouri, "were never allowed to talk with white people other than their masters or someone their masters knew, as they were afraid the white man might have the slave run away. The masters aimed to keep their slaves in ignorance. . . ."[8] Another former slave whose remembrances of slavery are recorded in the Fisk University study *Unwritten History of Slavery* says that as children he and his friends were not allowed "to even look at the po' white children."[9]

Secret or unsupervised meetings where blacks could exchange information, views of their slave condition, and knowledge of the larger world were outlawed. "A slave," writes Kenneth Stampp, "was not to preach, except to his master's own slaves on his master's premises in the presence of whites. A gathering of more than a few slaves (usually five) away from home, unattended by a white, was an 'unlawful assembly' regardless of its purpose or orderly decorum."[10]

Besides limiting the slaves' knowledge of the world by restricting their direct contact with it and their conversation with others who knew of it, most planters also attempted to cut off all access to the information that might be gained from books, pamphlets, and newspapers. The law in all slave states save Kentucky forbade anyone, even the master, to teach a slave how to read or write. A slave able to read or write not only could forge passes for himself and his friends but could read incendiary literature. Judge Lumpkin of the Supreme Court of Georgia, speaking in favor of his state's antiliteracy laws, said: "These severe restrictions . . . have my hearty and cordial approval. Everything must be interdicted which is calculated to render the slave discontent."[11] "Is there any great moral reason," asked the editors of the *Presbyterian Herald,* "why we should incur the tremendous risk of having our wives slaughtered in consequence of our slaves being taught to read incendiary publications?"[12] Speaking before the Virginia House of Delegates after that legislature had passed a bill prohibiting the "education" of blacks, one delegate declared: "We have as far as possible closed every avenue by which light may enter their minds. If we could extinguish the capacity to see the light, our work would be completed. . . ."[13]

The seriousness of the white purpose to keep slaves from independently learning of the outside world is revealed by the severity of the punishments facing black offenders. In most localities paid patrols of poor whites roamed the countryside with the legal authority to lay the biblically ordained thirty-nine stripes on the back of any slave caught off his home plantation without a pass. Slaves known to have the ability to read or write were sold or kept segregated from other slaves, as were blacks who had learned of the outside world through attempted escape.[14] Slaves who attempted to learn to read or write were severely whipped or threatened with the dismemberment of a finger or branding on the cheek as a sign to other blacks of the fate awaiting those who would learn forbidden skills and as a signal to whites to keep the marked slaves separated from other blacks.[15] Those who dared to teach others to read or write faced even greater penalties. Jamie Parker's grandfather, and fellow slave, Scipio, was put to death for attempting to teach Jamie to read and spell from the Bible.[16]

What to do with blacks who had successfully escaped and were later recaptured was occasionally an issue of debate among plantation authorities. Without fail such slaves were severely punished in front of a compulsory assemblage of other slaves. Some owners then preferred to sell them so that their knowledge of escape routes and their apparent "mania for freedom" could not contaminate the other blacks who were assumed to be content with their slave status. M. D. Conway, the son of a wealthy Virginia planter, reports that, at least in Virginia, "Every slave that tries to escape to a Free State was invariably sold if caught . . . and never suffered to return to the place from which he ran, lest he should tell others."[17] Ephraim Beanland, an overseer on the James Knox Polk plantation in Mississippi, believed that it was important to plantation discipline that all runaways be returned to the plantation in order to demonstrate to the others that successful escape was impossible and that unsuccessful escape would not result in a change of owner.[18]

Having taken all possible steps to seal off any means by which slaves could independently learn of the world beyond the plantation, plantation authorities drew for slaves a compensatory picture of the world as they wanted slaves to see and understand it. In their talks with their slaves the planters emphasized not only the impossibility of escape but also the wretchedness of black life elsewhere. "Slaveholders," observes Frederick Douglass, "sought to impress their slaves with a belief in the boundlessness of slave territory, and of their own limitless power."[19] Africa, if it was mentioned to slaves at all, was portrayed as a dark, uncivilized land of headhunters and cannibals where a small number of powerful princes enslaved the rest of the population who lived in a state of naked brutishness and ignorant immorality. On some plantations slaves were taught to thank God "for the institution of slavery which brought them from darkest Africa."[20]

The life of free blacks in the South was presented as one of hardship, insecurity, and poverty. Without the care of a rich and powerful white master, these deprived blacks were unable to provide for their own nourishment and medical care and were constantly exposed to the thievery and unrestrained harassment of the poor white population. To drive the point home, numerous stories were told slaves of "free coloreds" begging to be made slaves and to be taken under the protective wing of a sympathetic master.[21]

In the northern slave states whites taught blacks the horrors of the deep South, describing in vivid detail incessant labor in the rice swamps, the unbearably hot temperatures, incurable diseases, and constant hard usage by overseers unrestrained by absentee owners. James Williams, who was born on the Maryland plantation of William Hollingsworth in 1825, recalls being admonished when a child never to run away because if he did he would surely be caught and sent to Georgia, "where they will bore holes in your ears and plow you like a horse."[22] The deep South taught the horrors of the western slave states.

As the Civil War approached and it became apparent that the slave population had learned of the existence of free states and of Canada, masters warned their slaves of the extreme race prejudice of northern whites who did not "understand their darkies" and of the evils of falling into the hands of abolitionists or Canadians. The slaves on the Virginia plantation of M. D. Conway's father had their minds "systematically poisoned toward the North; they were told that the North would kill or sell them to foreign lands."[23] William and Ellen Craft, who labored as slaves in Georgia, report that they were taught to think of abolitionists as a "fearful kind of wild animal."[24] Lewis Clarke, a slave who escaped from a Kentucky plantation, attests to "horrid stories slaveholders tell about Canada. They assure the slave that, when they get hold of slaves in Canada, they make various uses of them. Sometimes they *skin* the *head,* and wear the wool on their coat collars—put them into the lead mines with both eyes out—the young slaves they eat—as for the Red Coats, they are sure death to the slave."[25]

After the beginning of the war, slaves were told of the evils that would befall them if they fell into the hands of Yankee troops. One of the more prevalent stories was that the northern side did not want any black people to remain in the United States and any blacks seized by the enemy would be transported to Cuba.[26] As a slave child in Arkansas Mittie Freeman was informed that Yankee soldiers had horns on their heads, and Andrew Boone, owned as a slave by a Protestant preacher in North Carolina, admits to having been "afraid of de Yankees cause de Rebels told us dat de Yankees would kill us. Dey told us dat de Yankees would bore holes in our shoulders and work us to carts. Dey told us we would be treated a lot worser den dey was treating us."[27]

In order to have slaves internalize a proper sense of their innate inferiority as Negroes and a concomitant belief in the natural superiority of whites, the planter class worked out a carefully constructed system of slavery laws, plantation rules, and social etiquette. Although these laws, rules, and points of etiquette differed from state to state and from plantation to plantation, they were fundamentally much alike throughout the ante-bellum South. Stampp concludes that at the heart of every state's slave code was "the requirement that slaves submit to their masters and respect all white men. The Louisiana code proclaimed this most lucidly: 'The condition of the slave being merely a passive one, his subordination to his master and to all who represent him is not susceptible of modification or restriction . . . he owes to his master, and to all his family a respect without bounds, and an absolute obedience, and he is consequently to execute all orders which he receives from him, his said master, or from them.' "[28]

Laws passed throughout the South made it illegal for a slave: to strike any white person except when in the act of protecting his master; to use abusive or insulting language; to be at large without a pass; to learn to read or write; to possess liquor without his master's consent; to trade without a permit; to gamble; to beat drums or blow horns; to possess guns; to own property; to testify against any white in court; to bring a legal suit; or, to be a party to any contract including that of marriage. No promise of freedom by a master to his slave was legally enforceable. Slaves could be traded or sold at the will of their master and could be punished with or without cause as long as said punishment was not calculated to produce permanent harm to life or limb. Though, in some ways, the law recognized the person of a slave, generally, "throughout the South the cold language of statutes and judicial decisions made it evident that, legally, the slave was less a person than a thing."[29] " 'Every distinction should be created,' wrote the memorialists to the South Carolina legislature, 'between the whites and the Negroes, calculated to make the latter feel the superiority of the former.' "[30]

Within the microcosm of the plantation itself, the training of the slave population frequently began at an early age. Mary Anderson, remembering her childhood days as a slave in North Carolina, recalls that "Marster didn't quarrel with anybody; Missus would not speak short to a slave, but both Marster and Missus taught slaves to be obedient in a nice quiet way. The slaves were taught to take their hats and bonnets off before going into the house, and to bow and say 'Good nornin' Marster Sam and Missus Evaline.' "[31] Jacob Stroyer recounts how as a child in South Carolina he and his companions were sent to the "sand-hill" in the summertime where they were taught how to greet and address their white owners. "The boys were required to bend the body forward with the head down and rest the body on the left foot, and scrape the right foot backwards on the ground while uttering the words, 'howdy Massa and Missie.' The girls were required to use the same words accompanied with a curtsy."[32] According to Lewis Paine, a white laborer who was jailed for aiding the escape of a slave, one of the first lessons given to slaves was "to obey everything that has a white skin. They are soon made to know that obedience is law and gospel."[33] Jermain Loguen, who grew up as a slave in Davison County, Tennessee, says that he "had been taught, in the severest school, that he was a thing for others' uses, and that he must bend his head, body and mind in conformity to that idea, in the presence of a superior race. . . ."[34]

In order to reinforce a sense of inferiority and dependence, many masters were careful to hand out the weekly rations personally and to distribute personally the yearly allotment of clothes, bedding, and other necessities." The *Southern Cultivator,* in an article on slave management, counseled slaveholders concerning the slave:

> You must provide for him yourself, and by that means create in him a habit of perfect dependence on you. Allow it once to be understood by a negro that he is to provide for himself, and you that moment give him an undeniable claim on you for a portion of his time to make this provision; and should you from necessity, or any other cause, encroach upon his time, disappointment and discontent are seriously felt.[35]

On most plantations, slaves were required to take the surname of their owner. On some plantations they were not allowed to name their children, who were instead given fanciful first names by some member of the white family. John Long, a white man whose father was a Maryland slaveholder, reports that "The males, like the dogs of their masters, are frequently called after the celebrated philosophers and generals of Greece and Rome. Almost every plantation has a Plato, Cato, Pompey and Caesar."[36] Occasionally, a favored slave family was allowed to name one of their children after the master and was given a present for doing so.[37]

Whatever his name, "every man slave is called boy til he is very old, then the more respectable slaveholders call him uncle. The women are all girls until they are aged, then they are called aunts."[38] Any other honorific titles were discouraged, as attested to by escaped slave William Grimes of Virginia, who was whipped for referring to a slave woman as "miss."[39] Commonly blacks were addressed by the less sophisticated whites as merely "nigger," "nigra," or "darkey." When referring to their slaves as a group, plantation whites invariably did so with the words "my people."

Deferential subservience on the part of the slave was rigidly enforced. On the Maryland plantation where Charles Ball spent part of his slave life the slaves "were always obliged to approach the door of the mansion, in the most humble and supplicating manner, with our hats in our hands, and the most subdued and beseeching language in our mouths. . . ."[40] Referring to his Louisiana master, Solomon Northup writes: "Ten years I was compelled to address him with downcast eyes and uncovered head—in the attitude and language of a slave."[41] "Whenever white folks had a baby born," remembers Harriet Robinson of her slave days in Texas, "den all de old niggers had to come through the room and the master would be over behind the bed and he'd say, 'here's a new little mistress or master you got to work for.' You had to say 'Yessir, Master,' and bow real low or the overseer would crack you."[42]

On most plantations slaves were not allowed to sing African songs, dance African dances, or speak African languages. The practice of conjuration was universally outlawed. The very word "African" was meant to invoke the image of ignorant savagery and the words "black" and "dark" (as in "darkey") carried connotations of evil, immorality, and ugliness. Blacks were taught that their skin was ugly, that their lips and noses were unaesthetic and malformed, and that they carried a natural smell that was offensive. Like sheep, negroes did not have hair but wool. "Mistress uster ask me," recalls a former slave, "what that was I had on my head and I would tell her, 'hair,' and she said, 'no that ain't hair, that's wool.' "[43] When they died slaves were buried in a separate graveyard set apart from the white burial grounds.

Although many whites, rich and poor alike, seemed to believe that physical labor was degrading, blacks were taught that to work as a slave was a privilege. They must, therefore, work with a happy contentment. Most planters felt, with a Virginia slaveholder, that slaves "must obey at all times, and under all circumstances, cheerfully and with alacrity. It greatly impairs the happiness of a negro, to be allowed to cultivate an insubordinate temper. Unconditional submission is the only footing upon which slavery should be placed."[44] Henry Banks, who was born a slave in 1835, remembers that he "was whipped once because the overseer said I looked mad: 'Come here, you d—d selfish son of a b—h, I'll please you by the time I've done with you.' Then he whipped me, so that I couldn't hollow."[45] Henry Watson, who was a slave in both Virginia and Mississippi, reports that "the slaveholder watches every move of the slave, and if he is downcast or sad,—in fact, if they are in any mood but laughing and singing, and manifesting symptoms of perfect content at heart,—they are said to have the devil in them. . . ."[46] Frederick Douglass, summing up many of the ways a slave could breach proper etiquette, writes:

> Does a slave look dissatisfied? It is said, he has the devil in him, and it must be whipped out. Does he speak loudly when spoken to by his master? Then he is getting high-minded, and should be taken down a button-hole lower. Does he forget to pull off his hat at the approach of a white person? Then he is wanting in reverence, and should be whipped for it. Does he venture to vindicate his conduct when censured for it? Then he is guilty of impudence,—one of the greatest crimes of which a slave can be guilty. Does he ever venture to suggest a different mode of doing things from that pointed out by his master? He is indeed presumptuous, and getting above himself; and nothing less than flogging will do for him.[47]

Besides the modes of proper etiquette, slaves were also taught a set of rules which they were expected to obey scrupulously, watched or not, and by which they were expected to regulate their free time. The following list of prohibitions, provided by a former slave of both South Carolina and Alabama, is similar to that drawn up on most ante-bellum plantations:

> Leaving home without a pass,
> Talking back—"sassing"—a white person,
> Hitting another Negro,
> Fussing, fighting, and rukkussing in the quarter,
> Lying,

Secular Training

Loitering on their work,
Taking things—the whites called it stealing.

Plantation rules forbade a slave to:
Own a firearm,
Leave home without a pass,
Sell or buy anything without his master's consent,
Marry without his master's consent,
Have a light on in his cabin after a certain hour at night,
Attend any secret meeting,
Harbor or in any manner assist a runaway slave,
Abuse a farm animal,
Mistreat a member of his family, and do
A great many other things.[48]

Little regard was paid by whites to the slave's privacy of home or person. The insides of quarter homes were shown to visitors without the consent of the inhabitants. A visit, announced or unannounced, to a quarter cabin by the master or a member of his family was expected to be received as an honor. Sudden, surprise searches for stolen food, weapons, or unapproved guests were made frequently. Some plantations even had a lookout tower from which the activities of the quarters could be observed.[49] Whether or not it was common practice on their plantation, whites made clear to their slaves that they, or their families, could be whipped, sold, or traded according to the will of their master. Like animals and other chattel property, slaves could be, and often were "bartered, deeded, devised, pledged, seized and auctioned . . . awarded as prizes in lotteries and raffles . . . wagered at gaming tables and horse races."[50]

Side by side with their attempt to have slaves internalize a belief in the benevolence and omnipotence of whites, slaveholders encouraged in their slaves a sense of loyalty to the master and his family even if this meant disloyalty to fellow slaves. Most masters attempted to stay informed about quarter happenings through the aid of loyal house servants and by rewarding those fieldhands willing to disclose the clandestine behavior of other quarter residents.[51] As one Fisk respondent recalls, the whites "taught us to be against one another. . . ."[52]

Planters also promoted a separating status hierarchy among

their slaves. Obedient fieldhands were taught they were better than the "bad nigger"—the malcontent or runaway. Drivers were taught they were better than common fieldhands; domestics, that they were better than any fieldhand; skilled tradesmen, that they were better than the average house servant. This hierarchy was reinforced by the granting of special material comforts to those higher on the scale. Most explicit was the status symbol of special clothes. A former Alabama driver reports that "It was the object of the overseer to separate me in feeling and interest as widely as possible from my suffering brethren and sisters. I had relations among the fieldhands, and used to call them my cousins. He forbid my doing so, and told me that if I acknowledged relationship with any of the hands I should be flogged for it."[53] The white Susan Eppes asserts that the hierarchy also included at the top those slaves who had been with a given master the longest and at the bottom those who had been bought most recently.[54]

On some plantations the master, at the summit of the hierarchy, promoted his dignity and prestige by never directly inflicting pain. In an article entitled "On the General Management of a Plantation," W. W. Hazard of Georgia wrote that he rarely whipped slaves himself, hoping to "remove from the mind of the servant who commits a fault, the unfavorable impression, too apt to be indulged in, that it is for the pleasure of punishing, rather than for the purpose of enforcing obedience and establishing good order that punishments are inflicted."[55] Rather it was the overseer or the black driver that were to be seen as the immediate oppressor. On many plantations, as on that in Mississippi where Henry Bibb spent part of his life as a slave, there was a black slave "whose business it was to watch and drive the slaves in the field, and do the orders of the overseer."[56] It was the driver's or overseer's role to punish, the master's to forgive.[57] By keeping aloof from the infliction of punishment the master was able, thus, to maintain his image as a benevolent, merciful father.[58]

Once tradition and practice had established any given plantation's pattern of operation, its rules, regulations, and social etiquette were enforced through a system of rewards as well as of punishments. Most plantation authorities intended blacks to feel that they stood to benefit if they were hardworking, cheerful, submissive, and obedient. On plantations where the task system prevailed, once fieldhands had successfully completed their assigned tasks they were frequently free to return to the quarters or, if they elected, to stay on in the fields and be paid for work completed beyond that assigned.[59] Often a Christmas dole was given to all the fieldhands to be split among them if the crop was abundant. On one Louisiana sugar plantation which Olmsted visited, the fieldhands were given one dollar for each hogshead of sugar produced during the preceding year.[60]

Sundays were universally days of rest. Occasionally, if a planter felt the slaves had shirked their work during the week, he required them to work Sunday as well.[61] Saturday afternoons off were offered frequently as an incentive to work hard during the week. Rest days during holidays celebrated by whites were not given as a matter of course but in return for work well done. Feasts, dances, cornshuckings, even funerals were to be seen as a direct result of the master's beneficence and his pride in their labors. Douglass perceives two motivations behind the awarding of these holidays:

> ... [K]eeping the minds of slaves occupied with prospective pleasure within the limits of slavery. ... Before the holidays there were pleasures in prospect; after the holidays they were pleasures of memory, and they served to keep out thoughts and wishes of a more dangerous character. These holidays were also used as conductors or safety-valves to carry off the explosive elements inseparable from the human mind when reduced to the condition of slavery. But for these the rigors of bondage would have become too severe for endurance, and the slave would have been forced to a dangerous desperation.[62]

On an individual basis slaves were given special favors—a piece of desired cloth, extra or special food, passes, the right to cultivate a garden, the right to use a knife or a hunting gun—not simply because they had done jobs assigned to them but because they had made a special effort to gain the trust of the white family and had demonstrated that the family's welfare was their first and greatest concern. Model servants, dressed in fine clothes and given privileges beyond those of the typical fieldhand, were held up as examples to the other slaves of what they too might become if they were assiduously faithful, obedient, and industrious. Some plantation owners, and indeed the slave codes themselves, even went so far as to let it be known that emancipation itself was not beyond the grasp of those slaves who demonstrated their unceasing loyalty and primary interest in the health, safety, and welfare of the white population.[63]

Just as the "carrot" was dangled as a reward for unquestioning and submissive obedience, so too was the "stick" ever ready to descend upon the backs of the sullen, the "uppity," and the disobedient. Most plantation owners tried to impress upon their black population not so much the severity of punishment awaiting deviance from expected slave behavior as its certainty. In the abstract, most planters seemed genuinely to prefer to induce obedience through habit-building, the furtherance of black self-interest, and the nurturing of a paternalistic relationship with their black "charges," than through punishment alone. At the same time, however, most slave owners agreed that all but the rarest slave was in need of occasional correction and that some needed to be dealt with quite severely.

> The mawkish sentimentalism that pronounces against all corporal punishment and deals in moral suasion only, must be deferred to the millennium. It does not suit the world as it is now, and human nature as it is. To resort to punishment as seldom as possible, and to administer it in such a manner as will best accomplish its purposes, individually and generally, is the master's duty. Correction and prevention are its legitimate goals.[64]

Many masters punished their slaves in the sincere belief that it was for their own moral good. Indeed, some masters went so far as to emphasize the righteousness behind their actions by requiring the culprit to express appreciation for his correction.[65]

Accordingly, the more enlightened planters were conscientious in insuring that the punishment followed directly upon a rule infraction and that it was not meted out in anger. Many slaveholders believed with Dr. J. C. Young, a Presbyterian minister of Kentucky, that "admonitions, rebukes, and personal chastisement produce a much better effect, both on children and servants, when inflicted with calmness."[66] Even the most ardent Southerners did not deny, however, that extreme physical abuse, and even torture, did sometimes occur. Both were probably more prevalent than the planter class realized; they set the policies but rarely carried out the punishments. Besides whipping, punishments mentioned most frequently in the slave narratives include being imprisoned in the stocks or "nigger box," fettered in irons and chains, hung from the feet or fingers, and having a cat "hauled" down the back. Pregnant women were beaten while made to lie over a hole in the ground.

Although it would be a mistake to suppose that very many planters employed the cruel and often sexually sadistic tortures used by some, most masters agreed on the necessity of making a frightening example of slaves who were thought by whites to have committed serious crimes.[67] Esther Easter, who was a slave in Tennessee, recalls having seen "one whipping and that enough. They wasn't no fooling about it. A runaway slave from the Henkin's plantation was brought back, and there was a public whipping, so's the slaves could see what happens when they tries to get away. The runaway was chained to the whipping post, and I was full of misery when I see the lash cutting deep into that boy's skin. He swell up like a dead horse, but he gets over it, only he was never no 'count for work no more."[68] Blacks suspected of rape, arson, murder, or insurrection faced even harsher punishments. These included: branding, having an ear, tongue, or finger cut off, being castrated, skinned, or burned alive. Or they could be staked to the ground and left for the crows and buzzards to eat.

Warning of punishment for serious crimes was often followed by the example made of a refractory slave in order to dissuade others from following his independent example. As the white son of one planter writes: "So far from a man's interest in his slave property being a guarantee against the laceration of that slave, such laceration may be, and frequently is, the only means of retaining him as property. 'Breaking their spirit' is a phrase as frequently used with regard to slaves as horses. Sometimes a slave must be killed, that the mastery of a hundred others may be secured. No large body of slaves could be held securely unless it was understood that there would be no hestitation in shooting any who should rebel."[69] And, as Eugene Genovese has so aptly observed:

> Sooner or later the masters fell back on the whip. If a master lacked the will to use it, he would have to sell his "incorrigibles," in which case someone else had to use it. "Were fidelity the only security we enjoyed," wrote a planter in the *Southern Patriot,* "deplorable indeed would be our situation. The fear of punishment is the principle to which we must and do appeal, to keep them in awe and order." On a well-run plantation the whip did not crack often or excessively; the threat of its use, in combination with other incentives and threats, preserved order. The whip, *Affleck's Cotton Plantation Record and Account Book* instructed overseers, ought to be used sparingly but cannot be dispensed with. From colonial times to the end of the regime intelligent masters tried to reduce their dependency on the whip but admitted they could not do without it.[70]

Thus, whatever their personal, private attitudes toward punishment, most slaveholders saw physical chastisement as one of several instruments with which they could maximize their efforts to have the slave learn "that his master is to govern absolutely, and he is to obey implicitly. That he is never for a moment to exercise his will or judgment in opposition to a positive order."[71] Indeed, many planters saw clearly that the need to punish frequently reflected poorly upon their ability as plantation managers and educators of their slaves. For, as one slave owner counseled his colleagues in a letter to the editor of *The Farmer's Register,* "The character of the negro is . . . like the plastic clay which may be molded into agreeable or disagreeable figures according to the skill of the molder."[72]

3

Religious Instruction

Hence is the Negro come, by God's command,
For wiser teaching to a foreign land;
If they who brought him were by Mammon driven,
Still have they served, blind instruments of Heaven;
And though the way be rough, the agent stern,
No better mode can human wits discern,
No happier system wealth or virtue find,
To tame and elevate the Negro mind:
Thus mortal purposes, whate'er their mood,
Are only means with Heaven for working good;
And wisest they who labor to fulfill,
With zeal and hope, the all-directing will,
And in each change that marks the fleeting year,
Submissive see God's guiding hand appear.

> William J. Grayson,
> from a poem en-
> titled "The Hireling
> and the Slave"

Slaves, be obedient to those who are your earthly masters, with fear and trembling, in singleness of heart, as to Christ.

Ephesians 6:5

The arguments for religious training were persuasive and usually fell into one of three categories: those which appealed to the planter's pocketbook; those which appealed to his sense of Christian responsibility; and those which assuaged his fear of slave rebellion. Those arguments which were profit-related were based upon the idea that religious training had the effect of making slaves more content, more hardworking, more obedient, and more submissive than they would be without such instruction. "You will find," wrote Thomas Affleck in his *Cotton Plantation Record and Account Book,* "that an hour devoted every Sabboth morning to their moral and religious instruction would prove a great aid to you in bringing about a better state of things amongst the Negroes. It has been thoroughly tried, and with the most satisfactory results, in many parts of the South. As a matter of mere interest it has proved to be advisable, to say nothing of it as a point of duty."[1] A meticulous student of the plantation records, Ulrich Phillips concludes that: "From all quarters the expression was common that the promotion of religion among the slaves was not only the duty of masters but was to their interest as well in that it elevated the morale of the workmen and improved the quality of the service they rendered."[2]

The utility of this argument, though most often promulgated by agricultural journals and essays on plantation management, was not lost upon Southern churchmen. In their eagerness to gain a foothold upon the plantation, churchmen were quick to point out that "other things being equal, the plantation which enjoys religious instruction will do better for the interest of its owner than it did before it enjoyed such instruction."[3] Not only were religious slaves guaranteed to be harder working, but lying, stealing, and running off were argued to be virtually unknown among slaves made dutifully reverent by the proper religious instruction.

Those arguments which appealed to the planter's sense of moral duty drew their strength from the recognition that blacks, however biologically and culturally inferior, were members of the human race possessing souls in need of eternal salvation. Because blacks on the plantation were thought to have no means of seeking or providing for their own religious instruction, it was doubly incumbent upon all Christian masters to take upon themselves the biblical responsibility of spreading the Gospel to their servants and thus providing them with the possible eternal salvation of their souls. Roman Catholic slaveholders were all but ordered to instruct their black population:

44

Religious Instruction

... [M]asters must provide for the salvation of the slaves, whose conduct deprives them of the opportunity of seeking help to salvation. These helps the master must supply, seeing to it that the slaves are instructed in the rudiments of religion and have the services of priests for the reception of the sacraments. Furthermore ... masters sin gravely if they are so intent on their own gains that they neglect to instruct the slaves, or do not provide them with the opportunity of receiving the sacraments, or fail to safeguard their morals.[4]

Besides its intrinsic moral righteousness, religious instruction was recognized by most of its advocates as having potential political benefits. "The most formidable weapon in the hands of the abolitionist," wrote the editor of the *Presbyterian Herald* in 1846, "is the indifference which he charges to the Christian slaveholder toward the spiritual welfare of the slave under his control. Disarm him of this weapon and you have done much to render him powerless."[5] Most churchmen, and an increasing number of politicians, began to share the belief of a noted South Carolina divine that the good work of Christianizing should go on until every slave knew Jesus. "Then they might turn back that tide of indignation which the public opinion of the world then had."[6]

The third set of arguments were given special emphasis in the years following the Nat Turner rebellion in 1831. Many planters feared that it was religion that had sparked the revolt, since Nat Turner was a black preacher. Many openly wondered if religious instruction might be better banned altogether. To this worry, advocates of religious instruction countered that Turner "was not himself a member of any Christian church; nor had he any followers who received sound and systematic religious instruction; or was connected with any church having a white man for a pastor or teacher."[7] Furthermore, plantation authorities were cautioned not to leave their slaves free to come to their own religious beliefs and potentially dangerous conclusions. "All men," it was philosophically argued, "will have some notions of religion, and if they will not be correct notions they will be erroneous, wild, fanatical, superstitious, or in some way highly dangerous."[8] The only way to prevent improper teaching from reaching black ears or sinful notions from occurring to black minds was for the planters themselves to tend to the religious training of their slaves. Only by being in direct personal control of the organization, curriculum, and proceedings of supervised church services and Sabbath schools could the planter be sure who the teachers of blacks were and *"what* and *when* and *where* they were taught."[9] "Intelligent masters," concluded the Alabama Baptist Association at its annual meeting in 1850, "with the light of experience before them will regard the communication of sound religious instruction as the truest economy and the most efficient police and as tending to the greatest utility, with regard to every interest involved."[10]

Not all slaveholders were convinced by these arguments. In colonial times and at the beginning of the nineteenth century when the South, at least among its speculative thinkers, was still somewhat divided on the question of eventual abolition, many planters feared that the conversion and baptism of their black servants might be used as an argument for slave emancipation.[11] Even after the courts had clearly put an end to such fears, some owners continued their practice of doing nothing to provide for the religious instruction of their slaves. Some whites avowed that blacks were not members of the human race and had no souls in need of salvation. Jenny Proctor, who was a slave in Alabama, recalls that there was no church for the slaves on her plantation and that they were told to "obey your master and mistress, 'cause what you git from them here in this world am all you ever going to git, 'cause you just like hogs and the other animals—when you dies you ain't no more, after you been throwed in that hole."[12] Henry Box Brown, who was born in Louisa County, Virginia in 1816, remembers one slaveholder who forbade his slaves religious instruction, informing them that "negroes have nothing to do with God."[13]

Other slaveowners believed that the practice of religion would take the minds of their slaves off their work and that if slaves got religion they would insist on "singing and dancing in their cabins, til dawn of day, and utterly unfit themselves for work."[14]

Religious Instruction

Still others "objected that they saw little use in training their slaves religiously since it was expensive to hire teachers, introduced men and principles that were liable to cause trouble, took up too much of the slaves' time, and at last, did little or no good, since the Negroes would be hypocrites or worse after conversion, and further that baptism really meant "little more than the difference between a Negro wet and a Negro dry.""[15]

Perhaps the most common argument against religious instruction was that it tended to make blacks insubordinate by implying that they were as worthy as whites in the eyes of God.[16] Andrew Moss, who worked as a young slave on the large Georgia plantation of George Hopper, relates that if a master saw one of his slaves on his knees, "He say, 'What you prayin' about?' And you say, 'Oh, Marster, I'se prayin' to Jesus 'cause I wants to go to Heaven when I dies.' And Marster says, 'You's my Negro. I get you to Heaven. Get up offen your knees.' De white folks what owned slaves thought that when dey go to Heaven de colored folks would be dere to wait on 'em."[17]

All planters were well aware of the potentially disquieting effect a full knowledge of the tenets of Christianity might have upon slaves. For this reason, some slaveholders preferred no religious instruction at all to the risk of slaves' learning "more than was good for them."

Despite exceptions, however, most students of the history of plantation slavery in the American South are agreed that in the period 1831–1865, the majority of the South's big plantation owners were of one mind concerning the efficacy of ensuring the religious instruction of their slaves.[18] "The great majority of planters were actively interested in the religious life of their slaves and provided chapels for them. On Sunday, strictly observed as a holiday on most plantations, the slave children were usually taught by some member of the owner's family; church members might worship at a neighboring church, but more often services were held on the plantation."[19] Indeed, most historians who have studied the question of religious training on the plantation report confidently that the zeal for such instruction increased continually right up to the time of the Civil War.

Deep Like the Rivers

Faithfulness, obedience, and integrity would become rules of living for the negro, and so would substitute moral obligation for fear in his relationship to his master. To teach the practical points of morality—as honesty, sobriety, chastity and industry—would not only improve the slave, but would tremendously enhance his economic value. . . . Hence the indifference or hostility of the earlier period gave way to the willing, and ever increasing activity of the master to secure religious instruction for his negroes.[20]

Once a planter had become convinced of the utility and/or moral rightness of providing his slaves with some form of religious instruction, he had to decide exactly what he wanted his servants to learn about God and the teachings of Jesus. Most plantation heads reached the two-pronged conclusion that blacks should be taught enough to ensure their heavenly salvation while at the same time increasing the fruits of their labor on earth. "As one prominent leader of the movement explained, 'human happiness does not so much depend upon the cultivation of the intellect as on the improvement of the disposition and the heart.' When the slave was informed on points essential to his salvation the whole duty of the instructor was complete."[21] Although individual nuances were added by each planter in his effort to improve both his slaves' dispositions and their chances for salvation, the fundamentals of the religious curriculum were the same from plantation to plantation.

The first task of the religious instructor was to impress upon his black pupils the supreme power and authority of the God of Christianity. God was the supreme master of mankind and obedience to His will, as interpreted from carefully selected passages of the Bible, was pronounced to be the only path to eternal salvation. The fiery torments of an everlasting hell were vividly contrasted with the eternal peace and blessedness of heaven. Bethany Veney remembers the very images used by her mistress, who impressed upon her as a child that *"some time* all this world that we saw would be burned up—that the moon would be turned to blood, the stars would fall out of the sky, and everything would melt away with a great heat, and that everybody, *every little child* that had told a lie, would be cast into a lake of fire and brimstone, and would burn for ever and ever, and what was more, though they should burn for ever and ever, they would never be burned up."[22] "The great end to which religion is there made to minister," writes Henry Box Brown of his experience in the slave South, "is to keep the slaves in a docile and submissive frame of mind, by instilling into them the idea that if they do not obey their masters, they will infallibly go to hell. . . ."[23]

Few slaveholders, however, permitted the benefits of obedience to God's holy will to be regulated solely to the hereafter. Most held out to their slaves the promise of earthly happiness— a happiness won only by the obedient Christian, secure in the knowledge of God's love and his own eventual salvation. He who goes against God's will "merely appears to be happy. In reality he struts and swaggers through life on a hellbound road, and: 'Before long he'll be weeping, and wailing, and gnashing his teeth, because God is angry with him forever . . .' that is, if he makes it through his ill-fated life without falling victim (as is usually the case with sinners) to sickness and infirmity of the mind and body."[24]

Once the omnipotence of God and the fateful importance of obeying His will had been imparted, the next task of plantation religious instruction was to teach slaves what God intended for them as black persons under slavery. Slaves were taught that it was God's design, as decreed by the Holy Scriptures, that they, as the sons and daughters of Ham, be the servants of whites into eternity. The life of a hewer of wood and a carrier of water was not to be thought of as a curse, however. Rather it was to be recognized as blessing in disguise; God's means of providing a road to salvation for the pagan African. Lunsford Lane recalls how as a child in Virginia he and the other slaves were "often told by the minister how good God was in bringing us over to this country from dark and benighted Africa, and permitting us to listen to the sound of the gospel."[25] Another former slave who lived on a large plantation in Queen Anne's County, Maryland, asserts slaves were informed by their religious instructors that:

> . . . [W]hen we were in our native country, Africa, we were destitute of Bible light, worshipping idols of sticks and stone, and bar-

barously murdering one another. God put it into the hearts of these good slaveholders to venture across the bosom of the hazardous Atlantic to Africa, and snatch us poor negroes as brands from the eternal burning, and bring us where we might sit under the droppings of his sanctuary, and learn the ways of industry and the way to God. "Oh, nigger! How happy are your eyes which see this heavenly light; many millions of niggers desired it long, but died without the sight!"[26]

Not only had God thus ordained slavery, but in so doing He had likewise sanctioned the relationship between master and slave. Just as blacks were placed on earth to fulfill their role as slaves, certain whites were placed on earth to fulfill their obligations as God's earthly lieutenants. Thus it was the master's duty to feed, clothe, protect, and instruct his slaves and the slave's duty to serve, honor, and obey his master as he would God Himself. James Roberts, who experienced slavery in Maryland and Louisiana, asserts that a master's sermon usually contained words such as the following: "O, how you should love the precious truths of the Lord, my servants; they are so wise and so adapted to your condition. For, by obeying your master you obey God."[27] "The first commandment impressed upon our minds was to obey our masters," recalls Lane, "and the second was like unto it, namely, to do as much work when they or the overseers were not watching us as when they were."[28]

Since slavery was presented as a condition of God's grace, then obedience must be accompanied by a "cheerful alacrity." As the Right Reverend William Meade, Episcopal bishop of Virginia, admonished in a sermon:

> Take care that you do not fret, or murmur, or grumble at your condition, for this will not only make your life uneasy, but it will greatly offend Almighty God. Consider that it is not yourselves; it is not the people that you belong to; it is not the men that have brought you to it; but it is the will of God, who hath by his wise providence made you servants, because, no doubt, he knew that condition would be best for you in this world and help you better towards heaven, if you do your duty in it; so that any discontent at your not being free, or rich, or great as some others, is quarreling with your Heavenly Master, and finding fault with God himself.[29]

Even punishment was to be borne cheerfully; for when deserved, it was a proper form of correction sanctioned by God's own word: "He that knoweth his master's will, and doeth it not shall be beaten with many stripes." In those rare cases where punishment was undeservedly meted out, "there is this great comfort in it, that if you bear it patiently and leave your cause in the hands of God, he will reward you for it in heaven; and this punishment you suffer unjustly here, shall turn to your exceeding great glory hereafter."[30]

Though obedience and cheerful submission were stressed as the most important commandments, whites also taught blacks a host of others, among them, the sinfulness of stealing, lying, vandalism, harming whites, and suicide. Peter Randolph recalls that the favorite white sermon on the Edloe plantation in Virginia could be summarized in the words: "Servants, obey your masters. Do not *steal* or *lie,* for this is very wrong. Such conduct is sinning against the Holy Ghost, *and is base ingratitude to your kind masters who feed, clothe, and protect you.*"[31] Lucretia Alexander, who lived as a slave in both Mississippi and Arkansas, remembers that when the white preacher came to the quarters, "He'd just say, 'Serve your masters. Don't steal your master's turkey. Don't steal your master's chickens. Don't steal your master's hogs. Don't steal your master's meat. Do whatsomeever your master tells you to do.' Same old thing all de time."[32]

Suicide was pictured as a particularly monstrous sin. Those who committed such a crime were "always branded in reputation after death, as the worst of criminals; and their bodies are not allowed the small portion of Christian rites which are awarded the corpses of other slaves."[33]

Regular plantation rules were frequently imbued with religious sanctions. Emma Tidwell, who was a twenty-two-year-old fieldhand when the Civil War began, recounts that when she and her fellow slaves were preached to, the commandments became: "Mind yo mistress . . . Don't steal der potatoes; don't lie bout nothin' an don't talk back tuh yo boss; ifn yo does yo'll be tied tuh a tree and stripped neckid. When dey tell yuh tuh do somethin run an do hit."[34] John Blassingame offers this list of what he calls the "slave beatitudes": "Blessed are the patient, blessed are the faithful, blessed are the cheerful, blessed are the submissive, blessed are the hardworking, and above all, blessed are the obedient."[35]

Most planters agreed in theory that the best system of religious instruction "was one in which the master himself assumed the responsibility for the religious life of his slaves. Gathering his 'people' around him on the Sabbath he preached to them from one of the handbooks or read to them from Scriptures."[36] Often it was the planter's wife who took the primary responsibility for organizing the religious instruction of the plantation's slave population. When Israel Campbell's master's new wife arrived at the Kentucky plantation, "She established family prayer, and at night all the slaves were called upon to participate in the devotion—master reading the Bible and Miss Sally singing a hymn and praying."[37] The Rev. T. D. Ozanne asserts that on many southern plantations "The ladies of the family visit, every Sunday evening, in the 'quarter,' the aged and infirm who may not be able to attend church; they read and explain to them several chapters in the Bible, and teach the little ones who are gathered around the old people."[38]

In practice, however, few planters were as personally and intimately involved in the religious instruction of their quarter slaves as those portrayed by Campbell and Ozanne. Although many did pray with and instruct their house servants, most planters, especially those on the larger plantations, were content to leave the religious instruction of their fieldhands in the care of a paid missionary of the Southern Church. Though this instruction had to be requested by the planter and was often observed by him, it was the preacher/missionary who created the curriculum, did the actual preaching and instructing, organized prayer meetings and pastoral visits, and was generally responsible for the content and method of the religious instruction that reached most blacks in the quarters.

Because of the delicate politics of their teaching position, a position they attained and remained in solely at the pleasure of the planter, only missionaries who empathized with the South's general view of slavery and had been carefully trained by the Southern Church were sent to the plantations by church authorities. Susan Fickling points out that "As religious instruction was entirely separated from civil status, it was necessary to select as missionaries only men tried and true, for the slightest indiscretion would have been fatal to the whole movement."[39] Jones counseled his fellow churchmen that "missionaries should be *Southern men,* or men no matter from what country, yet *identified* in views, feelings and interests with the South, and who possess the *confidence of society.*"[40] Such men were considered to have a better understanding of the conditions, relations, and necessities of plantation life and therefore better qualified to preach the gospel to southern slaves.

Once sanctioned by the Southern Church, and invited by a planter or group of planters, most missionaries attempted to perform a wide gamut of religious functions: preaching on Sundays at both the white and black services, holding weekday prayer meetings or lectures, setting up and teaching Sabbath schools, visiting the sick, attending funerals, performing marriage services and baptisms, and presiding over the moral discipline of his flock. Often a given missionary served a group of smaller plantations, traveling between them and sometimes conducting joint services.

In carrying out their duties, most missionaries were careful to have nothing to do with the civil condition of the slaves they instructed. Their calling was strictly a spiritual one—to illuminate the gospel and the road to salvation, not to comment upon social relationships or politics. Once within the plantation itself, a churchman was instructed to "avoid making himself the repository of tales and difficulties between individuals and on plantations, and hear no tales at all respecting owners and matters which belong to their civil condition."[41] "There is hardly a word in Bumpus's private journal," writes Genovese, "or in Cornish's diary, or in the private papers even of the most dedicated ministers, about the worldly hopes, fears, sorrows, aspirations, and travail of those slaves whom they felt it a duty to attend. They dared not concern themselves."[42]

The actual instruction methods devised and employed by these missionaries and other white teachers consisted mainly of oral instruction and repetition. "By this method the instructed was called upon to repeat verbally by rote certain sentences or passages given by the instructor. It was the catechistical method of old, common to the Christian Church except that the slave usually must not or could not do any reading from the catechism in the role of instructor."[43] Jones advises that two plans were to be used in giving oral lessons: "First, the teacher asking the question, and stating the answer and then requiring the *whole* school, or his whole class to answer *together*. Second, the teacher requiring the scholars in his class, or school to answer the questions, *one by one,* one after another, until it is apparent the whole know it. Let *both plans* be united."[44]

Of course the content of the catechistical books, of the scriptural passages selected for reading, and of all extemporaneous instruction was carefully selected. The master class understood that only a carefully censored version of the Bible and Christianity could have the desired effect of making slaves faithful, obedient, and content. "As long as the slaves communed with whites, their religious instruction was circumscribed. The planters, in spite of their piety, insisted that slaves not learn any of the potentially subversive tenets of Christianity (the brotherhood of all men, for instance). Consequently, no white minister could give a full exposition of the gospel to the slaves without incurring the wrath of the planters."[45]

If mentioned at all, the figure of Jesus was spoken of only in a special context. Slaves were taught of a meek and submissive Jesus who had urged his followers to become like little children in order to enter the kingdom of heaven. They were taught to imitate Jesus and to bear their burdens and obey God's will without question just as he had done.[46] Sermons frequently left out any mention of Jesus for, as with religious instruction generally, the figure of Jesus confronted white instructors with the strategic question of determining what truths could be safely imparted to blacks and which would be better withheld.[47] As Kemble points out, all religious teachers were forced to differentiate between how much blacks "may learn to become better slaves and how much they may not learn, lest they cease to be slaves at all."[48]

Most missionaries attempted to couch their sermons in the

simplest of terms, making frequent reference to the actual experiences of black life under slavery. A white preacher was advised to study "the character of the Negroes ... their habits of thought, superstitions and manners ... so that he might adapt his preaching to them."[49] For most preachers this meant speaking to their black parishioners as if they were children while not oppressing them with knowledge of their ignorance. Since heavy theological exegesis was met with snores and a decrease in attendance the following Sunday, simple stories, parables, and stern but short injunctions were the principal fare of white sermons to blacks. Even the songs to be taught slaves were to be primarily those "of the infant school and Sunday school hymns, written expressly for children. . . ."[50]

> In order to preserve and nurture the "good" qualities of the "Negro," it was deemed necessary both by theologian and aristocrat to make certain allowances for the childlike demeanor of this creature. No doubt Southern churchmen managed to convince themselves that they were actually bringing genuine salvation to the heathen Blacks. But after all, they were by nature children; and so, of course, they received salvation at the hands of their mentors *as children*.[51]

Although most ministers sought to instruct their slave congregations in terms they thought easily understood by blacks, few thought it beneficial to employ "negroisms" in their addresses and conversations. "His *language* should be as pure Saxon as he can make it: and not accommodated in any degree whatever to their *broken English,* if he would escape contempt."[52] Furthermore, the most rigid decorum was to be maintained inside the church or during worship services or Sabbath school classes. "The *strictest* order should be preserved at all the religious meetings of the Negroes, especially those held on the Sabbath day, and punctuality observed in commencing them at the appointed hour. No *audible* expression of feeling in the way of groaning, cries, or noises of any kind, should be allowed."[53] Most missionaries believed it beneficial to allow a carefully trained black preacher or "watchman" to occasionally address the slave congregation. This black preacher, whose character and life history were always thoroughly examined before he was licensed to preach under the supervision of the white minister, "became, more often than not, something of a repository of 'Negro' virtue. He was displayed by his master, and held up as the model to which the young, especially were supposed to aspire. This was what-a-'Negro'-could-be-if-he-worked-hard nineteenth century style."[54] Besides acting as symbol, showpiece, and mouthpiece for the white instructor, the other duties expected of the black preacher, and other elders of "approved discretion and piety," were to "watch over" the activities of those of their own color and "report on their general conduct from time to time."[55]

Despite what may appear with historical hindsight to be calculated self-interest, the planters and missionaries should not be thought of as outright or self-conscious hypocrites. A reading of their diaries and letters leaves the firm impression that few plantation authorities were being devious when they taught slaves that God had ordained slavery. Rather they were only teaching blacks what they themselves believed. Most slaveholders were convinced that God quite clearly sanctioned slavery in the Bible.[56] And, because they did not believe in a "progressive God" who "changes his mind, as the politicians do about the availability of their candidates," they felt certain that slavery continued to be morally justified.[57] Indeed, few whites who had grown up on a slave plantation even thought to question the morality of slavery. "It must be remembered," wrote Harriet Martineau, "that the greater number of slaveholders have no other idea than of holding slaves."[58] Like Victoria Clayton and her husband, they:

> . . .[N]ever raised the question for one moment as to whether slavery was right. We had inherited the institution from devout parents. Slaves were held by pious relatives and friends and clergymen to whom we were accustomed to look up. The system of slaveholding was incorporated into our laws, and was regulated and protected by them. We read our Bible and accepted its teachings as the true guide in faith and morals. We understood literally our Lord's instruction to His chosen people, and applied them to our circumstances and surroundings.[59]

Religious Instruction

Nor were most planters conscious of any hypocrisy when they taught that slavery was a blessing for blacks. Most plantation whites sincerely believed that not only was slavery the means by which blacks were offered the possibility of salvation and moral refinement but that under its protective wing they were better off than "nine out of ten of the poor in every kingdom of Europe."[60] "The plain truth," believed R. Q. Mallard and the other members of the planter class, "is just this, that *no tillers of the soil, in ancient or modern times, received such ample compensation for their labors*. He was not paid down, it is true, in cash, but he was amply compensated for his toil in free quarters, free medical attention, free food, free firewood, free support of sick, infirm and young. . . ."[61]

Not only did slavery provide for the slave's physical wants and needs, but in return for "obedience, fidelity and industry," he was insured of "*peace, plenty, security,* and the indulgence of his social propensities—freed from all care for the present, or anxiety for the future with regard to himself or his family."[62] Like James C. Coggesball, a rich planter from Tennessee, most slaveholders believed that "slavery is a blessing to the slave in the largest extent, produced by the wisdom of God, and retained as such by his overruling providence, and that the Christian slaveholder is the true friend of the black man."[63]

Slavery was to many slaveholders a profoundly paternalistic institution involving reciprocal obligations and responsibilities. "The master, as the head of the system, has a right to the obedience and labor of the slave, but the slave has also his mutual rights in the master; the right of protection, the right of counsel and guidance, the right of subsistence, the right of care and attention in sickness and old age."[64]

> Our lot is not more implicated in theirs, than their lot in ours; in our mutual relations we survive or perish together. The worst foes of the black race are those who have intermeddled in their behalf. We know better than others that every attribute of their character fits them for dependence and servitude. By nature the most affectionate and loyal of all races beneath the sun, they are also the most helpless: and no calamity can befall them greater than the loss of that protection they enjoy under this patriarchial

system. . . . My servant, whether born in my house or bought with my money, stands to me in the relation of a child.[65]

Finally, slaveholders and other plantation whites felt they were only fulfilling their religious obligation in modifying religious instruction so that it would be "appropriate" for slaves. Most whites sincerely believed that they taught blacks all that they were capable of understanding—all that, as overgrown children, it was right for them to hear. Like Bishop Elliott of Georgia, they righteously felt that in providing instruction for their slaves they were "educating these people as they are educated nowhere else; that we are elevating them in every generation; that we are working but God's purposes, whose consummation we are quite willing to leave in his hands."[66]

To the planter and his missionary associate it seemed but moral common sense to believe that the black who had most nearly internalized values, attitudes, and feelings taught by white religious teachers became, through that education, not only the most perfect of slaves but the most perfect in the eyes of God. Few Southern whites could conceive of any but the most smiling, submissive slave partaking, with them, of the joys of heaven.

PART II

BLACK LEARNING:
THE CULTURAL THEMES
OF THE QUARTER COMMUNITY

Deep river, my home is over Jordan,
Deep river, Lord; I want to cross over into camp ground.

O, don't you want to go to that gospel feast,
That promised land where all is peace?

Deep river, my home is over Jordan,
Deep river, Lord; I want to cross over into camp ground.

Slave Spiritual

Introduction

The culture of black people under slavery in America can be likened to a deep river. Having as its source a great African well-spring, this ever moving ever changing river had by the 1850's a distinctly American appearance. As it flowed and deepened through its new land it both adapted to the contours of the American landscape and reshaped each bank it touched. It never lost its African undercurrents. For its people it was a healing river. Its waters refreshed them and helped them escape the torturous American environment. To the oppressed slave his culture was like a deep river; to immerse oneself in its waters was to commune with one's own cultural identity.

The following chapters deal with the deep river of slave culture and its nine strongest currents. Part I portrayed what, and how, whites taught their slaves. This part explores what it was that blacks under slavery actually learned. How did slaves understand and make sense of the world and their relationship to it? What were their most basic attitudes, values, feelings? In order to answer these questions Morris Opler's theory of themes in culture is applied to the slave data in steps similar to those which Opler describes he took in applying his theory to the Lipan Apaches of the American Southwest.*

The themes presented here are not given in any necessary order of importance. The expressions of some of them could be viewed equally well as expressions of others and, in fact, an occasional action or thought is viewed as an outgrowth of more than one theme. Though each theme is pictured as distinct and separable from each other theme, in reality they are incomplete without each other. For this reason, the individual themes depicted in the following pages should be seen as different parts of

* For a discussion of Opler's theory and how it is used in the present study, see the Appendix.

a larger whole; as nine strong currents in a deep river which interact with each other, expand upon and limit each other, blend and flow together, and, without each other, are neither complete nor fully understandable.

✦ 4 ✦

Theme 1: Communality: The Group Spirit, Identification, and Solidarity of the Quarter Community

We were social and affectionate and the ties of kindred were strong within us.

Isaac Williams

The tendency of quarter people to view themselves as a familial group, with a common life-style, common interests and problems, and a common need to stick together is a theme which appears frequently in the black source material. Whatever their personal jealousies and animosities, as a group the members of the quarter community identified each other as a distinct body of persons tied together by a common historical experience, by a common philosophical and behavioral approach to their world, and by their common struggle against the pressures and demands of slavery.

Perhaps the principal expression of the theme of communality was the quarter community's unwritten behavioral injunction never to betray the confidence of a fellow black or to expose the secrets of the quarter community. Blacks who betray their fellows are treated with almost universal scorn in the narratives, and those of the informants who admit to an occasional act contrary to the solidarity norm evince feelings of shame and guilt at their acts.

Whereas most white property was considered fair game, stealing from other slaves was considered to be a serious wrong. Lewis Clarke writes that a slave who stole from another slave was called "mean as master. This is the lowest comparison slaves knew how to use: 'just as mean as white folks.' "[1] John Brown states that he and his friends saw no wrong in cheating, lying, and stealing "so long as we were not acting against one another. I am sure that, as a rule, any one of us who would have thought nothing of stealing a hog, or a sack of corn, from our master, would have allowed himself to be cut to pieces rather than betray the confidence of his fellow-slave. . . ."[2]

Physical abuse of one quarter member by another was also seen as reprehensible. The narratives are full of blacks who when ordered to whip another slave refuse to do so or maneuver so that both executioner and accused can avoid punishment.[3] Other informants express great guilt at being part to the unjust punishment of another slave. Rarely would quarter members fight with each other in the presence of whites. When disputes had to be settled with fists it was most often done out of the sight of whites.[4] On the other hand, a slave who unfairly abused another black was ostracized by the community and found no succor when he himself met hard times.[5]

The thought of assisting the capture or sale of other slaves was abhorrent to most members of the quarter community. Campbell reports that nothing could cajole him to "consent to help to sell my fellow-mortals where I cannot follow.[6] Several narratives recount episodes in which an entire quarter community went to great lengths to aid and abet the flight of a fellow slave.[7] Commenting in general on the slaves' tendency to help each other, if possible, Susan Davis Rhodes, who lived as a slave in North Carolina, says: "People in my day didn't know book learning but dey studied how to protect each other, and save 'em from such misery as they could."[8]

The point here is not that quarter members never betrayed each other, or stole from each other, or even killed each other, but rather that most members understood that it was to their mutual advantage to protect each other and that such solidarity was a good which they believed to have moral force. Indeed, the sources suggest that they judged themselves and other blacks according to the extent to which they could be relied upon to put the interests of the quarter community above personal interests and, most importantly, above the interests of whites.

Black men and women were not automatically trusted by the

members of the quarter community on the basis of their skin color. Most members of the quarter community seemed to believe that, in the words of John Little, " 'tis not the skin that makes a man mean."[9] Although blacks who had grown up within a given quarter community were generally considered reliable by other members of the same quarters—unless they had demonstrated otherwise—newly arrived blacks, or blacks with a special relationship to whites, had to actively establish their loyalty before they would be counted among the number of the trusted membership. The house servant, the favored skilled artisan, the driver, the white-appointed preacher, the slave with obvious white blood, were not judged according to their position in the plantation hierarchy but rather, like all blacks, according to the extent to which they could be relied upon to place the welfare of the quarter community first. The mulatto who felt himself to be better than the full-blooded African, the house servant who tattled on other slaves, the driver who when forced to whip seemed to enjoy it, the preacher who actually believed the tenets of the white religious code and attempted to get other blacks to believe likewise are portrayed by the informants with a moralistic vehemence that goes well beyond a sense of purely personal betrayal. Speaking of these untrusted special servants, Steward writes:

> . . . [M]any of them are the most despicable tale-bearers and mischief-makers, who will, for the sake of the favor of his master or mistress, frequently betray his fellow-slave, and by tattling, get him severely whipped; and for these acts of perfidy, and sometimes downright falsehood, he is often rewarded by his master, who knows it is for his interest to keep such ones about him; though he is sometimes obliged, in addition to a reward, to send him away, for fear of the vengeance of the betrayed slaves.[10]

The fervor of the quarter community reaction against such men and women is explained by the fact that they were perceived by other slaves as transgressors of one of the quarter community's strictest behavioral principles—that of sticking together against whites. They had no esteem in the quarters and, as we shall see in more depth later, were severely ostracized by the community.[11]

There is more to the theme of communality, however, than

the notion of the moral good and behavioral necessity of sticking together as a group. In much of the narrative material and in many of the songs and stories there comes through a sense of common bonds, of mutual affection, of a kinship-like sense of group spirit.

Throughout the narratives and the folklore one finds expression of a constant longing to be among one's people engaged in group activities. Holidays, weekends, and nighttime were prized not only as periods free from labor but as times when slaves could congregate with one another.[12] Although some quarter members may have wished to work in the great house in order to enjoy the food and clothes available to house servants, most quarter members seemed to prefer work in the field where they could associate with the larger group free from the constant surveillance of the white master and his family. One Armstrong informant expressed the preference for field work over house work this way: "You is wid er crowd, an' can sing when you feel like it. Dat's much better'n wu'kin' off by yo'self somewhar."[13]

Similarly, the commonly expressed desire to work on a large plantation as opposed to a farm seems to have sprung as much from the desire for life within a quarter community, apart from whites, as it did from the hope for better food and living conditions. Solomon Northup records a song that expresses this sentiment as he heard it sung among the slaves of a Louisiana sugar plantation:

> Harper's creek and roarin' ribber,
> Thar, my dear, we'll live forebber;
> Den we'll go to de Ingin nation,
> All I want in dis creation,
> Is pretty little wife and big plantation.[14]

Not only did quarter members address each other with familial titles but they by and large accepted the virtue of behaving towards one another as brothers and sisters with quasi-familial reciprocal obligations. The narratives are full of examples of quarter members feeling obligated to share their food, to protect runaways, and to generally care for, succor, and protect each other with a familial warmth.[15]

Older quarter members accepted the responsibility for the discipline and protection of quarter children. As they grew up, younger slaves displayed, in turn, both a respect for their elders and a desire to care for those community members too old to care for themselves. Although older slaves were generally provided for by their masters, on those plantations where they were turned out to provide for themselves they were well cared for by the other quarter members, who shared their food, clothing, and often their cabins with these older slaves.[16] Douglass writes:

> Strange and even ridiculous as it may seem, among a people so uncultivated and with so many stern trials to look in the face, there is not to be found among any people a more rigid enforcement of the law of respect to elders than they maintain. . . . A young slave must approach the company of the older with hat in hand, and woe betide him, if he fails to acknowledge a favor, of any sort, with the accustomed "tank ee," etc.[17]

Besides attempting to care for each other, and stick together, the quarter theme of communality is also attested to by the countless expressions within the narratives of the pride which quarter members felt in each other's accomplishments. Hardly a narrative can be read which does not contain at least one account of a great black dancer, singer, or storyteller; of the learning of a slave who against all odds acquired skill in reading, writing, or mathematics; of the exploits of a successful hunter or athlete; of the wisdom and power of a black doctor, preacher, or conjuror; of the outrageous schemes of a black trickster; of the courage of a black rebel who dared to stand up physically to the power of whites. These accounts are told with such obvious relish that there can be little doubt of the pride and vicarious pleasure which the informants enjoyed through the exploits of their fellow quarter members.

The theme of communality was also expressed beyond the limits of the individual quarter community. The narratives give ample evidence of one quarter assuming a large part in taking care of neighboring slaves who were treated poorly by their owners. One Fisk informant recalls how the folks of his quarters would procure food for the often half-starved slaves of a neighboring plantation who frequently "slipped over for something to eat."[18] Fanny Johnson's Louisiana quarter community engaged in the common practice of supplying food to the women of another quarter.[19] Fugitive slaves in need of food, clothing, or shelter were almost always assisted.[20] Aunt Sally, who lived as a slave in North Carolina and Alabama and who herself was often forced to borrow food for her children from neighboring quarters, writes: "There is a strong community of feeling among the slaves, and they are always ready to assist those who are less fortunate than themselves."[21]

Slaves also universally planned occasions when they could get together with the members of other quarters. They went to elaborate lengths to get passes so that they could join the dances, cornhuskings, funerals, and religious meetings of other quarters or simply visit friends there. If no means could be found to obtain passes, quarter members usually elected "to take their chances" rather than to remain out of touch with the people of neighboring quarters. Often the members of adjoining quarters seemed to take pride in their common blackness. Few of the informants speak with any shame of being black and many narratives and songs evince great pride in being a full-blooded African. Adeline, who had been a slave in Tennessee but moved to Arkansas at age one, recounts that: "I had always been told from the time I was a small child that I was a Negro of African stock. That it was no disgrace to be a Negro and had it not been for the white folks who brought us over here from Africa as slaves, we would never have been here and would have been much better off."[22]

Two of the most vivid illustrations of the black communal spirit under slavery were the ambivalence which attachments to friends and quarter community caused in those slaves contemplating an escape attempt and the scenes of grief which accompanied the forced separation of quarter members from their homes and quarter group. When George Johnson was preparing to escape from slavery in Virginia he "felt disagreeably about leaving my friends."[23] When Douglass was preparing for his second escape attempt he was pained most by the thought of separation "from a circle of honest and warm-hearted friends. The thought of such a separation, where the hope of ever meeting again was excluded, and where there could be no correspondence, was very painful."[24] Bibb writes that even after he had decided to escape, "My strong attachments to friends and relatives, with all the love of home and birth-place which is so natural among the human family, twined about my heart and were hard to break away from."[25]

When slave traders came to buy some of the slaves from the Maryland plantation where William Parker grew up as a slave: "The men, women, and children were crying and general confusion prevailed. For years they had associated together in their rude way—the old counseling the young, recounting their experience, and sympathizing in their trials. . . ."[26] One of the chief regrets of many fugitive slaves was a longing to see their friends from the old quarters. "I feel much better satisfied for myself since I have been free, than when I was a slave," relates a former slave from Maryland, Robert Belt, "but I feel grieved to think that my friends are in slavery. I wish they could come out here."[27] "Although we were not properly housed," imparts George Buckner, an ex-slave from Kentucky, "properly nourished nor properly clothed we loved our cabin homes and were unhappy when compelled to part."[28] As sung in countless songs, heaven for most slaves would be no real heaven if it were not a place of reconciliation with old friends.

> If you get there before I do,
> Coming for to carry me home,
> Tell all my friends I'm coming too,
> Coming for to carry me home.[29]

Trying to explain the pervasiveness of the slave's affection for his friends and quarter community and why they so greatly feared being sold away, Douglass writes:

The people of the North, and free people generally, I think have less attachment to the places where they are born and brought up than had the slaves. Their freedom to come and go, to be here or there, as they list, prevents any extravagant attachment to any one particular place. On the other hand, the slave was a fixture; he had no choice, no goal, but was pegged down to one single spot, and must take root there or nowhere.[30]

Isaac Williams of Virginia provides a simpler explanation: "We were social and affectionate and the ties of kindred were strong within us."[31]

᪻ 5 ᪺

Theme 2. Antipathy Towards Whites: As a Group, the Interests of Whites Are Inimical to Those of the Quarter Community

White folks got a heap to answer for the way they've done to colored folks! So much they won't never pray it away.

—former slave

The sense of antipathy which quarter members felt towards whites in general is a thematic counterpoint to the theme of communality. Although specific white men and women were judged individually—some respected, some detested—the interests of whites as a group were seen as inimical to those of the quarter community. More importantly, whites in general, and members of the slaveholding class in particular, were held responsible for most of the sorrow that blacks experienced under slavery. In fact, the repulsion which quarter slaves felt towards whites was so strong that however much they may have envied white comforts, power, and freedom, most blacks of the quarters displayed little desire to be like whites or to adopt white standards and white ways. Indeed, far from wishing to emulate whites, the narratives suggest that many quarter slaves desired to be done with whites altogether. The prevalence of this theme and the great variety of its expressions suggest strongly that an aversion to whites was an attitude quite consciously held by quarter people and openly expressed among themselves.

The central component of the quarter theme of antipathy towards whites was the belief that whites could only be trusted in

71

those areas where, and to the extent which, they had consistently proven themselves trustworthy. This meant, first and foremost, never trusting an unknown—and therefore untested—white. Quarter members were trained to assume that the motives of strange whites were malign. Blacks felt that they risked unprovoked physical abuse at the hand of any white, and although most knew that many whites seldom executed such unpredictable behavior, blacks understood only too well the dire consequences of one miscalculation. In terms of practical behavior, therefore, unknown whites were simply to be avoided wherever and whenever possible.[1]

Just as untested whites were never to be trusted in anything, there were certain topics and confidences that were too explosive to be discussed with, or divulged to, even those whites most solicitous of the welfare of the quarter community. The kind and concerned white, except in very special circumstances, could be esteemed, and even perhaps loved, but never fully trusted. As Frederick Douglass relates, there was an established maxim among quarter people that "a still tongue makes a wise head."[2] The truth of what went on in the quarters after the all-in bell, what blacks thought about particular whites and whites in general, what they thought about freedom and life under slavery, were never revealed to any whites. Conversation with whites concerning these topics was to be avoided whenever possible and lied about if necessary. If asked directly for an opinion by a white, even the younger slaves thought it best to "suppress the truth rather than take the consequences of telling it."[3]

Aside from the general prescription to keep all whites as ignorant as possible concerning the quarter community, blacks categorized whites according to their relationship to the institution of slavery. Some whites were constantly and completely mistrusted on principle because they occupied positions which dictated that their interests conflict with the perceived interests of the quarter community. Members of the slave patrol were placed in this category, as were slave catchers and slave merchants. Although blacks believed that the best way of dealing with these whites was to stay clear of them altogether, and endless strategies were devised for doing so, they were spoken of by the large majority of informants as personal as well as political enemies. Lewis Clarke had these choice words for the captains of the slave patrol:

> They are the offscouring of all things; the refuse, the fag end, the ears and tails of slavery; the scales and fins of fish; the tooth and tongues of serpents. They are the very fool's cap of baboons, the echo of parrots, the wallet and satchel of polecats, the scum of stagnant pools, the exuvial, the worn-out skins of slaveholders; they dress in their old clothes. They are, emphatically, the servants of servants, and slaves of the devil; they are the meanest, and lowest, and worst of all creation.[4]

What quarter members thought about the class of poor whites in general depended upon the extent and nature of their contact with the whites in the immediate vicinity of their home plantation. Those blacks whose contacts with poor whites were limited to speculators, patrollers, and slave catchers, as well as white drunks and gamblers, feared, hated, and sometimes pitied them. Robert Anderson, for instance, writes that in his Kentucky quarters "the persons who would associate with the 'po' white trash' were practically outcasts, and held in very great contempt."[5] Peter Bruner, on the other hand, having gotten to know some whites in the mountains near his home in Clark County, Kentucky, realized that they were often as opposed to slavery as were blacks.[6]

Some quarter communities believed that the slave system created a degree of common interest between slaves and poor whites. At the very least poor whites were seen as a means of contact with the outside world through which news and forbidden goods could be attained and prohibited skills learned. Certainly most blacks were well aware of the planters' disdain for poor whites and some believed that this dislike was generated by the planters' fear that poor whites would make common cause with their slaves. "One reason for the prejudice which the plantation owners had against the poor white people in every community," writes William Singleton, who lived on a large plantation in North Carolina, "was that these poor white people naturally sympathized with us and the plantation owners were afraid that because of this they might teach us to read or might give us some information about what the North was trying to do."[7]

Overseers, too, were generally regarded by the quarter community as holding positions which, by definition, were opposed to quarter community interests. This was especially true on those plantations where overseers were hired on a yearly basis and paid a percentage of the crops produced. In such cases, blacks understood only too well that the overseer's interest lay in working them as hard as possible, whereas their own interest lay in doing only as much labor as necessary to avoid punishment. Unlike traders and speculators, however, the overseer was known personally by blacks, often more personally than any other white. Blacks were able to study each overseer, to see how far he would let them bend plantation rules, to learn his moods and temperament, and to determine what his weaknesses were and how to play on them. Occasionally, the quarter community found an overseer whom they thought fair and to whose authority they were willing to accommodate themselves. Most often, however, the relationship between overseer and the quarter community was a constant battle of wills and wits.[8]

Most blacks learned that they could trust those whites who, like themselves, were willing to risk the wrath and punitive power of the planter class. The white who, like Lewis Paine, was willing to risk imprisonment or worse, could be trusted with even the most seditious secrets.[9] The white who, like the neighborhood bootlegger, broke the law by selling whiskey to slaves could be trusted at least to the extent of maintaining the secrecy of the liquor transaction.

The attitudes of quarter members towards their masters and the members of their masters' families varied greatly. A study of the narratives reveals that the feelings for individual whites of the slaveholding class ran the gamut from resentment and hatred to genuine affection. Most of the informants who speak with more than casual warmth about their masters, however, experienced at least part of their lives under slavery as servants in the great house. It is usually house servants, like Josiah Henson, who was the "especial pet" of his master, who wrote passages such as the following:

> He was far kinder to his slaves than the planters generally were, never suffering them to be struck by any one. He was a man of good, kind impulses, liberal, jovial, hearty. No degree of arbitrary power could ever lead him to cruelty.[10]

For the blacks of the quarters, especially on the larger plantations, the master and his family were often remote figures.[11] For these slaves who had little or no direct contact with master and his family, a master was judged according to how well he treated his slaves in terms of food, clothing, shelter, work conditions, leisure time, passes, punishments, and sellings. A good master, "as masters go," was one who fed bountifully, set a fair task, whipped only when absolutely necessary, allowed quarter slaves to do as they wished with their leisure time, stayed out of their internal affairs, and refused to sell slaves in even the direst of circumstances. For such masters most quarter slaves were willing to work diligently, realizing perhaps that their interests were not mutually exclusive. It is of such masters that quarter slaves speak with real warmth.

Some of the narratives speak of master and master class with undisguised hatred. Sometimes the vehemence of this dislike seems the outgrowth of a specific case of abuse. "My ma was a slave in the field," relates Warren McKinney. "When I was little, Mr. Strauter whipped my ma. It hurt me as bad as it did her. I hated him."[12] William Street's mother used to show him the spot on the fence where her father had died when his mistress drove him out of the house, a sick man.[13] Often the hurt sustained during slavery was carried over many years. Anne Harris told her interviewer that she had not allowed a white person to set foot in her house for more than sixty years. "Don't 'low it. Dey stole my sister Kate. I saw it wid dese here eyes. Stole her in 1860, and I ain't seed nor heard of her since. Folks say white folks is all right dese days. Maybe dey is, maybe dey isn't. But I can't stand to see 'em. Not on my place."[14] Besides whippings and sellings the specific wrong mentioned most often in the narratives was that of making false promises, especially about freedom. This the slaves put to song:

> My ole Mistiss promise me,
> W'en she died she'd set me free.
> She lived so long dat 'er head got bal'.
> An' she give out 'n de notion a-dyin' at all.
>
> Ole Massar lakwise promise me,
> W'en he died, he'd set me free.
> But ole Massar go an' make his will
> Fer to leave me a-plowin' ole Beck still.
>
> Yes, my ole Massar promise me;
> But "his papers" didn' set me free.
> A dose of pizen he'ped 'im along.
> May di Devil preach 'is funer'l song.[15]

The attitudes of slaves towards their masters comes through clearly when they talk or write about their reaction to a master's death. Some of the slaves shed tears of real grief. For others they were tears of gladness or an outpouring of fear of possible sale. Austin Steward recognized all three sentiments among the slaves at the death of the plantation mistress. "The slaves were all deeply affected by the scene; some doubtless truly lamented the death of their mistress; others rejoiced that she was no more, and all were more or less frightened. One of them I remember went to the pump and wet his face, so as to appear to weep with the rest."[16]

Whatever their feelings for specific whites, however, most members of the quarter community evidence a resentment for general wrongs towards slaveholders as a class. Blacks of the quarters recognized that it was the planter class who had enslaved them, whose pocketbooks benefited most from their unpaid labor, and whose power perpetuated the hated institution of slavery. "Dey allus done tell us it am wrong to lie and steal but why," asked Josephine Howard, "did de white folks steal my mammy and her mammy? Dey lives clost to some water, somewheres over in Africy. . . . Dat de sinfulles' stealin' dey is."[17] Not only were planters resented for that original theft but for the continual theft of the slaves' labor. "Every slave," wrote John Brown, "works against his heart, because he knows he is laboring for the benefit of another man."[18] "The slaves work and the planter gets the benefit of it," complained an aged informant in Canada. "It is wrong for him to have the money for their labor, and if a man goes to him for ten cents, to be refused."[19] Again the resourceful slaves committed this attitude to song:

> We raise de wheat,
> Dey gib us de corn;
> We bake de bread,
> Dey gib us de crust;
> We sif' de meal,
> Dey gib us de huss;
> We peel de meat,
> Dey gib us de skin;
> And dat's de way
> Dey take us in;
> We skim de pot,
> Dey gib us de liquor,
> And say dat's good enough for nigger.[20]

Or, in a song recorded by William Wells Brown:

> The big bee flies high,
> The little bee makes the honey.
> The black folks make the cotton.
> And the white folks get the money.[21]

Nor were white folks content to steal the slaves' labor. They were constantly scheming to think up ways of making their slaves work harder:

> Ol' massa an' ol' missis,
> Sittin' in the parlour,

Deep Like the Rivers

Jus' fig'in an' a-plannin'
How to work a nigger harder.[22]

Whites were also felt to be liars and hypocrites in their relations with the quarters. The pious hypocrisy of slaveholders who preach one thing on Sunday and whip on Monday was a common topic of conversation around the quarters.[23] As we shall see in the following chapter, most members of the quarter community were scornful of the all too evident utility of white religious instruction and thought this one more example that the word of whites could not be trusted.

George Williams says he "felt mad every day when I thought of being kept a slave."[24] Henry Brant "felt wrathy at the white men" when he realized that "I was to live all my life subject to being driven about at the will of another."[25] The expression of this anger took many forms. Some slaves ran off, stole, organized work slowdowns, cursed at master behind his back, called him disparaging nicknames, and endlessly discussed and sang about their wrongs amongst themselves. Others exploded in physical retaliation, hitting back, burning, raping, murdering, and organizing armed rebellions. Still others, mindful perhaps of white power, swallowed their anger, at least temporarily, or took it out upon the nearest tree, their dogs, and, undoubtedly, themselves. In whatever way their anger was expressed, however, most slaves, even those who professed a strong and enduring love for him, still recognized their master as the ultimate oppressor.[26] Northup, observing the disappointment in the quarters at news of the United States victory in the Mexican War, commented:

> They are deceived who flatter themselves that the ignorant and debased slave has no conception of the magnitude of his wrongs. They are deceived who imagine that he arises from his knees, with back lacerated and bleeding, cherishing only a spirit of meekness and forgiveness. A day may come—it *will* come, if his prayer is heard—a terrible day of vengeance, when the master in his turn will cry in vain for mercy.[27]

78

Antipathy Towards Whites

Although it was the overseer who was more often personally hated, and physically attacked, in calmer moods most members of the quarter community understood the master to be ultimately responsible for the ills of slavery. Like John Little, they did not "put the blame of cruelty on the overseer: I put it on the master who could prohibit it, if he would."[28] Certainly most quarter members, as we shall see more fully later, believed that whites would have to pay for their crimes against blacks, if not in this world then in the hereafter. "White folks got a heap to answer for the way they've done to colored folks! So much they won't never *pray* it away![29]

❄ 6 ❄

Theme 3. True Christianity
Versus Slaveholding Priestcraft:
The Immorality of Slavery

*There are thoughtful days in the lives of children—at least
there were in mine—when they grapple with the great primary subjects of knowledge, and reach in a moment conclusions
which no subsequent experience can shake. I was just as
well aware of the unjust, unnatural, and murderous character
of slavery, when nine years old, as I am now. Without appeals
to books, to laws, or to authorities of any kind, I knew to
regard God as "Our Father" condemned slavery as a crime.*

Frederick Douglass

Perhaps the most pervasive religious theme of the quarter
community centered upon the immorality of slavery and the
necessity of distinguishing between the concepts of true Christianity and the falsehoods of the slaveholders' preaching.[1]
Douglass writes that all except one of his fellow slaves were
"quite clear from slaveholding priestcraft."

It was in vain that we had been taught from the pulpit at St.
Michaels the duty of obedience to our masters—to recognize God
as the author of our enslavement—to regard running away as an
offense, alike against God and man—to deem our enslavement a
merciful and beneficial arrangement—to esteem our condition in
this country a paradise to that from which we have been snatched
in Africa—to consider our hard hands and dark color as God's
displeasure, and as pointing us out as the proper subjects of
slavery—that the relation of master and slave was one of reciprocal benefits and that our work was not more serviceable to our

masters than our master's thinking was to us. I say it was in vain that the pulpit of St. Michaels had constantly inculcated these plausible doctrines. Nature laughed them to scorn.[2]

Quarter people made a distinction between the word of God and the words preached by white masters or their ministers.[3] Louis Hughes believed that it was strong evidence of the slaves' "native intelligence and discrimination that they could discern the difference between the truths of the 'word' and the professed practice of those truths by their masters."[4] "A white man—a Baptist," recalls James Simler of his slave days in Virginia, "used to preach to us. The white people took the communion in the morning, and we took it in the evening. The minister used to tell us not to be disorderly on taking the sacrament—I thought he was disorderly himself, for he kept slaves."[5] "I have often been asked," writes John Brown, "how we slaves, being so ignorant, come to know that holding a human creature as a slave is wrong and wicked."

> I say that, putting the cruelties of the system out of the question, we cannot be made to understand how any man can hold another man as a slave, and do right. A slave is not a human being in the eye of the law, and the slaveholder looks upon him just as what the law makes him; nothing more, and perhaps even something less. But God made every man to stand upright before him, and if the slave law throws that man down ... then the law unmakes God's work; the slaveholder lends himself to it, and not all the reasoning or arguments that can be strung together, on a text or on none, can make the thing right. I have heard long preachments from ministers of the Gospel to try and show that slavery is not a wrong system; but somehow they could not fix it right to my mind, and they always seemed to me to have a hard matter to bring it square to their own.[6]

William Craft expressed the sentiments of many slaves when he recorded that the conduct of whites towards their slaves gave him a "thorough hatred, not for true Christianity, but for slaveholding piety.[7]

So strong was the conviction concerning the falsehoods contained in the white preaching and religious instruction that most slaves did not put much stock in the Bible as they knew it from their masters. "They generally believe there is somewhere a real Bible, that came from God; but they frequently say the Bible now used is master's Bible, the most they hear from it being, 'Servants, obey your masters.' "[8]

One of the best evidences of the quarter community's attitude towards the gospel according to the planters was their reaction to the marriage ceremonies and baptisms performed by slave-holding ministers. The white practice of dropping the vow "till death do you part" from slave weddings did not escape the notice of many slaves. As Matthew Jarret remarked: "We slaves knowed that them words wasn't bindin'. Don't mean nothin' lessen you say, 'What God has jined, caint no man pull asunder.' But dey never would say dat. Jus' say, 'Now you married.' "[9] Many slaves had themselves remarried or rebaptized after emancipation. Bibb, speaking of the fugitive slaves he met in the North after his escape, writes that ". . . if they profess religion, and have been baptized by a slaveholding minister, they repudiate it after becoming free, and are rebaptized by a man who is worthy of doing it according to the gospel rule."[10]

For those slaves who knew more of Christianity than what they heard from slaveholders, the principal tenents of true Christianity revolved around the complementary principles that God intended all men to be free and that, therefore, slavery was wrong. "I think that God made all men to be free and equal," observed one time Missouri slave Alexander Hamilton, "not one to be a slave."[11] Whenever the narratives speak of the true gospel it is with an emphasis upon equality and deliverance. Like most slaves, Anthony Burns, who grew up in Stafford County, Virginia, was convinced that God "had made of one blood all nations of the earth, that there was no divine ordinance requiring one part of the human family to be in bondage to another, and that there was no passage of Holy Writ by virtue of which Col. Suttle could claim a right of property in him, any more than he could in Col. Suttle."[12]

Josiah Henson recounts the impact that a white religious meeting in Maryland had upon him when, at the age of eighteen, he first heard some of the Bible not often mentioned in the presence of slaves:

Christianity Versus Slaveholding Priestcraft

When I arrived at the place of the meeting, the services were so
far advanced that the speaker was just beginning his discourse,
from the text Hebrews II, 9: "That he, by the grace of God,
should taste of death for every man." This was the first text of the
Bible to which I had ever listened, knowing it to be such. I have
never forgotten it, and scarce a day has passed since in which I
have not recalled it, and the sermon that was preached from it.[13]

Henson goes on to tell how he heard for the first time that "the
death of Christ was not designed for the benefit of a select few
only, but for the salvation of the world"; and about how Christ
came to preach "deliverance to the captive"; and of the "liberty
wherewith Christ has made us free" and avowed that this new
knowledge awakened him to a "new life—a consciousness of superior powers and destiny to anything I had before conceived
of. . . ." Most importantly, Henson relates how these "little
glimmerings of light from another world" caused him to become
"an esteemed preacher" among the other slaves.[14]

John Thompson, whose father and mother were both fieldhands on the large Maryland plantation of James H. Wagar,
describes what happened when somehow the message of plain
evangelical Methodism found its way into the quarters before
the slaveholders organized special patrols to break up the meetings.

> This new doctrine produced great consternation among the
> slaveholders. It was something which they could not understand.
> It brought glad tidings to the poor bondman; it bound up the
> broken-hearted; it opened the prison doors to them that were
> bound, and let the captive go free.
> As soon as it got among the slaves, it spread from plantation to
> plantation, until it reached ours, where there were but a few who
> did not experience religion.[15]

Believing as they did that God intended all men to be free,
slavery could be nothing but sin. "By the law of Almighty God, I
was born free," dictated Aaron Siddles, "by the law of man a
slave."[16] Douglass states that at the age of nine he realized that
"to regard God as 'Our Father' condemned slavery as a crime."[17]
From the time he was a little boy Henry Banks never thought "it

83

was intended for any man to be a slave."[18] And to Henry Atkinson slavery was "the worst and meanest thing to be thought of. . . . God made all men—He is no respecter of persons—and it is impossible that He should, on account of color, intend that I should be a slave of a man, because he is of a brighter skin than I am."[19] Recalling a white minister who told his slave congregation "how good God was in bringing us over to this country from dark and benighted Africa, and permitting us to listen to the sound of the gospel," Lunsford Lane remarked, "To me, God also granted temporal freedom, which *man* without God's consent had stolen away."[20]

Writing in theoretical terms, Aaron, who experienced slavery in Maryland, Kentucky, and Virginia, sums up the general position of the quarters with regards to the morality of slavery:

> We believe slavery to be a sin—always, everywhere, and only sin. Sin in itself, apart from the occasional rigors incidental to its administration, and from all those perils, liabilities, and positive inflictions to which its victims are continually exposed. Sin is the nature of the act which created it, and in the elements which constitute it. Sin, because it converts persons into things; men into property; God's image into merchandise. Because it forbids men from using themselves for the advancement of their own well being, and turns them into mere instruments to be used by others solely for the benefit of the users. Because it constitutes one man the owner of the body and spirit of other men; gives him power and permission to make his pecuniary profit the very end of their being, thus striking them out of existence as beings, possessing rights and susceptibilities of happiness, and forcing them to exist merely as appendages of his own existence, in other words, because slavery holds and uses men as mere means for which to accomplish ends, of which end, their own interests are not a part. Thus annihilating the sacred and eternal distinction between a person and a thing; a distinction proclaimed an axiom of all human consciousness; a distinction created by God. . . .[21]

So strong was the quarter community's belief that the ideals of true Christianity and the will of God were contrary to the practice of slavery that the emancipation of his slaves was the only positive proof of a slaveholder's conversion to true Christianity. "This was proof to us that he was willing to give up all to God, and for the sake of God, and not to do this was, in our estimation, an evidence of hardheartedness, and was wholly inconsistent with the idea of genuine conversion."[22] One of the more famous story lines of slave folklore was the efforts of blacks under slavery to convert their masters to the principles of true Christianity. These stories always end in the emancipation of his slaves by the newly converted, true-believing master.[23] Jacob Stroyer, following a discussion of the quarter community's reaction to the Civil War, ends with the statement: "Thank God, where Christianity exists slavery cannot exist."[24] To the black men and women of the quarter community, slavery and Christianity were so antithetical that they did not think of the slaveholding South as a Christian land.

The quarter slaves' conviction of the immorality of the system of slavery under which they were forced to live caused them to place slaves and slaveholders in a special moral relationship both towards each other and towards God. It is a clear outgrowth of slave religion and a persistent attitude in the narratives that since slavery was a sin, those who practiced, sanctioned, or perpetuated it were sinners. Certainly most members of the quarter community seemed to believe that the cruel white would be judged by God and made to pay for his acts of cruelty. "Slaves," writes Douglass, "knew enough of the orthodox theology of the time to consign all bad slaveholders to hell. . . ."[25] After relating an incident in which a white cruelly murdered a slave baby, one Fisk informant gave such acts on the part of whites as the reason why he believed in hell. "I don't believe that a just God is going to take no such man as that into His Kingdom."[26] James Roberts expressed the belief that "the word of God being true that every man shall receive according to his deeds done in the body, deep, deep indeed must be their damnation."[27] Another ex-slave interviewed by the Fisk project recalls that on his plantation "when the white folks would die the slaves would all stand around and 'tend like they was crying but after they would get outside they would say, 'They going on to hell like a damn barrel full of nails.' "[28]

Cruel whites were not the only whites, however, consigned to hell by the religious creed of the quarter community. For quarter blacks the very act of holding slaves was sufficient to cause even the most benevolent master's soul to be damned. Though he loved his master "in health and in death," David West feared for his soul because, like most slaves, West believed that "no man can keep the laws of God and hold to slavery."[29] The members of the quarter community believed with Henry Brown in "a hell, where the wicked will dwell, and knowing the character of slaveholders and slavery, it is my settled belief, as it was while I was a slave, even though I was treated kindly, that *every* slaveholder will infallibly go to hell, unless he repents."[30]

Nor did the members of the quarter community believe that God was necessarily content to postpone the wrath of His judgment until the hereafter. Like the God of Israel, He sent suffering and sickness to plague the unrepentant, slaveholding South. The blacks on one ante-bellum plantation were convinced that the planter and his family "suffered a long line of reverses, culminating in the loss of the plantation, because old Massa would not allow meetings on his place."[31] When John Thompson's master was killed when his barn roof caved in, Thompson was sure that "God had overruled."[32] When Douglass heard of Nat Turner's rebellion and an outbreak of cholera, he remembers thinking that "God was angry with the white people because of their slaveholding wickedness, and therefore his judgments were abroad in the land."[33]

Just as the blacks of the quarters believed in an angry God of judgment for whites, they came to believe in a loving, healing God of mercy and salvation for those who had been forced to live and toil under slavery's yoke. It was a prime tenet of the Christianity of the slave quarters that unearned suffering is redemptive. Though the whips and scorns of slavery were not necessarily to be borne patiently on earth, they were a sure ticket of admission to heaven when presented at the pearly gates.[34] Charles Ball makes explicit the idea that "a revolution in the conditions of the whites and blacks, is the cornerstone of the religion of the latter. . . ."

It is impossible to reconcile the mind of the native slave to the idea of living in a state of perfect equality, and boundless affection,

86

with the white people. Heaven will be no heaven to him, if he is not to be avenged of his enemies. I know, from experience, that those are the fundamental rules of his religious creed; because I learned them in the religious meetings of the slaves themselves. A favorite or kind master or mistress may now and then be admitted into heaven, but this rather as a matter of favour, to the intercession of some slave, than as a matter of strict justice to the whites, who will, by no means, be of an equal rank with those who shall be raised from the depths of misery, in this world. . . . They are ready enough to receive the faith, which conducts them to heaven, and eternal rest, on account of their present sufferings; but they by no means so willingly admit the master and mistress to an equal participation in their enjoyments—this would only be partial justice and half way retribution.[35]

The belief of most members of the quarter community that God was a god of judgment primarily, if not solely, for white folks is further illuminated by the quarter attitude concerning their own moral situation as men and women held in slavery. Although some blacks, like James Pennington, believed it their "moral duty" to escape from slavery, most blacks felt that they would not be held morally responsible for acts committed while slaves and over which they had little or no control.[36] Thus, slaves who were forced by the master or overseer to whip other blacks, who could not provide for or protect their children, who were forced into sexual liaisons against their will, were not thought of as culpable in the eyes of God and were not morally judged by the quarter community.

However, if acts which might be considered "sinful" in freer circumstances, especially those against other blacks, were committed without coercion or fear of punishment, then the perpetuator was thought to be morally accountable even though his ultimate damnation depended largely on the enormity of the crime. The notion that even "sinful" blacks had already suffered enough on earth was a strong one, although a pampered, snobbish, traitorous slave might easily burn in hell along with the whites he appeared to love so well.

Acts which blacks committed against whites ("crimes" to plantation authorities) were not considered sins but justifiable acts of retaliation against an unfair system. For the members of the quarter community the immorality of the slave system suspended moral considerations with regard to action towards whites. Ball says that he was "never acquainted with a slave who believed that he violated any rule of morality by appropriating to himself anything that belonged to his master, if it was necessary to his comfort."[37] Bibb, in stealing an ass with which to attempt escape, justified his action with the reasoning that "if one piece of property took off another, there could be no law violated in the act; no more sin committed in this than if one jackass had rode off with another."[38] Douglass says that he perceived no immorality in stealing from his own master, it was merely a "question of removal—the taking of his meat out of one tub and putting it in another; the ownership of the meat was not affected by the transaction. At first he owned it in the tub, and last he owned it in me."[39] When "driving a mile or two into the woods a pig or a sheep and slaughtering it for the good of those whom Riley was starving," Henson writes that he was assured of the justice of the act and felt "good, moral, heroic."[40]

Even the murder of white adults (children of young age not being held responsible for the evils of slavery), especially in self-defense or in defense of a relative or friend, was but infrequently felt to be a sin.[41] As Douglass writes:

> The morality of free society could have no application to slave society. Slaveholders made it almost impossible for the slave to commit any crime, known either to the laws of God or to the laws of man. If he stole, he took but his own; if he killed his master, he only imitated the heroes of the revolution. Slaveholders I held to be individually and collectively responsible for all the evils which grew out of the horrid relation, and I believed they would be so held in the sight of God. To make a man a slave was to rob him of moral responsibility. Freedom of choice is the essence of all accountability.[42]

The quarter community's belief in the certainty of heaven for those who have endured slavery is also expressed in the quarter attitude towards death. Although the separation of death was dreaded on the one hand, on the other it was often greeted joyfully in the knowledge that it brought an escape from the suffering of slavery. Many of the narratives relate instances in which the news of a loved one's death caused the mingling of sorrow and joy within the hearts of the living.[43] Quarter funerals were always occasions of mixed sorrow and joy. Although the living inevitably mourned the departure of the company and love of their friend or relative, their grief was sweetened by the knowledge that the departed was free from the burdens of slavery in a heaven where:

> No more rain fall for wet you, Hallelujah,
> No more sun shine for burn you,
> Dere's no hard trial,
> Dere's no whips a-crackin'
> No evil-doers in de kingdom
> All is gladness in de kingdom.[44]

Furthermore, the estrangement from loved ones brought by death could be counted upon to be only of a temporary nature. This certainty of a heavenly reunion even mitigated the sorrow felt when friends and relatives were sold apart. Stroyer reports that when a slave was sold away from his home plantation, those remaining would sing "little hymns that they had been accustomed to for the consolation of those that were going away, such as:

> When we all meet in Heaven,
> There is no parting there;
> When we all meet in Heaven,
> There is no parting more.[45]

One of the clearest indicators of the quarter community's belief in the mercy and salvation which life under slavery earned for them was the minimal role which the issue of hell, fire, and damnation played in either their religious songs or religious services. Whereas poor whites of that day preached fervently about the tortures of a hell which awaited even those who thought themselves most righteous, slaves had little interest in hell except as an eternal depository for slaveholders. For the quarter community the ideas of mercy, comfort, rest, justice, and salvation were far more essential to their religion.

So great was the assurance of the members of the quarter community in their eventual salvation that many prayed for the hastening of the judgment day. During an eclipse of the sun Austin Steward remembers hoping it to be a sign that the judgment day had come. "I recollect well thinking, that if indeed all things earthly were coming to an end, I should be free from Robinson's brutal force, and as to meeting my Creator, I felt far less dread of that than of meeting my cross, unmerciful master."[46] "In violent thunderstorms," relates Moses Grandy, "when the whites have got between the featherbeds to be safe from the lightning, I have often seen negroes, the aged as well as others, go out, and, lifting up their hands, thank God that judgment was coming at last."[47]

7

Theme 4. Black Superiority

I fooled Old Master seven years,
    Fooled the overseer three.
Hand me down my banjo,
    And I'll tickle your bel-lee.

Slave song

The members of the quarter community thought of themselves not only as morally superior to whites but as superior on a
behavioral level as well. This theme is strongly documented in
both the slave narratives and the folklore of black life under
slavery. Whereas most slaves thought of themselves as competent, hard workers, whites in general were felt to be lazy and in-
competent, unable to hoe, plow, work in the sun, cook, or wash.
Some whites were so lazy, or inept, that they would not, perhaps
could not, tie their own shoes or comb their own hair. Most,
without blacks to work for them, would be incapable of running
a profitable plantation.

Recalling life under slavery in South Carolina, Josephine Bacchus concludes that ". . . white folks couldn' work den no more
den dey can work dese days like de colored people can."[1] When
freedom came to Texas, Felix Heywood and his friends
"thought we was goin' to be richer than the white folks, 'cause we
was stronger and knowed how to work, and the whites didn't,
and they didn't have us to work for them any more."[2] Ellen
Craft, when asked in London several years subsequent to her escape from a Mason, Georgia, plantation whether she thought
slaves were intelligent enough to care for themselves were they
to be set free, replied simply: "At present, they take care of
themselves and their masters too; if they were free, I think they
would be able to take care of themselves."[3] The quarter commu-

nity had a saying which succinctly sums up quarter disdain for pampered plantation whites: "It is a poor dog that won't wag its own tail."[4]

Slaves thought of each other, in the main, as men and women who, though often obstructed in their attempts, sincerely struggled to provide and care for their families.[5] White men, on the other hand, were seen generally as profligate philanderers who spent an inordinate amount of time away from home worrying about money or lavishly spending it.

> My master's habits were such as were common enough among the dissipated planters of the neighborhood; and one of their frequent practices was to assemble on Saturday or Sunday . . . and gamble, run horses, or fight game-cocks, discuss politics, and drink whiskey and brandy and water all day long. Perfectly aware that they would not be able to find their own way home at night, each one ordered a slave, his particular attendant, to come after him and help him home.[6]

"Dat dere fellow am as ill as if he were one of de white pop'-lation," remarked one old black man about another showing signs of syphilitic deformities.[7] Speaking of the antimiscegenation laws, one Fisk respondent said, in reference to white men generally, "He made the law himself and he is the first to violation."[8] White men were thought to be poor fathers who did not supervise the proper raising of their children, and poor husbands who did not look after their wives. Incredibly, to the quarter community, many were even willing to sell their own sons and daughters.[9]

White women were thought to be frail and uncommonly naive: unable to lift a finger for themselves, to raise their children, to make proper love to their husbands, to see what their husbands were up to at night in the quarters or, sometimes, in the great house itself. One ex-slave reported on a mistress who "couldn't get a glass of water for herself nor nuthin'," and the recounting of such stories was frequently pressed upon house servants when they visited the quarters.[10] The practice, however infrequent, of giving their children to black mammies to suckle, as well as to raise generally, further undermined white women in black eyes.

White children were viewed as disobedient, disrespectful tyrants whose ill-mannered behavior was restrained only by the strict training of their black mammies. Most quarter members believed that their own children were far better behaved than white children and certainly felt that they matured more quickly in their ability to care for themselves and shoulder family and community responsibilities. The fact that black children of a young age were called upon to care for white children of an equal age was not lost upon the quarter community.[11]

Most blacks were also of the opinion that the character of but few whites was strong enough to withstand the corrupting influence of slavery. The unlimited power which slavery gives the slaveholder over the slave "in almost every instance transforms the man into a tyrant; the brother into a demon" and "more than one, otherwise excellent woman, into a feminine monster."[12] "Under the influence of slavery's polluting power, the most gentle women become the fiercest viragos."[13] Each generation of slaveholding families was thought to become more and more debased. According to Pennington, "this decline of slaveholding families is a subject of observation and daily remark among slaves."

> There is no one feature of slavery to which the mind recurs with more gloomy impressions than to its disastrous influence upon the families of the masters, physically, pecuniarily, and mentally.
> It seems to destroy families as by a powerful blight, large and opulent slave-holding families often vanish like a group of shadows at the third or fourth generation. . . . As far back as I can recollect, indeed, it was a remark among slaves, that every generation of slaveholders are more and more inferior.[14]

Slaves also seem to have looked down upon whites for their style, or rather, for their lack of style. Although members of the quarter community often envied the potency of white wealth, they generally thought of themselves as more colorful dressers, more energetic dancers, more creative singers and storytellers, and better cooks. This conviction of their own stylistic superiority is expressed most clearly in the aversion shown by the quarter community for white church services. Quite aside from the distasteful theological content of these services, they were, bluntly, boring. Whites simply could not shout properly or preach like their own. "Mostly we had white preachers," recalls Anthony Dawson, who was a fieldhand on a large North Carolina plantation, "but when we had a black preacher that was Heaven."[15] "The whites preached to the niggers," asserts Lizzie Hughes of slave days in Texas, "and the niggers preached to theyselves."[16] As they did so often, the slaves introduced their attitude into song:

> White folks go to chu'ch,
> An' he never crack a smile;
> An' nigger go to chu'ch,
> An' you hear 'im laugh a mile.[17]

Perhaps most frequently, the black informants boast of the slaves' ability to outwit whites. The members of the patrol were often subjects of shrewd quarter planning. H. C. Bruce says that as a slave in Virginia he used to hear "of many jokes played on these patrols by slaves, tending to show how easy it was to fool them, because they were as a rule illiterate, and of course could not read. The slaves knowing this would take a portion of a letter picked up and palm it off on them as a pass when arrested."[18] Henry Green recounts for his interviewer how the slaves on his Alabama plantation would fool the patrol in order to court their sweethearts.

Yo' see, mos' all de wimmins, dey be er wukkin' at night on dey tasks dat dere old mis gib 'em ter do, er weavin' er de cloth. Dese wimmins would be settin' 'round de fire weavin' de cloth en de nigger be dar too er courtin' de gal, en all ter once here cum dem paddyrollers, some at der front door en some at de back door, en when de wimmins er hear 'em comin', dey raise er loose plank in de flo' whut dey done made loose fer dis bery puppus, en de nigger he den drop right quick down 'neath de flo' twix de jists, en de

94

wimmins den slap de plank right bak in place on top er de man ter hide him, so iffen de paddyrollers does cum in dat dey see dat dere ain't no man in dar. Dat wus de way dat de niggers used ter fool 'em heap er times.[19]

The ploy most often reported for outwitting the patrol was that of tying ropes, or vines, across their path to slow their pursuit of fleeing slaves.

I 'member once when we was gonna have a meetin' down in de woods near de river. Well, dey made me de lookout boy, an' when de paddyrollers come down de lane past de church—you see dey was 'spectin' dat de niggers gonna hold a meetin' dat night—well, sir, dey tell me to step out f'm de woods an' let 'em see me. Well, I does, an' de paddyrollers dat was on horseback come a chasin' arter me, jus' a-gallopin' down de lane to beat de band. Well I was jus' ahead of 'em, an' when they got almost up wid me I jus' ducked into de woods. Course de paddyrollers couldn't stop so quick an' kep' on 'roun' de ben', an' den dere came a-screamin' an' cryin' dat make you think dat hell done bust loose. Dem old paddyrollers done rid plumb into a great line of grape vines dat de slaves had stretched 'cross de path. An' dese vines tripped up de horses an' throwed de ole paddyrollers off in de bushes. An' some done landed mighty hard, cause dey was a-limpin' roun' an' cussin' an' callin' fo' de slaves to come an' help dem, but dem slaves got plenty o' sense. Dey lay in de bushes an' hole dere sides a-laughin', but ain't none o' 'em gonna risk bein' seen.[20]

Overseers were also the common target of slave jokes and plots. On those plantations where no tasks were set and field-hands were made to work as long as the sun shone, the tactics the slaves employed were simple ones. Anderson writes that the slaves in the fields "used our wits to escape from all the work we could, and would lag behind, or shirk when he was not looking."[21] John Brown recalls that blacks in Georgia would often "flag and rest if they got the chance. Whilst they do so, one of their number is usually set to watch the overseer, and when he sees him coming they have a signal, and all the hands fall to as fast as they can."[22] As a boy in Texas, Richard Carruthers was posted by his fellow quarter blacks as such a "look-out": "I kept an eye on the niggers down in the cotton patch, sometimes they lazy around and if I see the overseer comin' from the Big House

I sings a song to warn 'em so they no get whipped, and it go like this:

> Hold up, hold up, American Spirit!
> Hold up, hold up, H-O-O-O-O-O-O-O!"[23]

Among themselves slaves would also sing:

> You may call me Raggedy Pat
> 'Cause I wear this raggedy hat,
> And you may think I'm a workin'
> But I ain't.[24]

Many schemes were also employed for the purpose of insuring the freedom to come and go as they pleased after working hours. Though the overseer usually went from cabin to cabin at about nine o'clock to make sure that the fieldhands were all in bed, many slaves would "git up an' have some fun" after he made his rounds.[25] On those plantations where plantation authorities locked the slaves in at night, slaves used their chimneys or a hole dug under the cabin walls for exits. Passes were obtained by any means possible: they were forged or updated by members of the community who could write, bought from free blacks or poor whites, or, less frequently, cajoled from young whites willing to forge their father's name.

Slaves delighted in telling stories about how they had outsmarted the overseer by stealing food. Milton Clarke writes of Aunt Peggy, who was a "master at stealing little pigs."

With a dead pig in the cabin and the water all hot for scalding, she was at one time warned by her son that the Phillistines were upon her. Her resources were fully equal to the sudden emergency. Quick as thought, the pig was thrown into the boiling kettle, a door put over it, her daughter seated upon it, and a good thick quilt around her, the overseer found little Clara taking a steam bath for a terrible cold. The daughter, acting well her part, groaned sadly; the mother was busy in tucking in the quilt, and the overseer was blinded, and went away without seeing a bristle of pig.[26]

Black Superiority

Although the outwitting of master appears most often in the narratives of those slaves who were house servants, such stories were in great demand in the quarters. One ex-slave tells the story of a slave named old man Jack:

> Once the mistress wanted him to drive her to church on Sunday morning. When the message came to him, he swore he wouldn't drive and she sent for him. We all laughed at him because we thought he surely would have to go. But while he was talking to her he let his knife slip and cut his hand right between the first finger and the thumb. "There now I have ruined my hand standing here whittling." Mistress excused him from driving. He went back to his house and such laughing I never heard as he told us how he outwitted her.[27]

Peter Randolph tells how a slick bodyservant made fun of his master right to his face, after the master had carefully dressed himself for a fight, and asked how he looked.

> "Oh massa, mighty!" "What do you mean mighty, Pompey?" "Why massa, you look noble." "What do you mean by noble?" "Why, sar, you look just like one lion." "Why, Pompey, where have you ever seen a lion." "I seen one down in yonder field the other day, massa." "Pompey, you foolish fellow, that was a *jackass!*" "Was it, massa? Well, you look just like him."[28]

Fieldhands often took a more direct hand in the fooling of master. Cornelius Carney of Virginia boasted of his father.

> Father got beat up so much that after a while he run away an' lived in de woods. Used to slip back to de house Saddy nights an' sometime Sundy when he knowed Marse and Missus done gone to meetin'. Mama used to send John, my oldes' brother, out to de woods wid food fo' father, an' what he didn't git fum us de Lawd provided. Never did ketch him, though ole Marse search real sharp.
>
> Father wasn't the onlies' one hidin' in de woods. Dere was his cousin, Gabriel, dat was hidin' an' a man name Charlie. Niggers was too sharp fo' white folks.[29]

Often fieldhands would rub garlic or red onions on their feet to keep the dogs off their trail.[30] "Some of de black folks," asserted

Hilliard Johnson of his slave days in Alabama, "knowed how to git away from dem nigger dogs jes' lac dey wa'n't dere."[31]

Frequently slaves took advantage of the absence of whites to do a little visiting. Reverend Ellis Jefson recalls a song sung in Virginia that made this point:

> Master and mistress both gone away,
> Gone down to Charleston to spend the summer day.
> I'm off to Charleston early in the mornin'
> To spend another day.[32]

And often, of course, in stealing, slaves fooled master as often as they fooled the overseer. One ex-slave in the Fisk study recalled how his father used to trade with Mr. Dodge, his master's uncle, who owned a hotel in town. "He would buy anything my pa brought to him; and many times he was buying his own stuff, or his nephew's stuff."[33]

Josie Jordan, who had been a slave in Tennessee, recalls her mother's tale of the day "malitis" struck amongst master's hogs.

> I remember Mammy told me about one master who almost starved his slaves. Mighty stingy, I reckon he was.
>
> Some of them slaves was so poorly thin they ribs would kinda rustle against each other like corn stalks a-drying in the hot winds. But they gets even one hog-killing time, and it was funny, too, Mammy said.
>
> They was seven hogs, fat and ready for fall hog-killing time. Just the day before Old Master told off they was to be killed, something happened to all them porkers. One of the field boys found them and come a-telling the master: "The hogs is all died, now they won't be any meats for the winter."
>
> When the master gets to where at the hogs is laying, they's a lot of Negroes standing round looking sorrow-eyed at the wasted meat. The master asks: "What's the illness with 'em?"
>
> "Malitis," they tells him, and they acts like they don't want to touch the hogs. Master says to dress them anyway for they ain't no more meat on the place.
>
> He says to keep all the meat for the slave families, but that's because he's afraid to eat it hisself account of the hogs' got malitis.
>
> "Don't you all know what is malitis?" Mammy would ask the children when she was telling of the seven fat hogs and seventy

lean slaves. And she would laugh, remembering how they fooled Old Master so's to get all them good meats.

"One of the strongest Negroes got up early in the morning," Mammy explained, "long 'fore the rising horn called the slaves from their cabins. He skitted to the hog pen with a heavy mallet in his hand. When he tapped Mister Hog 'tween the eyes with that mallet, 'malitis' set in mighty quick, but it was a uncommon 'disease,' even with hungry Negroes around all the time."[34]

Slaves also deceived whites through the artful use of words and gesture. Often they were able to communicate seditious thoughts to each other under their master's very nose. A white man, the Reverend J. G. Williams, recorded the sermons of a Gullah preacher by the name of Brudder Coteny. In one of these sermons he ends with reference to the biblical declaration that God would separate the sheep from the goats on the Judgment Day. "What the Reverend Mr. Williams apparently missed," according to Genovese, "was that black folklore assigns a special meaning to goats: they are white people. He ought not have missed the special meaning assigned by ante-bellum whites to sheep: they were akin to blacks since both had 'wool,' not hair. The slaves did not miss the reference, for they roared back at Brudder Coteny, 'Bless de Lawd, we nigger know who hab de wool.'"[35]

Often the songs of the slaves carried with them hidden thoughts or special messages. One such song carries the very idea illuminated by Genovese in the preceding paragraph:

1. And de moon will turn to blood,
    > And de moon will turn to blood,
    > And de moon will turn to blood,
    > In dat day—O-yoy,* my soul!
    > And de moon will turn to blood in dat day.

2. And you'll see de stars a-fallin'.
3. And de world will be on fire.
4. And you'll hear de saints a-singin'.

*"A sort of prolonged wail" (Mrs. C. J. B., in Allen, *Slave Songs*).

5.   And de Lord will say to de sheep.
6.   For to go to Him right hand.
7.   But de goats must go to de left.[36]

The quarter community theme of black superiority is expressed, however, not only by the countless stories of successful scheming but by the endless telling and retelling of these tales and by the obvious satisfaction they imparted. This point is made well in a scene from *Army Life in a Black Regiment* in which Thomas Higginson overhears a black soldier entertaining his comrades with the story of how he escaped to the Yankees:

> "Den I go up to de white man, berry humble, and say, would he please git ole man a mouthful for eat?"
> "He say he must hab de valeration ob half a dollar."
> "Den I look berry sorry, and turn for go away."
> "Den he say I might gib him dat hatchet I had."
> "Den I say," (this in a tragic vein) "dat I must hab dat hatchet for defend myself *from de dogs!*"
> [Immense applause and one appreciating auditor says, chuckling, "Dat was your *arms,* ole man," which brings the house down again.]
> "Den he say de Yankee pickets was near by, and I must be very keerful."
> "Den I say, 'Good Lord, Mas'r, am dey?' "
> Words cannot express the complete dissimulation with which these accents of terror were uttered—this being precisely the piece of information he wished to obtain.[37]

Some slaves, convinced perhaps by their success in outwitting whites, believed that whites blocked their learning because whites had recognized the superior intelligence of blacks. "I was never sent to school, nor allowed to go to church," observed Mrs. James Seward. "They were afraid we would have more sense than they."[38]

Often, of course, slaves were successfully tricked by whites. Furthermore, they realized, as we shall see in the next chapter, that they lived in a world where their political power was simply inferior to that of whites most of the time. Despite the awareness, however, of the handicap with which they labored as slaves, most members of the quarter community believed that they were generally able to get the better of whites in a battle of wits. They believed with Ball that even "the utmost caution and severity of masters and overseers, are sometimes insufficient to repress the cunning contrivances of the slaves."[39] They were convinced of the truth of the old Gullah saying which went: "De buckruh hab scheme, en de nigger hab trick, en ebry time de buckruh scheme once, de nigger trick twice."[40]

Theme 5. White Power:
The Great Relative Power
of White People, Backed by the Force
of the State, Makes Them Persons
to be Dealt with Carefully,
if Not Fearfully

There is nothing which a white man may not do against a black one, if he only takes care that no other white man can give evidence against him.

Moses Grandy

Side by side, but in opposition to the theme of black superiority, is that of white power. However much slaves believed in their own moral and behavioral superiority to whites, they were well aware of the superior political power which whites held as a group and of the potential for harming blacks which this power gave to individual whites. Although slaves reacted differently to their awareness of white power, they all were quite aware of its implications. Whites were to be handled carefully. Slaves knew that the laws created by white society provided little if any protection for black persons, families, or property. Slaves knew with Douglass that "A mere look, word, or motion—a mistake, accident, or want of power—are all matters for which a slave may be whipped at any time."[1]

"The law," asserts John Brown, "says you may give a slave thirty-nine lashes if he is found roaming about without a pass. I warrant that ten with the bull-whip, properly laid on, will cut any man's life out; and this is twenty-nine licks within the law. . . . There is no cruelty under the sun that hard-hearted men can devise, that has not been employed to bring 'niggers' into subjection."[2] Most slaves, if they had not experienced severe abuse themselves, had witnessed enough abuse of other blacks, both free and slave, to agree with Grandy: "There is nothing which a white man may not do against a black one, if he only takes care that no other white man can give evidence against him."[3]

Aware of their vulnerability to white power, a large number of blacks fairly lived in fear. This was especially true of those with cruel masters. Fear of the whipping post prompted William Grimes to pray constantly to God "to protect and defend me in this adversity."[4] Lewis Clarke walked in his sleep due to his fear of being flogged.[5] All the slaves on Henry Watson's Mississippi plantation were afraid of their mistress, who used the lash frequently, and Watson himself admits to feeling "perfectly terrified when she approached."[6] On the plantation in Maryland where Mrs. James Seward was a slave, all the slaves "were afraid of master: when I saw him coming, my heart would jump up into my mouth, as if I had seen a serpent."[7] Jermain Loguen reports that under a cruel master the slave's "highest aim was to dodge the lash of the tyrant—his daily prayer, that his mother, sisters and brothers might not be subjects of new wrongs."[8]

One did not have to have a cruel master or mistress, however, to experience anxieties over the adverse potentiality of white power. Even the kindest master was occasionally forced to sell his slaves or to divide them in his will. Henry Brown remembers the deep impression made upon his mind when his mother told him at an early age that slave children were often taken by tyrants, just as, in autumn, "leaves are stripped from the trees of the forest."[9] Harriet Tubman says that as a child she "was not happy or contented: every time I saw a white man I was afraid of being carried away."[10]

Many of the narratives relate the anxiety of slave parenthood. Bibb writes that he could never look upon the face of his daughter "without being filled with sorrow and fearful apprehensions, of being separated by slaveholders. . . ."[11] Jones states that his "dear parents were conscious of the desperate and incurable woe of their position and destiny: and of the lot of inevitable suffering in store for their beloved children.

> They talked about our coming misery, and they lifted up their voices and wept aloud, as they spoke of our being torn from them and sold off to the dreaded slave-trader, perhaps never again to see them or hear from them a word of fond love. I have heard them speak of their willingness to bear their own sorrows without complaint, if only we, their dear children, could be safe from the wretchedness before us. And I remember, and *now* fully understand, as I did not *then,* the sad and tearful look they would fix upon us when we were gathered round them and running on with our foolish prattle.[12]

The theme of white power was also evidenced in the feeling of helplessness which slaves often felt in the face of white abuse. When one Fisk informant's older sister was tied up in the back yard and whipped, none of her family dared come to her assistance. "There stood mother, there stood father, and there stood all the children and none could come to her rescue."[13] Austin Steward writes of his feelings while watching a white man whip his sister:

> The God of heaven only knows the conflict of feeling I then endured; He alone witnessed the tumult of my heart, at this outrage of manhood and kindred affection. God knows that my will was good enough to have wrung his neck; or to have drained from his heartless system its last drop of blood! And yet I was obliged to turn a deaf ear to her cries for assistance, which to this day ring in my ears. Strong and athletic as I was, no hand of mine could be raised in her defense, but at the peril of both our lives.[14]

One of the most frequently mentioned reasons for the slaves' preference for marrying wives of another plantation was the fact that by living apart slaves did not have to stand by and witness the abuse of their loved ones. "If my wife," wrote Henry Bibb, "must be exposed to the insults and licentious passions of wicked slavedrivers and overseers; if she must bear the stripes of the lash laid on by an unmerciful tyrant; if this is to be done with impunity, which is frequently done by slaveholders and their abettors, Heaven forbid that I should be compelled to witness the sight."[15] According to Moses Grandy, "no colored man wishes to live at the house where his wife lives, for he has to endure the continual misery of seeing her flogged and abused, without daring to say a word in her defense."[16]

Most slaves were apparently of the opinion that slavery itself could not exist without this slave fear of white power. "Cruelty," reflects John Brown, "is inseparable from slavery, as a system of forced labor; for it is only by it, or through fear of it, that enough work is got out of slaves to make it profitable to keep them."[17] H. C. Bruce says there were many slaves "who, though they knew they suffered a great wrong in their enslavement, gave their best services to their masters, realizing, philosophically, that the wisest course was to make the best of their unfortunate situation."[18] Like Henry Banks, they "tried to do the work faithfully that was assigned me, not because I felt it a duty, but because I was afraid not to do it. . . ."[19] "It is a mistake to suppose that the Southern planters could ever retain their property, or live amongst their slaves, if their slaves were not kept in terror of the punishment that would follow acts of violence and disorder."[20]

Often this fear persisted even after escape from slavery. John Seward, for example, was scared when he met abolitionists after his escape to the North: "They used me so well, I was afraid of a trick. I had been used so ill before, that I did not know what to make of it to be used decently."[21] During his escape, John Brown, though he was nearly starving, was unable to eat the meal offered by a kindly Quaker family because they insisted that he eat with them at their table: "I was so completely abashed, and felt so out of my element, that I had no eyes, no ears, no understanding. I was quite bewildered. As to eating, it was out of the question."[22]

The significance of the theme of white power is perhaps best attested to by the large amount of time which slaves spent figuring out how to deal with whites. Quarter child-raising gave special attention to the training of children in how to interact with whites.[23] Slaves might come to different conclusions about how to deal with white power; or the same slave might come to different conclusions at different times; few slaves took the problem lightly.

Some slaves stood up to whites and openly defied white power and authority. These were the men and women who resisted being whipped, who physically intervened in the abuse of spouse, parent, or child, who refused to obey orders to brutalize another black, who were willing to fight the white man in order to protect their individual and group dignity, who escaped from slavery only to return for other slaves, who organized and executed slave rebellions. William Wells Brown cites the example of a man named Randall: "He had been on the plantation since my earliest recollection, and I had never known of his being flogged. No thanks were due to the master or overseer for this. I have often heard him declare that no white man should ever whip him—that he would die first."[24] Douglass writes:

> They prefer to whip those who are the most easily whipped. The doctrine that submission to violence is the best cure for violence did not hold good as between slaves and overseers. He was whipped oftener who was whipped easiest. The slave who had the courage to stand up for himself against the overseer, although he might have many hard stripes at first, became while legally a slave virtually a freeman. "You can shoot me," said a slave to Rigby Hopkins, "but you can't whip me," and the result was he was neither whipped nor shot.[25]

Even the knowledge of sure death if caught did not stop some slaves from fighting, and sometimes killing, a white in the act of brutalizing a slave. Solomon Northup relates the story of a young black man who was so maddened at the injustice of his overseer that "seizing an axe" he literally "chopped the overseer in pieces." Later "he was led to the scaffold, and while the rope was around his neck, maintained an undismayed and fearless bearing, and with his last words justified the act."[26]

Occasionally escaped slaves would join together in bands and elude or fight off all attempts at recapture for years.

> Sometimes groups of runaway slaves, of eight, ten and even twenty, belonging to different owners, got together in the woods, which made it very dangerous for slave hunters to capture those

whom they were hired to hunt. In such cases sometimes these runaways killed both hunters and dogs. The thick forests in which they lived could not be searched on horseback, neither could man or dog run in them. The only chance the hunters had of catching runaway slaves was either to rout them from those thick forests or attack them when they came out in the opening to seek food.[27]

Some slaves organized a group to stand up to whites together. Steward tells of the actions of one such individual at a quarter community dance:

The patrol was nearing the building, when an athletic, powerful slave, who had been but a short time from his "father-land," whose spirit the cowardly overseer had labored in vain to quell, said in a calm, clear voice, that we had better stand our ground, and advised the females to lose no time in useless wailing, but get their things and repair immediately to a cabin at a short distance, and there remain quiet, without a light, which they did with all possible haste. The men were terrified at this bold act of their leader; and many with dismay at the thought of resistance, began to skulk behind fences and old buildings, when he opened the door and requested every slave to leave who felt unwilling to fight. None were urged to remain, and those who stood by him did so voluntarily.

Their number was now reduced to twenty-five men, but the leader, a gigantic African, with a massive, compact frame, and an arm of great strength, looked competent to put ten common men to flight. He clenched his powerful fist, and declared that he would resist until death, before he would be arrested by those savage men, even if they promised not to flog him. They closed the door, and agreed not to open it; and then the leader cried, "Extinguish the lights and let them come! We will meet them hand to hand!" Five of the number he stationed near the door, with orders to rush out, if the patrol entered, and seize their horses, cut the bridles, or otherwise unfit them for use. This would prevent them from giving an alarm and getting a reinforcement from surrounding plantations. In silence they waited the approach of the enemy, and soon the tramping of horses' feet announced their approach, but when within a few yards of the house they halted, and were overheard by one of the skulking slaves, maturing their plans and mode of attack. . . .

They stepped up to the door boldly, and demanded admittance but all was silent; they tried to open it, but it was fastened. Those inside, ranged on each side of the door, and stood perfectly still.

> The patrol finding the slaves not disposed to obey, burst off the slight fastening that secured the door, and the chief of the patrol bounded into their midst, followed by several of his companions, all in total darkness!
>
> Vain is the attempt to describe the tumultuous scene which followed. Hand to hand they fought and struggled with each other, amid the terrible explosion of firearms, oaths and curses, mingled with the prayers of the wounded, and the groans of the dying![28]

Despite such occasional heroics, however, many slaves, convinced as they were of the superiority of white power, thought of such resistance as foolish or dangerous. According to Northup he and his fellow slaves more than once discussed "in serious consultation" the idea of insurrection. "Without arms or ammunition, or even with them, I saw such a step would result in certain defeat, disaster and death, and always raised my voice against it."[29] "You know white folk would just as soon kill you as not," asserted one ex-slave, "and you had to do what they said."[30] Another former slave argued that most slaves didn't run off to the woods because they had stood up to white power but because they feared the consequences of doing so. "They didn't do something and run. They run before they did it, 'cause they knew that if they struck a white man, there wasn't going to be a nigger. In them days, they run to keep from doing something."[31]

The majority of slaves, it would seem from the narratives, developed more indirect ways of dealing with whites. Most of the members of the quarter community adopted the general posture that it was the better part of wisdom to appear to give the master and his family what they wanted within the bounds of a limited physical and psychological effort. If master wanted happiness, act happy; piety, appear pious; penitence, ask for forgiveness; childlike behavior, play the part of Sambo. For most blacks who worked in the fields and lived in the quarters, and whose interactions with the master were infrequent and brief, such acquiescence to white notions of proper slave behavior required no great psychological strain and saved them from the risk of considerable physical anguish. "As a master," observes Douglass, "studies to keep the slave ignorant, the slave is cunning enough to make the master think he succeeds."[32] Aware as he was that "public opinion and the law" was against him and that "resistance in many cases is death to the slave," Henry Bibb felt that it was "useless for a poor helpless slave to resist a white man in a slaveholding State." Like other slaves he concluded that "the only weapon of self-defense that I could use successfully, was that of deception."[33]

Another means of handling white power was to manipulate whites into positions where blacks held some real power in their relationship. Overseers, for example, were sometimes maneuvered into a situation where the quarter community was able to maintain an approximate, if not equal, balance of power. In most cases such a relationship was built upon mutual interest and mutual fear of the white planter. Charles Ball tells the marvelous story of how he and his companions outwitted the overseer of their special fishing project. They allowed the overseer to sleep while they secretly did their own fishing and trading with the local steamboat captain, as well as attending to their owner's nets. Even if the overseer had caught them in the act, he could have done nothing without risking the loss of his job. For Ball could expose the overseer's laxity on the job and this possibility placed the overseer "at least as much in my power as I was in his."[34]

Although Ball's example may be uncommon because completely successful, blacks under slavery spent much time establishing some similar degree of power over whites. One of the most frequently used practices was that of setting the power of different whites in opposition to each other. The narratives are full of examples of slaves using mistress against master, white child against parent, master against overseer, and planter against planter. Other tactics included running off, breaking tools, labor slowdowns, "sick-outs," and stealing. By such action slaves demonstrated their awareness of the power which their bodies and their labor gave them over any master concerned with his own pecuniary self-interest.

To counteract white power, blacks became students of white mood and personality. They learned to be sensitive to the nuances of white behavior: to detect shifting moods, to anticipate anger, to play on fear, and to sense by a word or expression the fine line between what would be tolerated and what would be punished. Blacks learned that the proper stance to assume when dealing with any individual white differed not only from personality to personality but from mood to mood and circumstance to circumstance. John Brown says he trained himself to "watch the changes in my master's physiognomy, as well as those of the parties he associated with, so as to frame my conduct in accordance with what I had reason to believe was their prevailing mood at any given time."[35]

However infrequently quarter slaves encountered whites, there was always an inherent danger in the latter's power. Whatever the form of their final behavior, the words and deeds of the members of the quarter community make clear the seriousness of their determination to deal effectively with the white man's power.

❄❈ 9 ❈❄

Theme 6. The Importance
of the Family

"If you knock de nose, de eye cry." (That meant) *"if you hurt one of the family, you hurt them all."*

Black proverb
from S. Carolina

Although, as we shall see in Chapter 13, the black family under slavery took many forms, the importance to slaves of family ties and affections is paramount. Such is the testimony of the overwhelming majority of the narratives and of the songs of slavery. It is one of the central themes of the quarter community.[1] Scarcely a narrator speaks of his slave experience without dwelling upon the ways in which a specific family member or the family as a unit "kept him up" during hard times.

Mother is spoken of most frequently. She is depicted nursing, hugging, washing, cooking, disciplining, instructing, and generally caring for and loving her family. She is talked of with pride: "My mother was the smartest black woman in Eden. She was as quick as a flash of lightning, and whatever she did could not be done better. She could do anything."[2] And always with affection: "The first thing I recollect is my love for my Mother—I loved her so and would cry when I couldn't be with her, and as I growed up I kept on loving her just that a-way even after I married and had children of my own."[3]

Nowhere is the quarter community's understanding of the crucial role of mother more vividly expressed than in the sorrow of the spiritual "Sometimes I feel like a Motherless Child." To most black people under slavery it was difficult to imagine a more sorrow-filled and lonely life than that of the motherless

111

child "a long way from home." So strong was the bond between slave mother and child that many an older black felt desolation at his mother's death or sale.

> When my old mammy died a-shoutin',
> All de friend I had done died and gone.
> She died a-prayin', she died a-prayin'.[4]

Several of the slave spirituals also speak of the longing to be reunited with mother in heaven.[5]

Some blacks even expressed the belief that death itself could not keep mother from watching over and helping them. Throughout his life during which he was a slave in both Virginia and Missouri, Archer Alexander continued to remember his mother "like yesterday. Seems like I never forgets her, nohow. 'Specially when trouble comes, and I've had a heap of that—thank the Lord—seems like she allays comes to me—not close up to me, but jess like she was when I seed her the last time; and she's allays a-prayin' for me. That's what keeps me up."[6]

Father is also spoken of with pride and affection. "My father," wrote John Thompson, "lived an exemplary life, and died a triumphant death, leaving to posterity a bright evidence of his acceptance with God."[7] Austin Steward speaks of his father as "a kind, affectionate husband and a fond, indulgent parent."[8] James Mars admired and loved his father because he was "a man of considerable muscular strength, and was not easily frightened into obedience."[9] Elijah Marrs' father "was always my friend when I thought trouble was in the air; he was my only refuge; when he failed to plead for me my hopes fled."[10] "I loved my father," says one ex-slave who saw his father only once a week during slavery. "He was such a good man. He was a good carpenter and could do anything."[11]

In more than portraits of specific fathers, however, the narratives give clear evidence of the importance which the quarter community gave to the role of fatherhood. Most men, when circumstances made it possible, took seriously their obligations as fathers. The narratives are full of fathers supplying their fami-

The Importance of the Family

lies with extra food, material comforts, protection, instruction, and love. "Poor as the slave is, and dependent at all times upon the arbitrary will of master, or yet more fickle caprice of the overseer, his children look up to him in his little cabin, as their protector and supporter."[12]

The narratives also give countless examples of the ties of duty and affection that existed between husbands and wives, brothers and sisters, grandparents and grandchildren, uncles, aunts, nieces, nephews. Separation through sale or death sometimes could make impossible the fulfillment of felt familial obligations; it could not always nullify the ties of affection. Informant after informant describes the "wretched disconsolateness" of slaves at the separation of family members. Ball remembers that when all the members of his family but him and his father were sold, "My father never recovered from the effects of the shock, which this sudden and overwhelming ruin of his family gave him. . . . After this time I never heard him laugh heartily, or sing a song. He became gloomy and morose in his temper, to all but me."[13] After his sale to a plantation thirty miles from that of his mother and siblings, Lewis Clarke wept over the occasional apple or sugar plum his mother was able to send him, but he "scarcely ever ate them—they were laid up and handled and wept over till they wasted away in my hand. My thoughts continually by day and my dreams by night were of mother and home. . . ."[14] Northup reports hearing mothers who had been separated from their children talking to them as if they were standing right next to them.[15]

The deep sorrow felt by slaves at the separation of their families finds ample embodiment in their songs:

> My dear wife un one chile, (Oho! Oho!)
> My poor heart is breaking; (Oho! Oho!)
> No more shall I see you, (Oho! Oho!)
> Oh! No more foreber! (Oho! Oho!)[16]

William Wells Brown learned this song from slaves being carried to New Orleans for sale:

113

See these poor souls from Africa
Transported to America;
We are stolen, and sold to Georgia,
Will you go along with me?
We are stolen, and sold in Georgia,
Come sound the jubilee!

See wives and husbands sold apart,
Their children's screams will break my heart;—
There's a better day a coming,
Will you go along with me?
There's a better day a coming,
Go sound the jubilee![17]

According to the narratives one of the greatest hardships of life under slavery was the knowledge that one's family might be separated. James Smith told his interviewer that "The fear of being sold away from the family or having the family sold kept the slaves in constant uneasiness. If a slave was called to the house by the owner or overseer and the cause was not known by the rest of the slaves they invariably guessed that a 'deal' had been made and the person in question had been sold."[18] John Brown relates the feelings within the quarter community concerning their coming distribution among mistress and her now grown and married daughters:

I remember well the grief this caused us to feel, and how the women and men used to whisper to one another when they thought nobody was by, and meet at night, or get together in the field when they had an opportunity, to talk about what was coming. They would speculate, too, on the prospects they had of being separated; to whose lot they and their children were likely to fall, and whether the husbands would go with their wives. The women who had young children cried very much. My mother did, and took to kissing us a good deal oftener. This uneasiness increased as the time wore on, for though we did not know when the great trouble would fall upon us, we all knew it would come, and were looking forward to it with very sorrowful hearts.[19]

The Importance of the Family

Another sign of the importance and strength of family ties within the quarter community is the frequency with which they are the primary reasons behind a slave's decision to run off. Though he was whipped each time he did it, Ben Brown ran away three times to see his sister who was "sold to a plantation some miles away."[20] Henry Williamson recalls: "My wife's sister was sold at private sale to a trader to go south, and was carried away. Her father and mother were dissatisfied with this, and concluded to go to Canada. I concluded to start with them with my family."[21]

Not infrequently the narratives tell of a slave who, having already successfully escaped, decided to go back into the land of slavery for his family. Despite the counsel of his friends in the North who feared that "I might be caught and sold off from my family into slavery forever," Henry Bibb returned to Kentucky several times in a vain effort to retrieve his wife and daughter.[22]

Conversely, family ties were also frequently given by informants as the reason for not attempting to escape from slavery, or waiting so long before they did it. Only after his wife died did George Johnson set out to fulfill his childhood ambition of becoming free.[23] After the death of his mistress and his impending sale away from his family Henry Atkinson "at last found an opportunity to escape, after studying upon it a long time. But it went hard to leave my wife; it was like taking my heart's blood. . . ."[24]

Charles Ball lived under slavery without attempting escape for fifty years because he placed a higher value upon the joys of living with his beloved family than he did upon freedom. In a beautifully illustrative passage Ball tells how the thought of being rejoined with his wife and little ones enabled him to endure and persevere through months of hardships and peril as he traveled hundreds of miles at night through woods and swamps to reach his home plantation after being sold to the deep South. Once he had attained his goal and was under his wife's roof, with his children around him, though not yet free from slavery, the drive and power to continue on to the free states, for the moment, left him.[25]

115

Pennington writes movingly of one of "the two great difficulties that stood in the way of my flight:

> I had a father and mother whom I dearly loved—I had also six sisters and four brothers on my plantation. The question was, shall I hide my purpose from them? Moreover, how will my flight affect them when I am gone? Will they not be suspected? Will not the whole family be sold off as a disaffected family, as is generally the case when one of its members flies?[26]

Nowhere is the theme of the importance of the family better expressed than in the quarter community's efforts to sanction and protect the bonds of marriage. Marriage ceremonies are invariably described by black informants as important occasions taken seriously by slaves if not by their masters. Henry Bibb observed that "there are no class of people in the United States who so highly appreciate the legality of marriage as those persons who have been held and treated as property."[27] And John Warren declared, "The slaves have no particular rules, except in regard to marriage: they try to make it as near lawful as they can."[28]

Though the quarter community does not seem to have been especially concerned about the sexual practices of their young slaves, once they married quarter members were expected to be faithful. "De women," observed Susan Snow, "had to walk a chalk line, I never heard tell o' wives runnin' round with other men in dem days."[29] According to H. B. Holloway, "There was a lot of old souls that came out of slavery times that lived together and raised children that never was married (except by word of mouth), just got together. But they made out better and were better husbands and wives and raised better families than they do now."[30]

Thus, although there can be little doubt that the realities of life under slavery could, and often did, cause the separation of family members and lend a measure of instability to the nuclear slave family, slavery, at the same time, may have actually increased the meaningfulness with which slaves imbued their family relationships. Slavery was full of trials and tribulations, and a large proportion of whatever human relationships and pleasures slaves were able to enjoy came in family assemblage. "It seems to me," writes Thomas Jones, "that no one can have such fondness of love and such intensity of desire for *home* and home affections, as the poor slave. Despised and trampled upon by a cruel race of unfeeling men, the bondman must die in the prime of his wretched life, if he finds no refuge in a dear home, where love and sympathy shall meet him from hearts made sacred to him by his own irrepressible affection and tenderness for them."[31]

10

Theme 7. The Reality and Significance of the Spirit World

> Every time I feel the spirit
> Moving in my heart I will pray.
> Every time I feel the spirit
> Moving in my heart I will pray.

> Slave Spiritual

> I do believe without a doubt
> That a Christian has a right to shout.

> William E. Barton,
> *Old Plantation Hymns*

As portrayed in the narratives, many, if not most, members of the quarter community believed in a spirit world which played an active role in the earthly world. At the same time, quarter members believed that they could, at least partially, control and affect spiritual forces. Indeed, far from separating the spirit world from the world of physical reality, many slaves thought in terms of one world in which spiritual and physical forces were equally convincing realities. And for at least some slaves, spiritual forces had the undisputed upper hand.

It is the rare informant who omits any mention of a widespread belief in witches, ghosts, and spirits in general.[1] Stroyer says that there was a rampant belief in witches among slaves.[2] William Wells Brown observed that a large number of slaves had an implicit faith in conjuration.[3] Ball asserted that "the negroes of the cotton plantations are exceedingly superstitious; and they are indeed, prone, beyond all other people that I have ever known, to believe in ghosts, and the existence of an infinite number of supernatural agents. No story of a miraculous character can be too absurd to obtain credit with them; and a narrative is not the less eagerly listened to, nor the more cautiously received, because it is impossible in its circumstances."[4]

Many of the narrators tell of their own personal experiences. Douglass tells how he was induced by an old black man named Sandy to wear a certain root on his right side as a protection from white whipping.[5] Bibb recounts numerous times in which he appealed to conjurors for assistance in helping to court a pretty girl.[6] William Grimes writes of his fear of the spirits of several slaves whom he believed to have been poisoned to death in the spinning room.[7] Abram Harris relates how he detected the presence of spirits:

> When yo is gwine long de road en feel sum warm air, den dat is whar de spirits hes jes been. De wings er de daid has done fanned dat air till hits hot, en when I is gwine er long en hits dat hot air, den I knows dat sum spirit er hant hes been er long dat same route, kase hit sho is hants in dis worl, yit en still dey don't walk en act lak natchal people.[8]

Even those informants whose Christianity prompted them to deny the existence of a spirit world inadvertently express their belief in it. "Us all de time heard folkses talkin' about voodoo, but my grandma was powerful religious, and her and Ma tell us children voodoo was a no 'count doin' of de devil, and Christians was never to pay it no attention."[9] "But I'm a believer, and this here voodoo and hoodoo and spirits ain't nothin' but somebody died outen Christ and his spirit ain't at rest, just in a wandering condition in the world."[10]

The strength of the quarter community's belief in the reality and power of the spirit world is clearly expressed by the way quarter people viewed those blacks believed to have special ability in controlling the forces of the spirit world. On one plantation the quarter community's faith in the prophetic powers of Sinda, a female conjuror, caused them to refuse to work because she had convinced them that the millennium was at hand.[11] An Armstrong informant tells of a case in which "an old gran'pap" led the rest of the community in a revolt against the especially dreaded overseer. "He knew conjur, and night after night he made the rounds of the cabins, chanting incantations against the overseer and passing on instructions for a meeting to be held soon." When the overseer fell off his horse and died a few days after the meeting, every slave on that plantation believed that "gran'pap's conjur was powerful indeed.[12] Henry Piles tells of a conjuror who used to make hoodoo hands for the young slaves. "Old Bab Russ was coal black, and he could talk African or some other unknown tongue, and all the young bucks and wenches was mortal 'fraid of him!"[13] H. C. Bruce writes that "I have known of cases where these conjurors held whole neighborhoods, as it were, in such mortal fear, that they could do unto the Colored people anything they desired, without the least fear of them telling their masters."[14]

Sometimes the slaves' belief in the power of the spirit world was used by the quarter community as a means of social control. Jacob Stroyer says that the slaves of his plantation had three ways of detecting thieves amongst themselves. The first two ways involved elaborate processes in which the accused was forced to hold a stick through the loop of a string tied to a Bible or a sieve. If the Bible or sieve turned he was thought to be guilty.

The third way of detecting thieves was taught by the fathers and mothers of the slaves. They said no matter how untrue a man might have been during his life, when he came to die he had to tell the truth and had to own everything he had ever done, and whatever dealing those alive had with anything pertaining to the dead, must be true, or they would immediately die and go to hell to burn in fire and brimstone. So in consequence of this, the graveyard dust was the truest of the three ways in detecting thieves. The dust would be taken from the grave of a person who had died last and put into a bottle with water. Then two of the men of the examining committee would use the same words as in the case of the Bible and the sieve, "John stole that chicken," "John did not steal that chicken," and after this had gone on for about five minutes, then one of the other two who attended to the Bible and the sieve would say, "John, you are accused of stealing that chicken that was taken from Sam's chicken coop at such a time." "In the name of the Father and the Son and the Holy Ghost, if you have taken Sam's chicken don't drink this water, for if you do you will die and go to hell and be burned in fire and brimstone but if you have not you may take it and it will not hurt you." So if John had taken the chicken he would own it rather than take the water.[15]

Slaves did not feel, however, completely at the mercy of spirit world forces. They believed that if they took special precautions and observed special rites they could ward off any evil. Young children wore different kinds of greegrees and charms upon the body to ward off diseases. Will Sheets and his siblings wore asafetida sacks around their necks as did many other children.[16] In Amanda McCray's quarters it was the custom for the infants to wear "moles' feet and pearl buttons around their necks to insure easy teething and had their legs bathed in a concoction of wasp nest and vinegar if they were slow about learning to walk."[17] Often the older slaves wore voodoo bags. According to Louis Hughes this custom "was handed down from generation to generation."[18] The purpose of these bags was to keep witches away, asserts Josephine Anderson, describing how they were made: "You take a little pinch o' dried snake skin an some graveyard dirt, an' some red pepper an' a lock o' your hair wrapped roun' some black rooster feathers. Den you spit whiskey on em an' wrap 'em in red flannel an' sew it into a ball 'bout dat big. Den you hand it under your right armpit, an' ever' week you give it a drick o' whiskey, to keep it strong an' powful."[19]

Some slaves took special precautions not to laugh at or be scared by any animal while pregnant under the belief that if they did so their baby would be born looking like that animal.[20] Doc Quinn asserts that "A practice that was quite common in antebellum days was for each member of the family to extract all their teeth, in the belief that in doing so the family would never disagree."[21] Sometimes graves were carefully decorated to insure the safe journey of the dead one's spirit.[22]

Curses presented special difficulties. If all preventive measures failed one could always, as a last resort, turn to a conjuror to have the curse removed. In some such cases a conjuror would willingly heal but would not return a curse. "Can't you put this same thing back on her?" H. B. Halloway asked Cain the conjuror after he had cured Halloway's wife from a disease sent by a neighbor. "He said, 'Yes, but it would kill my hand.' He meant that he had a curing hand and that if he made anybody sick or killed them, all his power to cure would go from him."[23]

A further expression of their belief that they could interact and affect the spirit world was the slaves' conviction that they could foretell the future through the reading of signs and dreams. Many of the informants tell how the slaves read various signs. If a rooster crows outside your door, visitors are coming. A tree frog's holler is a sure signal of coming rain. The sound of a screech owl means death, as does a dog howling at night. If your right eye itches it's a sign of good luck; if your left, a sign of bad luck. If you sneezed while at table that was bad luck and you would have to get up without eating anything.[24]

The slaves also placed great significance in dreams as prophecy of the future. "De slaves wuz natur'ally superstitious," Ellis Kannon informed his interviewer, "en b'leeved in dreams, ole sayings en signs."[25] Pastsy Hyde says simply: "In slavery time peoples b'leeved in dreams."[26] Many of the informants tell of their own personal belief in dreams. One of the Fisk studies contains the following testament:

> When I was small I used to dream a lot. I remember one night I dreamt that I saw Uncle Link, Uncle Jake and Uncle Peter skinning a cow and cutting her open. A lot of women and children were sitting around and seemed to be crying. I told my mother about it the next morning. She said it was a sign of death to dream about fresh meat. Sure enough that very evening Uncle Peter Price died. I used to dream so much that the old heads got so they took special notice of me and nearly every time it would come true.[27]

Isaac Williams gave this account to Benjamin Drew:

> On a Thursday evening, came a trader from the south, named Dr. _____. He looked at Henry, and at a man named George Strawden, and at me, but did not purchase, the price being too high. I dreamed that night that he took us three. Next morning I told Henry, "That man is coming to take you, and George, and me, just as sure as the world; so Henry, let's you and me make a bargain to try and get away; for I'm never deceived in a dream— if I dreamed master was going to whip me, he surely whip somebody next day." That's as good a sign in the south as ever was.[28]

The Reality and Significance of the Spirit World

The theme of the importance of the spirit world and of its constant interaction with the physical world was also expressed in many of the religious practices and beliefs of the quarter community. Many slaves believed that before one could become a true believer one had to be touched deeply and powerfully by the spirit. "I tell you, honey," testified one Fisk informant, "you got to be touched from the inside and to be struck by his hand like I was 'fore you feel that holy uplifting spirit."[29] A. P. Watson, who gathered over fifty accounts of this conversion process, was given various personal testimonies of how the converted: first heard the voice of God calling to him in the fields; learned to hear God with the spiritual ear and see him with the spiritual eye; was struck dead with the power of God and fell out on the floor flat on her back; began to moan on the inside and fall in her tracks; was shown visions of heaven and hell; and, always, was filled with the spirit and rose, talking, shouting, and praising God.[30]

Many of the informants tell of their conversion experiences in terms that suggest that it was the spirit which was seeking them and not necessarily vice versa.[31] Certainly most slaves believed that "God was a time God." "He don't come before time. He don't come after time. He comes just on time."[32] "He spoke to me once after I had prayed trying to hurry Him and get religion. He said, 'I am a time-God. Behold, I work after the counsel of my own will and in due time I will visit whomsoever I will.' "[33] "When God got through with me I spoke out of a full heart and said things that I didn't know I had in me. God has His own time and way of taking hold of His people and His works are more than we read and think about. He is a time-God and He won't make haste."[34]

Although God always would take His own good time, seekers often were able to influence His timing of the sending of the spirit. Henry Brown reports that many slaves felt they could influence the spirit by shaving the hair from their heads.[35] Most slaves felt that if they shouted zealously and prayed earnestly, they could not be denied. "The Lord said you gotta shout if you want to be saved," proclaimed Cornelius. "That's in the Bible."[36] Many of the slave spirituals tell of earnest seekers praying, fast-ing, spending time in the valley, and even wrestling like Jacob in order to be born again in the spirit.

> Hunt till you find him, Hallelujah,
> And a-huntin' for de Lord;
> Till you find him, Hallelujah,
> And a-huntin' for de Lord.[37]

> My brudder, want to get religion?
> Go down in de lonesome valley,
> Go down in de lonesome valley,
> Go down in de lonesome valley, my Lord;
> Go down in de lonesome valley,
> To meet my Jesus dere.[38]

> And I had a mighty battle like-a Jacob and de angel,
>   Jacob, time of old;
> I didn't 'tend to lef' 'em go
>   Till Jesus bless my soul.[39]

The importance of the spirit was also recognized in the religious services of the quarter community. Indeed, the service was somehow incomplete unless all had been touched by the spirit. Many a night it was not until the first signs of daybreak that the last believer "got happy" with the Holy Spirit.[40] Mary Gladdy says: "Practically always, every Negro attendant of these meetings felt the spirit of the Lord 'touch him (or her) just before day.' Then, all would arise, shake hands around, and begin to chant the canticle . . . :

> My sister, I feels 'im, my sister I feels 'im;
> All night long I've been feelin' 'im;
> Jest befoe day, I feels 'im, jest before day I feels 'im;
> The spirit, I feels 'im, the spirit I feels 'im.[41]

The spirit, however, was too powerful, too omnipresent, and too wonderful to be confined to conversion experiences or worship services. It could make you shout anywhere at any time. Martha Colquitt tells the story of her shouting grandmother.

> My grandmother was a powerful Christian woman, and she did love to sing and shout. . . . Grandma would git to shouting so loud she would make so much fuss nobody in the church could hear the preacher, and she would wander off from the gallery and go downstairs and try to go down the white folks' aisles to git to the altar where the preacher was, and they was always locking her up for 'sturbing worship, but they never could break her from that shouting and wandering round the meeting after she got old.[42]

Emoline Glasgow tells the story of one slave whose master offered to buy him a new pair of boots if he would stop his hollering in church. Everything went well until the middle of the service when he caught the spirit: "Boots or no boots, I gwine to shout today."[43] Fannie Moore gave this account of how her mother got the spirit while plowing:

> One day she plowin' in de cotton fiel. All sudden like she let out big yell. Den she sta't singin' an' a-shoutin', an' a-whoopin' an' a-hollerin'. Den it seem she plow all de harder. When she come home Marse Jim's mammy say: "What all dat goin' on in de fiel's? Yo' think we sen' you out there jes' to whoop and yell? No siree, we put you out there to work and you sho' bettah work, else we git de overseeah to cowhide you ole black back." My mammy jes grin all over her black wrinkled face and say: "I's saved. De Lawd done tell me I's saved. Now I know de Lawd will show me de way, I ain't gwine grieve no more. No matter how much yo' all done beat me an' my childun de Lawd will show me de way. An' some day we never be slaves." Ole granny Moore grab de cowhide and slash mammy cross de back but mammy nebber yell. She jes go back to de fiel' a singin'.[44]

Often during their private religious meetings out in the woods slaves would get so full of spirit that they imperiled the secrecy of the meeting. Richard Carruthers recalls that some of his fellow members used to get "so joyous they starts to holler loud and we has to stop up they mouth. I seen niggers get so full of the Lord and so happy they drops unconscious."[45] During most secret meetings "if anyone became animated and cried out, the others would quickly stop the noise by placing their hands over the offender's mouth."[46]

Many of the slaves' religious songs also tell of the uncontrollable movement of the spirit!

> O shout, O shout, O shout away,
> And don't you mind,
> And glory, glory, glory in my soul!

> And when 'twas night I thought 'twas day,
> I thought I'd pray my soul away,
> And glory, glory, glory in my soul![47]

> Big bells a-ringin' in de army of de Lord;
> Big bells a-ringin' in de army.
> I'm so glad I'm in de army of de Lord;
> My soul's a-shoutin' in de army.[48]

One of the sure ways that slaves told whether or not someone had true religion was if it was clear that his heart had been stirred by the spirit. To the people of the quarters religion was not something to be thought with the mind. Rather it was to be felt with the heart. Like Wes Woods of Kentucky, quarter people believed in "heart-felt religion and prayer" in which God would instruct them by the spirit in their heart.[49] "I can rise and tell you about God the darkest hour of midnight," proclaimed a Fisk informant. "The law is written in my heart and I don't need no book."[50] For the slaves, as for many blacks after emancipation, "Wisdom in the heart is unlike wisdom in the mind."[51]

Nor was heartfelt religion something that could be donned on Sunday and discarded on Monday. To have truly felt the spirit and to still be mean and unhappy was an impossibility. This was one of the chief reasons why slaves distrusted the religious convictions of their masters. One could not be truly filled with the spirit and remain a slaveholder. "White folks can't pray right to de black man's God," asserted Virginia ex-slave Henrietta Percy. "Cain't nobody do it for you. You got to call on God yourself when de spirit tell you to and let God know dat you been washed free from sin."[52] Another ex-slave from Virginia believed that: "Ole white preachers used to talk wid dey tongues widdout sayin' nothin', but Jesus told us slaves to talk wid our hearts."[53] Cordelia Jackson declared: "I stays independent of what white folks tells me when I shouts. De spirit moves me every day, dat's how I stays in. White folks don't feel sech as I does; so dey stays out."[54]

Two songs expressed this sentiment well:

> You call yourself church-member,
> You hold your head so high,
> You praise God with your glittering tongue,
> And leave all the heart behind.
>
> Hypocrite and concubine,
> Living among the swine;
> They run to God with the lips and tongue,
> And leave all the heart behind.[55]

For the quarter community, to pretend to religion without being truly moved was one of the few sure sins. "Ef I sing an' it doan move me any, den dat a sin on de Holy Ghost; I be tell a lie on de Lord."[56]

The quarter community, then, did not distinguish between the spirit world and the physical word. Many slaves believed that the Devil, God, and Jesus clearly and decisively intervened directly in the affairs of quarter people. For some slaves, according to William Wells Brown, "the devil was a real being, sporting a club-foot, horns, tail, and a bump on his back."[57] Old Satan roamed the earth on a constant lookout for ways to trick the slave into backsliding sin. But though the Devil was a force to be personally dealt with, and his presence feared, his power was no match for that of God and Jesus.

> Ole Satan thought he had a mighty aim;
> He missed my soul and caught my sins.
> Cry Amen, cry Amen, cry Amen to God!

127

Deep Like the Rivers

He took my sins upon his back;
Went muttering and grumbling down to hell.
Cry Amen, cry Amen, cry Amen to God![58]

Old Satan is one busy ole man;
   He rolls dem blocks all in my way;
But Jesus is my bosom friend
   He rolls dem blocks away.[59]

One could turn to God and Jesus not only as protection from sin and the Devil but as close personal friends and constant companions for the sick, the weary, the lonely, and the abused slave. God was prayed to at the whipping post, in the fields, in the mountains and forests, in the cabins, at morning, noon, or night. Often He spoke to His children directly: "Morte! Morte! Fear not, my little one, for behold! I come to bring you a message of truth."[60] "O William! O William! O William! Go preach my Gospel to every creature and fear not for I am with you, an everlasting prop. Amen!"[61] Orleans Finger who was a slave in Arkansas credits God with healing him. "I had a hurting in my leg, and I couldn't walk without a stick. Finally, one day I went to go and pick some turnips. . . . My leg hurt so bad that I talked to the Lord about it. And it seemed to me, He said, 'Put down your stick.' I put it down, and I ain't used it since."[62]

Frequently the slaves' faith in God enabled them to lose their fear of whites. William Webb says that "As soon as I felt in my heart that God was the Divine Being that I must call on in all my troubles, I heard a voice speak to me, and from that time I lost all fear of men on this earth."[63] This sentiment is expressed in song:

No fearin, no doubtin
While God's on our side.
We'll all die er shoutin'
De Lawd will provide.[64]

God's prompting could be felt, as we shall see in dealing with theme nine, even in the greatest of undertakings, the slave's escape.

The Reality and Significance of the Spirit World

Signs and dreams often signified God speaking to his children. "Seldom does anything happen in my family but that I get a warning," asserted one Fisk informant. "God knows what He is about and the best that any of us can do is to follow as He directs us through the spirit."[65]

> . . . I's always interested in the working of the signs. When I's a little pickaninny, my mammy and other folks used to talk about signs. I hears them talk about what happens to folks 'cause a spell was put on them. The old folks in them days know more about the signs that the Lord uses to reveal His laws than the folks of today. It am also true of the colored folks in Africa, they native land. Some of the folks laughs at their beliefs and says it am superstitition, but it am knowing how the Lord reveals His laws.[66]

Jesus, also, was a great source of friendship and comfort. "Nobody knows the trouble I've had, nobody knows but Jesus," was sung by many slaves in moments of suffering and sorrow.[67] Because Jesus, too, had experienced pain and grief, he of all persons would understand and bring comfort to the suffering slave. He too, had been " 'buked and scorned" just as they. He, too, had felt the whip, worn the crown of thorns, and borne the burdens of the cross. He had even been crucified, defiantly refusing to utter "a mumbling word."* For this reason, the quarter community felt a special kinship towards Jesus and were positive that he shared these feelings towards them and would share their suffering, ease their burdens, and cure their sicknesses. When one of the Fisk informants had a swollen leg, "The spirit directed me to get some peach-tree leaves and beat them up and put them about my limbs. I did this and in a day or two that swelling left me and I haven't been bothered since. . . . Dr. Jesus tells me what to do."[68]

The close personal friendship which slaves felt towards Jesus is revealed in many of the songs they sang. Nettie Van Buren's mother's favorite song was one entitled "Oh How I Love Jesus because He First Loved Me." At dawn slaves recognized His presence:

---

* The spiritual "they crucified my Lord, and He never said a mumbling word" reflects the admiration slaves felt for Jesus and for those of their own community who were able to bear a whipping without making a sound or begging for mercy.

Deep Like the Rivers

> In de mornin' when I rise,
> Tell my Jesus huddy, oh;
> I wash my hands in de mornin' glory,
> Tell my Jesus huddy, oh.[69]

At meetings in the valley they sang of His comfort and leadership:

> We will march thro' the valley in peace,
> We will march thro' the valley in peace;
> If Jesus himself will be our leader,
> We will march thro' the valley in peace.[70]

Many of the spirituals talk of "going home to Jesus," and some of the familial relationship slaves expected to enjoy with Jesus and his disciples in Heaven:

> A-settin' down with Jesus
> Eatin' milk and drinkin' wine
> Marchin' round de throne
> Wid Peter, James, and John.[71]

And often their conviction of His power and earthly presence gave them the strength to "fear no man but Jesus."[72]

> Walk in, kind Savior, No man can hinder me!
> Walk in, sweet Jesus, No man can hinder me!
> O no man, no man, no man can hinder me!
> O no man, no man, no man can hinder me!
>
> See what wonder Jesus done,
> O no man can hinder me. . . .
> Jesus make de dumb to speak.
> Jesus make de cripple walk.
> Jesus give de blind his sight.
> Jesus do most anything.[73]

❦ 11 ❧

Theme 8. The Desirability
of Learning to Read and Write

> You got a right,
> I got a right,
> We all got a right to the tree of life.

Slave Spiritual

By 1860 about five percent of the slaves had learned to read.[1] Many slaves were deterred from attempting to read or write by their awareness of the severe penalties they faced if discovered. A still greater number simply had no learning opportunity. Despite these facts, however, the black sources attest to a strong belief in the desirability of learning to read and write among the slave community.

Many informants speak of an unfulfilled longing to learn. "Dar is one thing I surely did want to do," asserts Mary Ella Grandberry, despite the fact she was illiterate while a slave, "and dat was to learn to read and write."[2] Booker T. Washington writes that he had no schooling whatever while a slave, although he remembers carrying his young mistress' books to the schoolhouse door. "The picture of several dozen boys and girls in a schoolroom engaged in study made a deep impression upon me, and I had the feeling that to get into a schoolhouse and study in this way would be about the same as getting into paradise."[3]

Of those slaves who did learn to read and write, many were taught by whites, especially by the sons and daughters of their masters. Moses Grandy observed that despite the laws against doing so, "A few well-disposed white young persons, of the families to which the slaves belonged, have ventured to teach them, but they dare not let it be known they have done so."[4] James

Graham told his interviewer that although they did so on the sly, "When the white children would come from school, my mother's people would get instruction from them."[5] James Sumler, who was able to buy a book with a ninepence that a man gave him for holding a horse, "hid in a hayloft on Sunday and got the younger white children to teach me."[6] John Thompson relates his own story:

> When about eight years of age, I was sent to the schoolhouse with the white children, to carry their dinners, it being a distance of two miles, and therefore too far for them to go home for them. There were two of these children relatives of my master, whose father had once been rich, but who, through misfortune, left his children almost penniless at his decease.
>
> Little Henry, one of the children, was one morning, while walking leisurely to school, repeating over his lesson, when I said to him, "How I would like to read like you." "Would you?" said he, "Then I will learn you." I told him, if his Uncle knew it, he would forbid it.
>
> "I know it," he answered, "But I will not tell him; for he would then stop you from going with me, and I would have to carry my own dinners!" Thereupon we made a mutual promise to reveal our secret to no person.
>
> Henry was about my own age, being the elder of the two children; his sister, Jane, being about five years old. He commenced teaching me from his book my letters. We sometimes started an hour or two before school time, that we might have more leisure for our undertaking. We had a piece of woods to pass on our way, which also facilitated the practical operation of our plans, as we could, by going into them, escape the observation of the other school children, or of passers by in the road. We even sometimes took Jane to the schoolhouse, leaving her to play with the other children, while we returned to our school in the woods, until the school bell rang.[7]

Some few masters appear to have taken an active interest in the education of a select few slaves. J. H. Curry's father was taught to read and write by his master who was a doctor so that he could take the addresses of visiting patients.[8] After Marrs was baptized his master "removed all objections to my learning how to read, and said he wanted all the boys to learn how to read the Bible. . . ."[9]

Often slaves learned to read from other slaves. Noah Davis learned to read and write from his father, as did others.[10] "Gate-eye" Fisher learned the alphabet from his mother, who had learned it from listening to the white children recite their ABC's.[11] Louis Hughes learned to write by imitating the writing of his friend, Thomas, the coachman.[12] Will Capers, an ex-slave from St. Helena Island, told Laura Towne in 1862 he had "conducted a secret night school for men during plantation days."[13] Douglass relates the following story of his own attempts to operate a clandestine school:

> As summer came on and the long Sabbath days stretched themselves over our idleness, I became uneasy and wanted a Sabbath-school in which to exercise my gifts and to impart to my brother-slaves the little knowledge I possessed. A house was hardly necessary in the summer-time; I could hold my school under the shade of an old oak tree as well as anywhere else. The thing was to get the scholars, and to have them thoroughly imbued with the idea to learn. Two such boys were quickly found in Henry and John, and from them the contagion spread. I was not long in bringing around me twenty or thirty young men, who enrolled themselves gladly in my Sabbath-school, and were willing to meet me regularly under the trees or elsewhere, for the purpose of learning to read. It was surprising with what ease they provided themselves with spelling-books.[14]

Impressive efforts were also made by individual slaves on their own behalf. W. E. Northcross tells of spending all of his Sundays without food on the mountain struggling to learn to read from his blue-back speller.[15] Steward "managed to purchase a spelling book, and set about teaching myself to read, as best I could. Every spare moment I could find was devoted to that employment, and when about my work I could catch now and then a stolen glance at my book, just to refresh my memory with the simple lesson I was trying to learn."[16] The first idea Noah Davis ever received of how to write "was from trying to imitate my employer, who used to write the names of his customers on the lining of the boots and shoes, as he gave them out to be made. So I tried to make letters, and soon succeeded in writing my name, and then the word Fredericksberg, and so on."[17] Douglass began his writing by copying the initials which the carpenters in the boatyard wrote on the timber they were preparing.[18] Bibb writes:

> Whenever I got hold of an old letter that had been thrown away, or a piece of white paper, I would save it to write on. I have often gone off in the woods and spent the greater part of the day alone, trying to learn to write myself a pass, by writing on the backs of old letters; copying after the pass that had been written by Whitfield; by so doing I got the use of the pen and could form letters as well as I can now, but knew not what they were.[19]

Often their attempts met with serious difficulty. When the little daughter of his mistress chanced upon Titus Byrnes practicing his letters on the ground, she informed on him. He was called before his mistress and told that if he was caught writing again his right arm would be cut off.[20] The mistress of Lewis Clarke made an even uglier threat. Upon being informed that Lewis had learned to spell, she "jumped up as though she had been shot. 'Let me ever know you to spell another word, I'll take your *heart* right out of you.'"[21]

Leonard Black, who experienced slavery in Maryland, had his first book for only one week "when the old man saw it in my bosom, and made inquiry as to what it was. He said, 'You son of a b---h, if I ever know you to have a book again, I will whip you half to death.' He took the book from me and burnt it."[22] Thompson was whipped and threatened with sale when he accidently handed his master a piece of paper containing a sample of his own writing.[23] Douglass Dorsey's alphabet and numbers were proceeding admirably with the help of one of the white children named Willie, when Willie's mother learned of their efforts.

> One morning after breakfast she called her son Willie to the dining room where she was seated and then sent for Douglass to come there too. She then took a quill pen the kind used at that time, and began writing the alphabet and numerals as far as ten.

The Desirability of Learning to Read and Write

> Holding the paper up to Douglass, she asked him if he knew what they were; he proudly answered in the affirmative, not suspecting anything. She then asked him to write them, which he did. When he reached the number ten, very proud of his learning, she struck him a heavy blow across the face, saying to him, "If I ever catch you making another figure anywhere I'll cut off your right arm."[24]

Ferebe Rodgers recalled a black man by the name of Enoch Golden who could read and write. "On his dyin' bed he said he had been de death o' many a nigger 'cause he taught so many to read and write."[25]

Often, however, the efforts of the white community to discourage the learning attempts of their slaves only strengthened the slaves' resolve. After several futile attempts at securing a book, Thomas Jones was finally successful. "I was a slave; and I knew that the whole community was in league to keep the poor slave in ignorance and chains. Yet I longed to be free, and to be able to move the minds of other men with my thoughts. It seemed to me now, that, if I could learn to read and write, this learning might—nay, I really thought it would, point out to me the way to freedom, influence, and real, secure happiness."[26] Later Jones received a severe whipping rather than divulge to his master where he had hidden the "dear book."[27]

The flogging which Austin Steward was given when found studying a book

> . . . [I]nstead of giving me the least idea of giving it up, only made me look upon it as a more valuable attainment. Else, why should my oppressors feel so unwilling that their slaves should possess that which they thought so essential to themselves? Even then, with my back bleeding and smarting from the punishment I had received, I determined to learn to read and write, at all hazards, if my life was only spared.[28]

When Frederick Douglass' master delivered a forceful lecture in which he forbade his wife from teaching Douglass to learn, "his iron sentences, cold and harsh, sunk like heavy weights deep into my heart, and stirred up within me a rebellion not soon to be allayed."

Deep Like the Rivers

This was a new and special revelation, dispelling a painful mystery against which my youthful understanding had struggled, and struggled in vain, to wit, the white man's power to perpetuate the enslavement of the black man. "Very well," thought I. "Knowledge unfits a child to be a slave." I instinctively assented to the proposition, and from that moment I understood the direct pathway from slavery to freedom. It was just what I needed, and it came to me at a time and from a source whence I least expected it. Of course I was greatly saddened at the thought of losing the assistance of my kind mistress, but the information so instantly derived, to some extent compensated me for the loss I had sustained in this direction. Wise as Mr. Auld was, he underrated my comprehension, and had little idea of the use to which I was capable of putting the impressive lesson he was giving to his wife. He wanted me to be a slave; I had already voted against that on the home plantation of Col. Lloyd. That which he most loved I most hated, and the very determination which he expressed to keep me in ignorance only rendered me the more resolute to seek intelligence. In learning to read, therefore, I am not sure that I do not owe quite as much to the opposition of my master as to the kindly assistance of my amiable mistress.[29]

Evidence of the slaves' belief in the desirability of learning to read and write comes not only from the many stories of individuals struggling for learning. More importantly, in terms of the slave community as a whole, this theme finds expression in the pride with which informants talk of other slaves who learned to read or write and in the esteem in which they were held, in the intensity and the frequency of the anger at slavery for limiting their educational opportunities, and in the efforts of the fugitive and newly emancipated slaves to secure schooling for themselves and their children.

One stimulus to learning was the recognition received from one's fellow slaves. Bruce says that to the slaves "A colored man who could read was a very important fellow."[30] Not only could such persons keep the other slaves abreast of the news, write them passes, and read to them straight from the Bible, but they disproved the racist notion promulgated by whites that blacks were incapable of such learning. Stories of literate slaves traveled quickly from plantation to plantation and were a source of great satisfaction within the quarters. Douglass writes that while he was a slave, "I was loved by the colored people, because they thought I was hated for my knowledge, and persecuted because I was feared. . . . My knowledge was now the pride of my brother slaves. . . ."[31]

A motive for learning to read could be disgust at the very prohibitions against slave learning and the sense of unfairness of having "to steal" their formal education. Alexander Hamilton says that he was not used badly as a slave "except that I was not taught to read nor write. . . ."[32] One of the chief reasons why William Troy decided to attempt escape was that "I could not educate my children there, and make them feel as women and men ought—for, under those oppressive laws, they would feel a degradation not intended by Him who made of one blood all the people of the earth."[33] Isaac Riley hated slavery because his son would be forced to "grow up in ignorance" and liked Canada because "My children can get good learning here."[34] One Fisk respondent explained why she did not want to return to slavery days despite the good life she had experienced on the plantation: "You see, children couldn't go to school in dem days."[35] "There is one sin that slavery committed against me," professed Pennington, "which I will never forgive. It robbed me of my education. . . ."[36]

Perhaps the most dramatic expression of the quarter community's great longing for education came after emancipation. When supervising the first "contrabands" at Fort Monroe in 1861, Edward L. Pierce "observed among them a widespread desire to learn to read."[37] In *Rehearsal for Reconstruction* Willie Lee Rose states that "By the end of 1862 more than 1,700 children were attending school on St. Helena, Ladies, and Port Royal Islands alone. . . . Conceived originally as a means of gaining the confidence of the colored people, teaching became an exciting goal in its own right, and the readiness and eagerness of the Negroes to learn to read was the subject of endless comment."[38] "The Negroes . . . ," wrote one observer of the Port Royal experiment, "will do anything for us, if we will only teach them."[39] Recalling the times directly after the end of the Civil War, Booker T. Washington paints a vivid picture of the great slave yearning for the ability to read and write:

Deep Like the Rivers

Few people who were not right in the midst of the scenes can form any exact idea of the intense desire which the people of my race showed for education. It was a whole race trying to go to school. Few were too young, and none too old, to make the attempt to learn. As fast as any kind of teachers could be secured, not only were day-schools filled, but night-schools as well. The great ambition of the older people was to try to learn to read the Bible before they died. With this end in view, men and women who were fifty and seventy-five years old, would be found in night-schools. Sunday-schools were formed soon after freedom, but the principal book studied in the Sunday-school was the spelling-book. Day-school, night-school, and Sunday-school were always crowded, and often many had to be turned away for want of room.[40]

◄⊗ 12 ▷◄

Theme 9. Freedom Is Something
of Great Value

*Though freedom was yearned for by some because the treatment
was so bad, others, who were bright and had looked into the matter,
knew it was a curse to be held a slave—they longed to stand out in
true manhood—allowed to express their opinions as were white
men. Others still desired freedom, thinking they could reclaim a
wife, or a husband, or children. The mother would again see her
child. All these promptings of the heart made them yearn for freedom.*

Louis Hughes

The theme that cut most deeply across the varying personalities and roles of quarter members was probably the theme of
freedom. Both the narratives and the songs and stories of the
slave community leave little doubt that slaves were united in a
common valuing of, and longing for, an "indescribable something called freedom." The black informants, with but rare exceptions, agree that while they were slaves the notion of freedom
occupied a central place in their thoughts and feelings.[1]

One of the best evidences of the quarter community's great
evaluation of freedom is the large amount of time which slaves
spent praying and planning for their freedom. Lunsford Lane
asserts that although "I saw no prospect that my condition would
ever be changed . . . I used to plan in my mind from day to day,
and from night to night, how I might be free."[2] Louis Hughes
and his friend named Thomas "used to get together every time
we had a chance and talk about freedom."[3] Clayborn Gantling
reports having heard "slaves morning and night pray for deliverance. Some of 'em would stand up in de fields or bend over

139

cotton and corn and pray out loud for God to help 'em. . . ."[4] On Laura Abromson's parents' plantation, as on many, the slaves had secret places where "they met and prayed for freedom."[5] John Thompson recalls that when he got hold of a newspaper containing a speech of John Quincy Adams, regarding a "petition of the ladies of Massachusetts, praying for the abolition of slavery in the District of Columbia," he read and reread it both to himself and in the quarters "until it was so worn that he could scarcely make out the printing."[6]

Slave conceptualizations of freedom and their reasons for desiring it varied greatly. When "too young to fully understand the meaning of freedom," Willis Dukes "wanted very much to go away to some place where he could earn enough money to buy his mother a dress."[7] Mary Reynolds tells how her family and the other slaves used to pray in secret "for the end of tribulation and the end of beatings and for shoes that fit our feet."[8] During his youth, Alexander Hensley's idea of freedom was "that it was a state of liberty for the mind—that there was a freedom of thought, which I could not enjoy unless I were free—that is, if I thought of anything beneficial for me, I should have the liberty to execute it."[9]

One of the most common reasons given for desiring freedom was the wish to end the unfairness of working without pay for the gain of another. "There is no one," writes Steward, "I care not how favorable his condition, who desires to be a slave, to labor for nothing all his life for the benefit of others. I have often heard fugitive slaves say, that it was not so much the cruel beatings and floggings that they received which induced them to leave the South, as the idea of dragging out a whole life of unrequited toil to enrich their masters."[10] Henry Blue asserts that "I should have been perfectly miserable to have had to work all my life for another man for nothing. As soon as I had arrived to years of discretion, I felt determined that I would not be a slave all my days."[11] James Williams viewed the leisure of the whites on his plantation as the "difference between freedom and slavery" and made up his mind that "when I was old enough I would run away."[12]

Freedom

Sometimes slaves sang of their longing to be free from the "hard trials of slavery, from wetting rain, and burning sun, from whips a-crakin, and dribers' dribing, from massa's hollering and missus' scolding."[13]

> Working all day,
> And part of the night,
> And up before the morning light.
>
> Chorus: When will Jehovah hear our cry,
> And free the sons of Africa?[14]

Often a desire for uninhibited religious expression was given as the reason for a yearning for freedom. Despite the fact that he was sold away from his parents at the age of ten, Tom Robinson remembers how his mother "used to take us children and kneel down in front of the fireplace and pray. She'd pray that the time would come when everybody would worship the Lord under their own vine and fig tree—all of them free. It's come to me lots of times since. There she was a'praying, and on other plantations women was a'praying. All over the country the same prayer was being prayed."[15]

Frederick Douglass was customarily philosophical about his personal reasons for desiring to be rid of slavery. "The thought of being only a creature of the *present* and the *past* troubled me, and I longed to have a *future*—a future with hope in it."[16]

Like many other black men and women who experienced slavery, Louis Hughes understood clearly that the reasons for cherishing the hope of freedom were many.

> Though freedom was yearned for by some because the treatment was so bad, others, who were bright and had looked into the matter, knew it was a curse to be held a slave—they longed to stand out in true manhood—allowed to express their opinions as were white men. Others still desired freedom, thinking they could then reclaim a wife, or a husband, or children. The mother would again see her child. All these promptings of the heart made them yearn for freedom.[17]

Deep Like the Rivers

In the narratives the most frequently mentioned freedoms are: the freedom to enjoy family life; the freedom to worship as one chooses, where and when one chooses; the freedom to come and go as one wishes and to freely associate with other blacks; the freedom to learn to read and write and to teach one's children; the freedom to express one's opinion without fear; the freedom from white supervision and abuse, and from the fear of that abuse; the freedom from forced labor for another man's profit; the freedom to decide on one's own occupation, level of exertion, and general life style.

Some of the informants suggest that on those plantations where slaves were kept in perpetual fear of the whip, or worse, where they were scantily fed and poorly clothed, and where infant mortality was high and disease commonplace, they most frequently talked about how to free themselves from fear, abuse, and hunger. Give a slave a bad master, argues Douglass, "and he aspires to a good master; give him a good master, and he wishes to become his own master. Such is human nature. You may hurl a man so low beneath the level of his kind, that he loses all just ideas of his natural position, but elevate him a little, and the clear conception of rights rises to life and power, and leads him onward."[18] Steward asserts that the more he and his friends "knew of freedom the more we desired it, and the less willing were we to remain in bondage."[19]

At the same time Northup offers his conclusion that even the most ignorant slaves valued the idea of freedom:

> They understand the privileges and exemptions that belong to it—that it would bestow upon them the enjoyment of domestic happiness. They do not fail to observe the difference between their own condition and the meanest white man's, and to realize the injustice of laws which place it within his power not only to appropriate the profits of their industry, but to subject them to unmerited and unprovoked punishment, without remedy, or the right to resist, or to remonstrate.[20]

And Webb recalls talking to the hungry, overworked, and constantly abused slaves of a neighboring plantation who nevertheless yearned for freedom: "They said they had been thinking they would be free, for a long time, and praying that they would live to see it. . . .[21]

Even more often than mention of specific freedoms, one finds in the narratives reference to Freedom in a generalized and idealized form. J. Vance Lewis recalls how as a boy of ten, he began to learn of a "mysterious something called freedom" which was longed for by the older blacks. "I observed them getting together in chimney corners and in other secret places whispering and talking earnestly and praying such prayers that I have never heard before, or since."[22] Henry Brown recollects "the thrills of exulting joy which the name of freedom caused to flow through my soul."[23] The thrill which could fill slaves at the very idea of being free is illustrated by Aaron in a story:

> A poor slave being on his death bed, begged of his master to give him liberty before he died, "I want to die free massa." His master replied, you are going to die soon, what good will your liberty do? "O master, I want to die free." He said to the slave, "You are free." "But do write it master, I want to see it on paper." At his earnest request he wrote that he was free, the slave took it in his trembling hand; looked at it with a smile and exclaimed, "O how beautiful, O how beautiful," and soon fell asleep in the arms of death.[24]

One gets a sense from the narratives that for many blacks freedom was not simply associated with the notion of escape from slavery, but that true Freedom consisted of all these lesser freedoms: freedoms, as we have seen, both from certain evils such as hunger, poverty, and white abuse; and freedoms to participate in certain desired goods such a family life, religious worship, self-employment. This notion of Freedom as the conglomeration of many lesser freedoms helps explain the skepticism on the part of many slaves concerning the possibility of true Freedom on earth as long as slavery continued. The great longing of the quarter community for Heaven can thus be seen, in part, as an expression of the slave understanding that while slavery continued, and the oppression of black men and women persisted, Freedom could be a reality only in Heaven; only there could blacks be free from white abuse.

The feeling that the closest approximation to Freedom which blacks could achieve on earth would come with the end of slavery rather than the escape from it can also be understood as an outgrowth of the quarter community's understanding of what black life in America was like for "free" blacks. Most members of the quarter community were well aware of the trials and troubles of the South's "free colored" population. This awareness, coupled with their ignorance concerning life in the North or Canada, caused them to question the certainty that they would enjoy more freedoms as so-called "freemen" than as slaves.[25]

The narratives do not leave the impression, however, that most of the quarter members thought of Freedom only in heavenly terms or were content to wait until their deaths to partake of its blessings. Although, as we have seen, the God of black folk religion was a comforter in the present and an assurance of better things to come in the hereafter, He is depicted most often and most powerfully as the God of Freedom who was working out His purposes right here on earth. Religious convictions and faith in God gave many slaves the needed courage to attempt escape. Archer Alexander reports that he heard the voice of God in a prayer telling him to flee.[26] Henry Brown credits God with the idea of his escaping in a box.[27] Thompson recalls being urged by three friends to accompany them on their escape attempt. One of these three was a black minister who particularly urged Thompson to come with them "saying he had full confidence in the surety of the promises of God, who had said that heaven and earth should pass away, before one jot of his word should fail; that he had often tried God, and never knew him to fail; consequently he believed he was able to carry him safely to the land of freedom, and accordingly he was determined to go."[28] William Webb writes that he "found that when I called on God in my trials he sent comfort to my heart, and told me the time would come, when I would be free in this world."[29]

Countless black men and women who did escape testify to their belief that had it not been for their faith that God sanctioned and protected their flight, their escape never would have been successful. The narratives are full of passages such as the following: "My escape was miraculous, and I attributed it all to

144

God."[30] "After more than twenty years of bondage, God delivered me from it, with a strong hand and an outstretched arm, as he did Israel of old."[31] ". . . it pleased the father of all mercy to look on me, and he sent a strengthening thought into my heart, which was this: that he that made the heavens and the earth, was able to deliver me."[32]

So strong was the belief that God intended slaves to seek freedom from slavery that those blacks who knew of the existence of the North Star were convinced "that the Lord had placed it there to lead people out of slavery."[33]

A significant number of blacks believed that it was their religious duty to free not only themselves but all of God's chosen people. Many of those slaves who assisted the escape of fellow blacks, or who returned into the land of bondage to lead others to freedom, did so not only out of friendship and love but out of a religious conviction that they had a moral responsibility to do so. It is no mere coincidence that in many of the so-called "slave rebellions" there emerged a black religious leader who felt called upon by God to become an instrument in the freeing of his people.

With the beginning of the Civil War, the quarter community's great longing for Freedom reached a crescendo. "The War was begun," recalls M. Anderson, "and there were stories of flights and freedom. The news went from plantation to plantation and while the slaves acted natural and some even more polite than usual, they prayed for freedom."[34] For the first time the dream of freedom from slavery without the loss of family or friends appeared to be a definite earthly possibility. "Ever since the beginning of the war, and the slaves had heard that possibly they might some time be free, they seemed unspeakably happy."[35]

Those slaves who were able to gain a correct understanding of the war's causes and potential ramifications believed that the Union army were none other than the soldiers of Christ and that the Day of Judgment was at hand for the slaveholder and the Day of Jubilee for the slave. "And though the South won victory after victory, and the Union reeled to and fro like a drunken man, the negroes never lost hope but faithfully supported the Union cause with their prayers."[36] William Adams relates what happened on his plantation after a white preacher had told the slaves that if they wanted to keep their homes and raise their children they had better pray for the South to win, and had made them agree to do so:

> That night all the slaves had a meeting down in the hollow. Old Uncle Mack, he gets up and says: "One time over in Virginia there was two old niggers, Uncle Bob and Uncle Tom. They was mad at one another, and one day they decided to have a dinner and bury the hatchet. So they sat down, and when Uncle Bob wasn't looking Uncle Tom put some poison in Uncle Bob's food, but he saw it and when Uncle Tom wasn't looking Uncle Bob he turned the tray around on Uncle Tom and he gets the poison food." Uncle Mack, he says: "That's what we slaves is gwine do, just turn the tray around and pray for the North to win."[37]

There was no way, believed the members of the quarter community, that Lincoln and his boys could lose. The God of Freedom was on their side and He "was using the Yankees to scourge the slaveholders just as He had, centuries before, used heathens and outcasts to chastise his chosen people—the Children of Israel."[38] When the other slaves told Angie Garrett about Mr. Lincoln, Angie thought "he was partly God."[39] "Slaves," asserted H. C. Bruce, "believed, deep down in their souls, that the government was fighting for their freedom, and it was useless for masters to tell them differently."[40]

And when the war was finally won, and the slaves received the message that they were "as free as master," jubilation filled the quarters as the slaves "cried and laughed and hollered and danced."[41]

> Niggers shoutin' an' clappin' hands an' singin'!
> Chillun runnin' all over de place beatin' tins an'
> yellin'. Ev'ybody happy. Sho' did some celebratin'.
> Run to de kitchen an' shout in de winder:
>
>> Mammy don't you cook no mo'
>> You's free! You's free!
>
> Run to de henhouse an shout:

Freedom

> Rooster, don't you crow no mo'
> You's free! You's free!
> Ol' hen, don't you lay no mo' eggs,
> You's free! You's free!

Go to de pigpen an' tell de pig:

> Ol' pig, don't grunt no mo'
> You's free! You's free!

Tell de cows:

> Ol' cow, don't you give no mo' milk,
> You's free! You's free!

An' some smart alec boys sneaked up under Miss
Sara Ann's winder an' shouted:

> Ain't got to slave no mo'
> We's free! We's free![42]

Nor did the quarter community leave any doubt about whom they believed to be ultimately responsible for their freedom. "One and all they remembered to thank God for their freedom. They immediately began to hold meetings, singing soul-stirring spirituals.

> T'ank ye Master Jesus, t'ank ye,
> T'ank ye Master Jesus, t'ank ye,
> T'ank ye Master Jesus, t'ank ye,
> Da Heben gwinter be my home.
> No slav'ry chains to tie me down,
> And no mo' driver's ho'n to blow for me
> No mo' stocks to fasten me down
> Jesus break slav'ry chain, Lord
> Break slav'ry chain Lord,
> Break slav'ry chain Lord,
> Da Heben gwinter be my home.[43]

De news come on a Thursday, an' all de slaves been shoutin' an' carryin' on till ev'ybody was all tired out. 'Member de fust Sundy of freedom. We was all sittin' roun' restin' an' tryin' to think what freedom meant a' ev'ybody was quiet an' peaceful. All at once ole Sister Carrie who was near 'bout a hundred started in to talkin':

147

Deep Like the Rivers

> Tain't no mo' sellin' today,
> Tain't no mo' hirin' today,
> Tain't no pullin' off shirts today,
> Its stomp down freedom today.
> Stomp it down!

An' when she says "Stomp it down," all de slaves commence to shoutin' wid her:

> Stomp down Freedom today—
> Stomp it down!
> Stomp down Freedom today.

Wasn't no mo' peace dat Sunday. Ev'ybody started in to sing an' shout once mo'. Fust thing you know dey done made up music to Sister Carrie's stomp song an' sang an' shouted dat song all de res' de day. Chile, dat was one glorious time![44]

We was dancin' an prancin' an' yellin' wid a big barn fire jus' ablazin' an' de white folks not darin' to come outside de big house. Guess dey made 'em up, 'cause purty soon ev'ybody fo' miles around was singin' freedom songs. One went like dis:

> I's free, I's free, I's free at las'!
> Thank God A'mighty, I's free at las'![45]

Conclusion

In the attempt to learn about the nature of life under slavery as understood and experienced by slaves themselves, the study of the themes of the quarter community help by giving relief to those postulates most central to the way quarter people saw their world. It is also possible to learn about the quarter community by noting the absence of certain other themes. For instance, there is little in the narratives to suggest that the quarter community made a strong delineation among people, either with respect to innate ability or role, according to their sex. One is struck by the absence of the familiar theme of male superiority and by the lack of evidence to support the view that the quarters was a female-dominated society. The black source material suggests, rather, a general equality between females and males.

Although plantation authorities generally observed a sexual bias in their appointment of slaves to certain tasks—men as drivers, artisans, butlers; women as cooks, sewers, nursery atten dants—no hard and fast role differentiation appeared in the quarters. While it is true that in most slave households women did the cooking, washing, sewing, and cleaning and men did the gardening, constructing, and hunting, roles were reversed often enough to suggest this was more a convenient division of labor than an expression of a societal norm that favored one sex over the other. Many of the narratives depict men cooking, sewing, and having primary responsibility for the care of children. Others give frequent examples of women who were champion cotton pickers, conjurors, doctors, storytellers, rebels, and re-vered community leaders. Even women preachers appear often enough, though admittedly less frequently than male preachers, to suggest that there was no community prohibition against their filling this crucial role. While it is true that more community dis-favor probably fell upon female than male adulterers, no signifi-cant community sanctions appeared concerning either female or male premarital chastity. Both the men and the women of the quarter community drank and smoked and there is no indication that the community felt this to be a pastime more suitable for one sex than the other.

In line with this lack of community discrimination between the sexes the narratives also suggest that the quarter community demonstrated little uptightness about their own sexual needs and forms of expression. Most slaves appear to have had little shame of nudity and to have viewed sex with a lack of guilt-ridden attitudes. Sex was seen as natural and pleasurable and, therefore, something meant to be enjoyed without either guilt or shame. "Two clean sheets can't smut," appears to have been one of the maxims of the quarter community. As explained by Rias Body, it meant that a virtuous man and woman were free to "indulge in the primal passion without committing sin."[1]

The black source material also displays an absence of any conscious thematic reference to Africa. However much their mode of communication, their carriage, their institutions, their beliefs, and the themes themselves might have been influenced by African antecedents, a conscious identification with things African is absent from the statements of all but a few of the informants. For most informants, America, for better or worse, was seen as home. For the slaves particularly, especially by the late years of slavery, home was their own quarter community. The informants do not, however, provide evidence that slaves wished to be disassociated from Africa or things African. On the contrary, many of the informants speak with pride of being full-blooded Africans.[2]

Thus the absence of certain themes such as sex discrimination and overt African loyalism itself suggests a theme. More positively one can study the interaction of themes as both limiting and supporting factors. The theme of true religion, for instance, by uniting slaves in the common consciousness of a just cause against the immorality of slavery, gave support to expressions of the theme of communality. By viewing slaves in a moral position superior to that of whites, it also encouraged expressions of the theme of black superiority.

The themes of communality, white power, and family all served to limit that expression of the theme of Freedom which

Conclusion

involved attempting to escape from slavery. The sadness at leaving their families and friends and the consciousness of the united determination of the white community to block such attempts, and make examples of those caught, were, as we have seen, major deterrents to the decision "to make the attempt." Concomitantly, other themes—antipathy to whites, and the desire to get away from them, true religion, and the conviction of the immorality of slavery, and the desire to read and write—were often the prime motivating factors in implementing the theme of Freedom by attempting to escape.

The interaction of themes could take complicated forms. At the same time that the theme of family was limiting expression of the theme of Freedom, the theme of Freedom was limiting expressions of the importance of the family. William Wells Brown, for example, refused to marry because he knew it would make escape more difficult.[3] Bibb would not marry until he had ascertained that the woman he loved was willing to attempt escape with him.[4]

The study of the nature of the themes provides some insight into the dynamic between the quarter community and the white world within which it existed. With few exceptions, the expressions of quarter community themes were not formalized expressions.[5] Rather most thematic expressions seem to be of the variety that Opler has called "unformalized expressions," "which test the resourcefulness, ingenuity, and originality of those who devise them" and "whose precise character, time, or place are not carefully defined by the culture."[6] The overt behavior of plantation blacks depended too often on the ever changing and varied restrictions placed upon it by plantation etiquette and white personality to permit the quarter community to be prescriptive about how themes were to be expressed. How the community expected the individual slave to express his loyalty to the quarter community, his antipathy to whites, his longing for Freedom, all varied according to possibilities within a given plantation. By and large how to express a theme was left up to the individual, who was expected to make quick judgments concerning the realities of his personal circumstances.

Indeed, an analysis of the themes suggests that the dynamic

tension between the world of whites and the world of the quarter community played a crucial role in shaping how slaves thought and acted. Each of the themes, either directly or by implication, is concerned with this dynamic. In the case of "true Christianity versus slaveholding priestcraft" the tension between the two societies has been incorporated within a single theme. The themes of "communality" and "black superiority," which might in another culture represent only a strong ethnocentrism, take on a whole other dimension when juxtaposed with the accompanying themes of "antipathy to whites" and "white power." The theme dealing with the spirit world is affected significantly by the slave belief in the inability of whites to participate effectively in the world of the spirit. The importance of Freedom to the quarter community is inexplicable without direct reference to the slaves' attitude towards the institution of slavery. Even the themes of "the importance of the family" and "the desirability of learning to read and write" are significantly shaped by the slaves' sense of the limitations placed upon them by their slave status in the eyes of the white world.

That the themes are all significantly influenced by the relationship between the quarter community and white society does not imply, however, that quarter culture was completely circumscribed by the institution of slavery or that slaves were obsessed with an awareness of their slave status and a fear of white power. At least four of the themes—communality, true Christianity, black superiority, and the spirit world—stand in direct opposition to the unlimited expression of the theme of white power. Slaves felt that they could contend with white power not only through their own individual maneuvering but with the aid of spiritual forces, including primarily the God of their religion, and with the aid of other slaves. The quarter conviction of the great power of God and the conviction of His unalterable opposition to slavery gave slaves a sense of the impotence of white power in God's ultimate scheme of things. Furthermore, the members of the quarter community, especially at night and during their leisure time, were able to create their own institutions within which whites had little, if any, influence.

Most importantly for the purposes of this book, the themes of

Conclusion

black life under slavery reveal dramatically just how little of white teaching was absorbed into the way members of the quarter community looked at the world. With the exception of the theme of white power, the themes of the quarter community imply values, attitudes, and beliefs quite different from those which whites attemped to inculcate in their black populations. Indeed, the most vivid picture of the quarter community which grows out of the themes is that of a people struggling with considerable success to create and maintain their own separate system of values and ways of understanding and dealing with the world.

PART III

THE EDUCATIONAL INSTRUMENTS
OF THE QUARTER COMMUNITY

I build my house upon de rock,
O yes, Lord!
No wind, no storm can blow 'em down,
O yes, Lord!

Allen, *Slaves Songs*

Introduction

In the preceding discussion of white teaching and black learning, I have argued that most members of most quarter communities learned to think and act in ways very different from those intended and taught by plantation whites. Although, as seen in Part I, whites used a variety of techniques in the attempt to mold their black population into obedient, docile, trustworthy, and grateful servants, Part II has shown that the adult members of the quarter community were able to transmit to their children and sustain in themselves a set of themes which were distinctly their own. How this was possible within a slave system which limited their forms of self-expression and organization is a question raised but left unanswered in Part II. The succeeding chapters seek to provide an answer by examining five slave institutions which provided quarter people a firm, rocklike foundation upon which to educate their children.

✺ 13 ✺

The Family

Don't you 'member what you promise de Lord?
Don't you 'member what you promise de Lord?
You promise de Lord that you would feed his sheep,
And gather his lambs so well.

Allen, *Slave Songs*

As was shown earlier, the nuclear family was the ideal family norm of the quarter community. Most blacks under slavery employed the term "family" in much the same way as did their white contemporaries, to mean the blood-relationship of father, mother, their common children and a possible grandparent, aunt, or uncle. Yet, despite the fact that they often donate their first few lines to an attempted outline of their blood-line family tree, most of the black narrators record the personalities and activities of people involved in a larger pattern of family associations and responsibilities. This larger family pattern included not only what is often referred to as the "extended family," but also other persons not necessarily related by blood or marriage. Such individuals might include step-parents, peer group members, community leaders, religious meeting brethren, nursery teachers, doctors, conjurors, special friends, and any other individuals who, for reasons other than kinship by blood, felt a familial responsibility to help nurture, protect, and educate any given black child. It is this larger grouping of persons which was the primary educational instrument of the quarter community and which was the quarter child's family under slavery.

Using such a definition of family, a blood-related parent—such as the white fathers of Frederick Douglass, William Wells Brown, Henry Bibb, and several others—who felt no responsi-

157

bility to nurture, protect, and educate is not considered a member of the child's family. A recently introduced fellow slave, as was Charles Ball when first placed in a quarter household after being sold away from his home quarters, who took a large part of the responsibility for feeding, sheltering, guarding and teaching a particular child becomes through the assuming of that responsibility a part of that child's family.[1] Under this definition it would thus be quite possible for two blood-tied brothers of the same household to have very different families.

This does not mean that any individual who might take such responsibility for a given child temporarily, or might tell her a story of Africa, place a charm around her neck, share his food, or save her from a snake or the blows of the overseer becomes by such deeds alone a member of that child's family. To become and remain a member of any family the member's adoption of responsibility must be of a sustained nature, unbroken by the normal rigors and regulations of plantation life. Furthermore, the relationship, depending on the age of the child, must be at least partially reciprocal. The child must feel not only that the individual can be relied upon but must have formed through personal contact a sense of attachment to him, identifying him with other family members and showing a growing concern for that member's welfare.

To be sure, family membership as here defined leaves somewhat blurred the distinction between the nature of the attachment formed between members of the same family and the duties and familial attitudes which most members of the quarter community had towards each other. Such a lack of clarity, however, is endemic to a situation in which, on many plantations, the family and the larger community became synonymous.[2] The indistinctness of the line between family and community, by rendering the predetermination of family lines and relationships impossible, reduces the question of family to a vital essential. What made a family were those individuals important to the child in terms of his nurture, protection, and education. Concern for the welfare of the dependent was added to, or could even become a substitute for, blood-relationships.

The Family

Mother was the central figure in the quarter family's educational role. From the time she first suckled her child at her breast, rocked him in her lap, or sang him to sleep, she began the process of transmitting values, beliefs, feelings, that would be reinforced later more deliberately. As a baby the black child of the quarters learned that comfort and security were to be found in black arms; that nurture came from black breasts; that drowsy tranquility accompanied the sounds of black music; that love was the caress of a black hand or the singing of a black voice. Many a slave's oldest and fondest memory was that of lying on his mother's lap, being "warmed in her bosom in the cold night of winter," and hearing her sing him to sleep with a lullaby. "Mamma was de good woman," recalls Lorenzo Ezell, "and I 'member her more than once rockin' de little cradle and singin' to de baby."[3]

> De moonlight, a shinin' star,
> De big owl hootin' in de tree;
> O, bye, my baby, ain't you gwinter sleep,
> A-rockin' on my knee?
>
> Bye, my honey baby,
> A rockin' on my knee,
> Baby done gone to sleep,
> Owl hush hootin' in de tree.
>
> She gone to sleep, honey baby sleep,
> A-rockin' on my, a-rockin' on my knee.[4]
>
> To a cabin in a woodland drear,
> You've come a mammy's heart to cheer,
>   In this ole slave's cabin,
> Your hands my heart strings grabbin'
> Jes lay your head upon my bres',
>
> Jes snuggle up close and res, and res,
> My little colored chile.[5]

159

Deep Like the Rivers

Often children were first introduced to the religion of the quarters through the songs of their mother. One ex-slave remembers that whenever he fell asleep over his supper his mother would pick him up and "set down wid me on the front stoop. Me in her arms. Singin' ter me, de songs she sing in church. . . . An' when Mammy sing an' rock, I hol' my haid tight 'gainst her breas'. She might keep on singing but I done gone to sleep."[6]

> Shout on, chil'en, you never die; Glory hallelu!
> You in de Lord, an' de Lord in you; Glory hallelu!
>
> Come on, chil'en, let's go home;
> O I'm so glad you're in de Lord.[7]

As the children grew older they learned from their mother how to care for themselves and their younger brothers and sisters. They were taught how to feed, watch over, and amuse the infants of their families; how to wash clothes in the wash house or in a nearby stream; how to comb black hair. "They had these combs that was just like cards you 'card' cotton with," remembers a Fisk interviewee, "and they would comb your hair with them."[8] Charley Williams learned how to make "pretty, long back-combs outen cow horn, and knitting needles outen second hickory."[9]

Girls, and less frequently boys, learned from mother how to sew, spin, iron, and clean. All children were taught how to stuff mattresses with moss, straw, or corn shucks; how to make candles from the fat of oxen and sheep; how to make buttons from dried gourds; how to color clothes with dye made from the juice of wild indigo, poke berries, and walnuts; and how to make home soap.[10] Lye for the soap was obtained by putting oak ashes in a barrel and pouring water over them. When the ashes had decayed by standing for several days, holes were drilled into the bottom of the barrel and the liquid lye drained off and trickled into a pot where the fat had been placed. The two were then boiled and, after cooking, cut into squares of soap.[11]

Both boys and girls were taught by their mothers how to cook. They were shown how to boil food in the pots hung out on long

160

The Family

hooks over the fire, fry food in the three-legged pans called "spiders," and cook vegetables wrapped in cabbage leaves and placed upon the coals.[12] Most slave children learned how to grind corn into meal, make coffee from parched potato peelings, brew tea from an assortment of herbs and leaves; procure baking powder from red corn cobs; fashion salt from sea water or the dirt from under the smokehouse meat; and distill whiskey, wine, and beer from any and all available vegetables.[13] Doc Quinn learned to make cotton seed and cornmeal mush by pouring corn-meal into a thick liquid produced by boiling cotton seeds for several hours.[14] Robert Grinstead was taught how to pound rice with mortar and pestle "until hulled and ready for cooking. This rice would be boiled with just salt and water and eaten as a great feast with delight."[15] Harriet Cheatam describes how Tennessee slaves used to cook chicken:

> When we roasted a chicken, we got it all nice and clean, stuffed him with dressing, greased him all over good, put a cabbage leaf on the floor of the fireplace, put the chicken on the cabbage leaf, then covered him good with another cabbage leaf, and put hot coals all over and around him, and left him to roast.[16]

One of the most artful cooking skills passed on to their children by quarter mothers was the routine for making the famous "hoe" or "ashcake." Austin Parnell gives this description of his grandmother's careful baking steps:

> She'd take a poker before she put the bread in and rake the ashes off the hearth down to the solid stone or earth bottom, and the ashes would be banked in two hills to one side and the other. Then she would put the batter down on it; the batter would be about an inch thick and about nine inches across. She'd put down three cakes at a time and let 'em stay there till the ashes were firm—about five minutes on the bare hot hearth. They would almost bake before she covered them up. Sometimes she would lay down as many as four at a time. The cakes had to dry before they were covered up, because if they were wet, there would be ashes in them when you would take them out to eat. She'd take her poker then and rake the ashes back on top of the cakes and let 'em stay there till the cakes were done. . . . Then she'd rake down the hearth gently, backward and forward, with the poker till she got

161

down to them and then she'd put the poker under them and lift them out. That poker was a kind of flat iron. It wasn't a round one. Then we'd wash 'em off like I told you and they'd be ready to eat. . . . Two-thirds of the water used in the ash cake was hot water, and that made the batter stick together like it was biscuit dough. She could put it together and take it in her hand and pat it out flat and lay it on the hearth. It would be just as round! That was the art of it![17]

More important, perhaps, than her teaching of household skills was the role which mother played in the transmission of religious beliefs, a longing for freedom, a desire to learn, a way of viewing and dealing with white people, and a sense of identification and solidarity with the other members of the quarter community. "What religious instruction I received on the plantation," asserts James Adams, "was from my mother."[18] Josiah Henson remembers his mother was "a good mother to us, a woman of deep piety, anxious above all things to touch our hearts with a sense of religion. . . . I remember seeing her often on her knees," and hearing her praying with "constant ejaculations, and the repetition of short phrases which were within my infant comprehension, and have remained in my memory to this hour."[19] One elderly preacher interviewed by the Fisk project reveals that "as a boy I lived close to my mother and she taught me how to live and pray and how to take care of myself." The seed of religion was planted in his heart by the prayers he heard and by "the joy and happiness that filled the older people's hearts . . . for I can never forget how my mother shouted and cried and wrung her hands for joy on the morning she was overcome by the Holy Spirit."[20] Another ex-slave says he learned to pray through imitation of his mother.

Me and my sister used to lazy around in the bed at night and listen to her and my aunt talk about what God had done for them. From this I began to pray like I heard them pray, I didn't know what it meant. I hardly knew what I said half the time, I just said something with the Lord's name in it and asked Him to have mercy on me.[21]

The Family

Often a young slave's incipient desire to be free was awakened by his mother and her prayers. Campbell recalls his mother praying three times a day "for mercy, deliverance, and protection."[22] Fannie Moore's mother was troubled in the heart about the way the overseer treated her children. "Every night she pray for de Lawd to get her an' her childun out ob de place."[23] Duncan Gaines remembers that his mother used to whisper to him and his brothers and sisters about the war and "fanned to a flame their desire to be free."[24] Booker T. Washington, who was only seven at the end of the Civil War, writes that he first learned he and his family were slaves and that freedom was a possibility "early one morning before day, when I was awakened by my mother kneeling over her children and fervently praying that Lincoln and his armies might be successful, and that one day she and her children might be free."[25]

Douglass attributed his love of letters to his mother, who had inspired him with her ability to read and her "earnest love of knowledge."[26] When one of her older sons learned to read from one of the white children, Bruce's mother made him teach the next oldest and so on.

> The older ones would teach the younger, and while mother had no education at all, she used to make the younger study the lesson given by the older sister or brother, and in that way they all learned to read.[27]

In families without grandparents it was frequently the role of mother to transmit the stories of Africa, and the folklore and songs of the quarter community which she had learned from her own parents or grandparents. These stories, as we shall see later, served not merely to transmit values and attitudes to each new generation but, by linking children to their ancestors, helped cement family ties. John Brown's mother used to repeat the story of John's grandmother and her capture in Africa:

> One day a big ship stopped off the shore and the natives hid in the brush along the beach. Grandmother was there. The ship men sent a little boat to the shore and scattered bright things and

163

trinkets on the beach. The natives were curious. Grandmother said everybody made a rush for them things soon as the boat left. The trinkets was fewer than the peoples. Next day the white folks scatter some more. There was another scramble. The natives were feeling less scared, and the next day some of them walked up the gangplank to get things off the plank and off the deck. The deck was covered with things like they'd found on the beach. Two-three hundred natives on the ship when they feel it move. They rush to the side but the plank was gone. Just dropped in the water when the ship moved away.

Folks on the beach started to crying and shouting. The ones on the boat was wild with fear. Grandmother was one of them who got fooled, and she say the last thing seen of that place was the natives running up and down the beach like they was mad. The boat men came up from below where they had been hiding and drive the slaves down in the bottom and keep them quiet with whips and clubs. The slaves was landed at Charleston. The town folks was mighty mad 'cause the blacks was driven through the streets without any clothes, and drove off the boat men after the slaves was sold on the market. Most of that load was sold to the Brown plantation in Alabama. Grandmother was one of the bunch.[28]

Sometimes slave mothers taught their children to resist white abuse physically. Richard Crump's mother inspired him to resist through her own example.[29] Lulu Wilson reports that her mother "could cuss and wasn't afraid. Wash Hodges tried to whip her with a cowhide and she'd knock him down and bloody him up."[30] Leonard Franklin tells of his mother and how she used to resist every whipping. "There wasn't many men could class up with her when it come to working. She could do more work than any two men. There wasn't no use for no one man to try to do nothing with her. No overseer never downed her."[31] Another mother deliberately instructed her children to resist.

The one doctrine of my mother's teaching that was branded upon my senses was that I should never let anyone abuse me. "I'll kill you, gal, if you don't stand up for yourself," she would say. "fight and if you can't fight, kick; if you can't kick, then bite."[32]

More often quarter mothers taught their children to be cautious in their dealing with whites: to run and hide at the sight of unknown whites and to be circumspect when forced to talk to any white. "My mother," relates a former slave, "used to teach me how to listen and hear and keep my mouth shut."

> Sometimes she would have a little meeting and some of the slaves from neighboring farms would come over. We children had better get out or at least make like we were not listening to what was being said and done. She used to call me to her and say, "Now don't you tell anybody that so and so was here, or that you saw me do so and so." She would caution me because she knew the white folks would be trying to pick some things out of me.[33]

To judge by the reports of the narrators, slave mothers were strict disciplinarians. Children were brought up not only to respect older blacks but to be polite in their presence and to obey their commands. Cora Armstrong's mother "did not allow us to sit around grown folks. When they were talking she always made us get under the bed."[34] Marriah Hines asserts that in slavery days "Children was mostly seen, not heard, different from youngens of today talking backward and foward cross their mamies and pappies. Chillen dat did dat den would git de breath slapped out on 'em."[35]

If children disobeyed they were sometimes cautioned with tales of haunts, spirits, and the slave bogey man, Raw-Head-and-Bloody-Bones. "Mother tole me a lot 'bout Raw Head an' Bloody Bones," remembers Jane Lassiter, "an' when I done mean she say, 'Better not do dat any more Raw Head an' Bloody Bones gwine ter git yo'.' "

> Don't talk! Go to sleep!
> Eyes shet an' don't you peep!
> Keep still, or he jes moans:
> Raw Head an' Bloody Bones![36]

More commonly they were threatened, or actually chastised, with the switch. "Mothers," writes Elijah Marrs, "were necessarily compelled to be severe on their children to keep them from talking too much. Many a poor mother has been whipped nearly to death on account of their children telling the white children things, who would then go and tell their mothers or fathers. My mother always told me what she was going to whip me for before commencing, and would talk to me while she was whipping me."[37] "Young people today don't know how to treat old folks," complained a Fisk informant. "In them days parents could just look at children and out their eyes at them and they would know what they meant. And if you said anything they would give you a back-hand lick without even looking at you."[38]

The relationship between most slave mothers and their children, however, does not appear to have been an irrationally harsh and disciplinary one. Though most slave mothers were forced to be authoritative they were seldom authoritarian.[39] By watching mother and through interacting warmly with her, most slave children learned not only what it meant to sacrifice but what it meant to feel loved. Sometimes mother's sacrifices were of an heroic nature. Peter Bruner recalls that his mother used to interfere physically with the master's abuse of her children.[40] One day J. T. Tims bit his mistress when she started to beat him for no apparent reason. His mistress then ordered another slave named William to come and beat him. "Ma had been peeping out from the kitchen watchin' the whole thing. When William come up to beat me, she come out with a big carving knife and told him, 'That's my child and if you hit him, I'll kill you.' "[41] J. W. Loguen's mother started a fire to save him from further torture after he had been beaten into a state of semi-consciousness.[42] In order to prevent her children from being sold, Moses Grandy's mother

> . . . [O]ften hid us all in the woods. . . . When we wanted water, she sought for it in any hole or puddle formed by falling trees or otherwise. It was often full of tadpoles and insects. She strained it, and gave it round to each of us in the hollow of her hand. For food, she gathered berries in the woods, got potatoes, raw corn, etc. After a time, the master would send word to her to come in, promising he would not sell us.[43]

More routine sacrifices provided slave children with equally great evidence of their mother's love. Though Sally Williams' mother was often somewhat stern, she trained her children "to the best of her ability in all industry and honesty. Every moment she could gain from labor was spent in spinning, and knitting, and sewing to keep them decently clothed."[44] Another former slave's mother worked all the time to keep her children clean and warm. "She would go around with her knitting in her pockets, and if she had to walk from the cabin to the house she would always knit whereever she walked to. Sometimes she would sit on top of the mule on her way to the field, knitting."[45] Harrison Beckett recalls that his mother, after working all day for her master in the fields and much of the night for her family in their cabin, would often be so tired that she would "go to bed without eatin' nothin' herself."[46] Ball's mother often divided her food among her children and went supperless herself.[47] Washington observed that the early years of his life, "which were spent in the little cabin were not very different from those of thousands of other slaves."

> My mother, of course, had little time in which to give attention to the training of her children during the day. She snatched a few moments for our care in the early morning before her work began, and at night after the day's work was done. One of my earliest recollections is that of my mother cooking a chicken late at night, and awakening her children for the purpose of feeding them. How or where she got it I do not know. I presume, however, it was procured from our owner's farm.[48]

Despite the fact that his mother kept a switch at hand to help raise her children, David Gullins remembers her as

> ... [O]ne of the best women God ever made. ... All through cold, bitter winter nights, I remember my mother getting up often to see about us and to keep the cover tucked in. She thought us sound asleep, and I pretended I was asleep while listening to her prayers. She would bend over the bed and stretching her arms so as to take us all in, she prayed with all her soul to God to help her bring up her children right.[49]

The educational impact of quarter families also depended greatly upon the role played by father. In most families, the father's role in the nurture, protection, and education of his children grew as the children grew. During infancy it consisted mainly of holding them, playing with them, and singing to them at night; of walking with them through the quarters on Sundays and holidays; and of planning for their future. Wash Ford's father used to bounce him up and down and roll with him on the floor.[50] Thomas Jones and his wife Lucinda "were never tired of planning to improve their [children's] condition, as far as might be done for slaves."[51]

As they grew older slave children were often indebted to their fathers for extra food and clothing.

> Little Boy, Little Boy, who made your breeches?
> Mama cut 'em out and pappa sewed de stitches.[52]

Many fathers tended their own garden patches on Sundays and at night. Mary Biddle's father used to set up "huge scaffolds in the fields which he burned" in order to produce light enough to work after dark.[53] Besides tending a garden many slaves raised their own chickens. Molly Ammond's father raised enough chickens to provide his family with eggs "nearly ev'ry mornin'."[54] Some slave fathers made cider, wine, whiskey, and even beer. West Turner describes how he made persimmon beer: "Jest stuck our persimmons in a keg with two or three gallons of water and sweet potato peelings and some hunks of corn bread and left it there until it began to work."[55]

Ball cites the example of a fellow slave who decided to go shoeless and to "lay out all his savings" in order to keep his wife and children warmly clothed and provide other "little necessities as were called for by his wife, from time to time."[56] Ball's own father kept his children supplied with "apples, melons, sweet potatoes, or, if he could produce nothing else, a little parched corn."[57] Sally was always glad to see her father come because "he brought us 'coons, an' 'possums, an' we had meat to eat."[58]

Ida May Fluker says that every Christmas her father would "bring me and my sister a red dress buttoned in the back."[59] Sometimes fathers supplied their children with clothes fashioned with the bounty of their hunting expeditions.

The Family

Bye baby buntin'
Daddy's gone a-huntin'
Ter fetch a little rabbit skin
Ter wrap de baby buntin' in.[60]

Slave fathers generally took the responsibility to make furniture and various other household articles, and in the process taught their older children. From their fathers quarter children learned how to make baskets of wooden splits, brooms of young white oak or hickory trees, mats of swamp rushes, horse collars of cornshucks, and hats of straw.[61] Most boys, and many girls, learned how to fix a gourd for drinking, hew wooden trays out of logs, and whittle dinner spoons and walking sticks.[62] They learned to make the beds, chairs, tables, and cabinets with which their cabin was furnished.

Sometimes besides providing the family with the articles themselves, these skills allowed family members to get a little money for extra family comforts. Pennington recalls how he "used to assist my father at night in making straw-hats and willow baskets, by which means we supplied our family with little articles of food, clothing and luxury, which slaves in the mildest form of the system never get from the master; . . ."[63]

Hunting and fishing were useful skills which fathers taught their sons, and not infrequently their daughters. Mittie Freeman, who experienced life as a slave in both Mississippi and Arkansas, was fishing with her father "the day freedom came."[64] Louisa Adams, who grew up on a large North Carolina plantation with her parents and eight brothers and sisters, says that "My old daddy partly raised his chilluns on game. He caught rabbits, coons, an' possums. He would work all day and hunt at night."[65] Robert Shepherd gives this description of how he learned to hunt rabbits while still a young slave in Georgia. "Marster didn't allow no huntin' with guns, so us just took dogs when us went huntin'. Rabbits was kilt with sticks and rocks 'cept when big snow come. Dey was easy to track to dey beds den, and us could just reach in and pull 'em out."[66]

As they grew old enough to be trusted, slave children began to accompany their fathers on late night "bagging" expeditions, and they were taught how to preserve excess meat until it could be safely eaten.

> I have seen pa go out at night with a big sack and come back with it full. He'd bring sweet potatoes, watermelons, chickens and tur-keys. We were fond of pig roast and sweet potatoes, and the only way to have pig roast was for pa to go out on one of his hunting trips. Where he went I cannot say, but he brought the booty home. The floor of our cabin was covered with planks. Pa had raised up two planks, and dug a hole. This was our storehouse.[67]

Those men talented or lucky enough to have learned a special skill were sure to attempt to pass it on to their children. Quarter fathers taught their sons and daughters how to read and write, how to doctor and conjure, how to dance, sing, tell stories and make and play a variety of musical instruments.[68] Often fathers played an important role in the transmission of the stories of the family history. W. Davis remembers his father who was proud and walked straighter than anybody he had ever seen. "He come from Congo, over in Africa, and I heard him say a big storm drove de ship somewhere on de Ca'lina coast."[69] Shack Thomas' father "used to spend hours after the candles were out telling him and his brothers about his capture and subsequent slavery.

> Adam was a native of the West Coast of Africa, and when quite a young man was attracted one day to a large ship that had just come near his home. With many others he was attracted aboard by bright red handkerchiefs, shawls, and other articles in the hands of the seamen. Shortly afterwards he was securely bound in the hold of the ship, to be later sold somewhere in America. Thomas does not know exactly where Adam landed, but knows that his father had been in Florida many years before his birth. "I guess that's why I can't stand red things now," he says, "my pa hated the sight of it."[70]

Fathers also transmitted the commonly shared songs and stories of the quarter community. At night when the day's work was done, Uncle Joe would tell stories of Br'er Rabbit and Br'er Wolf to his two sons Joe and Hector and "his sonorous voice could be heard throughout the quarters."[71] Ball's father, who lived on a neighboring plantation, "spent the greater part of the time, which his master permitted him to pass with us, in relating such stories as he learned from his companions, or in singing the rude songs common amonst the slaves of Maryland and Virginia."[72]

Often it was from their fathers that quarter children first began to learn the themes of true religion, freedom, communality, white power, and antipathy to whites. Many a slave father started his son or daughter in praying or in attending the secret meetings of the black church. Randel Lee informed his interviewer that his father woke early every morning, lit the tallow candle, "and fell upon his knees and prayed aloud for God's blessing and thanked him for another day."[73] L. Alexander used to accompany his father to some secret meetings where the slaves would have "some real preachin'."[74] Adeline Hodges believes that the seeds of religion were planted in her mind as she sat on a log in the woods listening to her father pray.[75] John Thompson gave thanks to heaven that his father's "prayers over me, a careless hardened sinner, were not as seed sown upon a rock, but as bread cast upon the waters, to be seen and gathered after many days."[76] Noah Davis' father "could read a little, and make figures, but could scarcely write at all. His custom, on those Sabbaths when we remained at home, was to spend his time instructing his children, or the neighboring servants, out of a New Testament sent him from Fredericksburg by one of his older sons."[77]

Jacob Stroyer's desire for freedom was stirred by his father's prayer.[78] Garret Buster's father inspired Garret with thoughts of freedom by naming him after a neighborhood acquaintance who was free "jes' lak we wants our l'il boy to be some day."[79] Archer Alexander was impressed not only with his father's words but with his daring in preaching freedom to the other slaves of the quarter.[80] A former slave interviewed by the Fisk project gives this description of his father's instructions to him upon his sale shortly after the beginning of the Civil War:

> My father came over and they prayed and sang over me. He gave me this advice. He knew more about what was going on than we

did. He had read about the war to free the Negroes. "When you get your freedom come back and look for us. But whatever you do, treat people right; respect the old; go to meetings; and if you never see us in this world, meet us in heaven."[81]

In their cabins at night all young blacks of the quarters were taught the rules of the white man's system, the habits and peculiarities of the whites in closest proximity, and the proper techniques for dealing with them. W. H. Robinson was taught by his father that he should die, if need be, in defense of his mother.[82] Joel Poinsett, a rich Southern planter, asserted that slave "children learn from their parents to regard white people with fear and to deceive them."[83] "The slave," writes William Wells Brown, "is brought up to look upon every white man as an enemy to him and his race. . . ."[84]

An important aspect of the father's role in the quarter family was to be ready to assume the double role of father and mother if and when the need arose. Though most quarter fathers were given much assistance by a grandparent, an aunt, or an older child at the death or sale of their wives, the primary obligation of taking over mother's role functions often was his. When Ball's mother was sold to a Georgia trader, Ball was raised mainly by his father and grandfather.[85] When Roxy Pitts' mother, who was part Indian, ran off, his father filled in and raised all the children.[86] Sometimes, of course, father assumed much of the primary care of his children without mother's death or sale. Lula Jackson says that her father raised not only all of his own children but those of his wife's first husband as well.[87] For three months every year Betty Guwn accompanied her mistress to the deep South while her husband "stayed at home to see after the family, and took them to the fields when too young to work under the task master, or over-seer."[88]

Far more important than the frequency of the contact between quarter children and their parents was the intensity and loving nature of those interactions they were able to have together. Irella Walker remembers how her father used to patiently rub her shoes with grease to make them more comfortable for her.[89] Margaret Nickerson's father tended to her beaten

The Family

legs.[90] Though he came to see them only on Sunday, the visit of Oscar Rogers' father was the high point of the week for Oscar and his brothers and sisters. "He came early and stay till bedtime. We all run to meet him. He kiss us all in bed when he be leavin'."[91]

Finally, by observing their father and his relationship with his wife, his own parents and brothers and sisters, and with them, the children of a quarter family learned the responsibilities and the value of membership in a strongly bound family. From their father they learned not only how to hunt, fish, grow crops, and "steal," but that it was expected of them to do likewise. From observing their father's efforts to provide for, protect, and educate his family, they learned not only the means but also the idea that they were responsible for each other's nurture, protection, and education.[92]

Some recollections show that not only the useful but the poetic clung to the mind. John Collins remembers how "Daddy used to play wid mammy just lak she was a child. He'd ketch her under de armpits and jump her up mighty nigh to the rafters of the little house us lived in."[93] Another ex-slave recalls how he loved his father:

> My mother just rejoiced in him. Whenever he sat down to talk she just sat and looked and listened. She would never cross him for anything. If they went to church together she always waited for him to interpret what the preacher had said or what he thought was the will of God. I was small but I noticed all these things. I sometimes think that I learned more in my early childhood about how to live than I have learned since.[94]

The role of father was not necessarily played by a child's biological father. Sometimes a grandfather accepted the duties of father towards his grandchildren. Sometimes an uncle or an older brother became the father of a child's family. And sometimes, father was a member of the larger community who was completely unrelated by blood but who, nevertheless, was willing to accept the responsibility of being father to a fatherless child.[95] From the time Mingo White was sold away from the rest of his family at age five, "the only carin' that I had or ever known anything 'bout was give to me by a frien' of my pappy. His name was John White. My pappy tol' him to take care of me for him. John was a fiddler an' many a night I woke up to find myse'f 'sleep 'twix' his legs whilst he was playin' for a dance for de white folks."[96] Although there seems to have been a substantial number of quarter children who lived in a household which did not contain both a biological mother and father, rarely did a quarter child lack a significant relationship with an older black man who felt and assumed responsibility to help nurture and protect him and who became instrumental in his education.

Another familial role important to the education of quarter children was that of grandparent. Although some grandparents maintained their own cabins until death, the general rule in most quarter communities was for single grandparents to move in with one of their married children after they became too old to work in the fields. In either case, one of the most common functions of grandparents was to care for family members while their mothers and fathers were working. Georgia Baker spent much of her early childhood in the company of her grandfather, who slept "on a trundle bed in the kitchen" and who tended Georgia and her siblings while their parents were in the fields.[97] By feeding, caring for, singing to, and playing with quarter children six days a week, many a grandparent became the effective grandparent of many more children than just his or her biological grandchildren.

Often grandparents, whether they lived with their family or not, helped provide material comforts for their children and grandchildren. Grandma helped to cook, wash, and make clothes.[98] Grandpa helped to supply wild nuts, garden produce, and meat for the family table.[99] Perry Jemison remembers that "My grandmother wuz named Snooky and my grandfather Anthony. I thought der wuzn't a better friend in all de world den my grandmother. She would do all she could for her grandchildren. Der wuz no food allowance for chillun that could not work and my grandmother fed us out of her and my mother's allowance."[100] Austin Grant's grandfather used to "tell us things, to keep the whip off our backs."[101]

The Family

It was often from grandparents that quarter children acquired most of their religious beliefs, their knowledge of signs and conjur, and their practice of herbal medicine. James Parker's grandfather not only taught him to read but gave him systematic religious instruction.[102] Sam Aleckson's grandmother, who cared for him during the day, patiently struggled "to impress upon my youthful mind the principles of a Christian life."[103] Eliza White recalls that "Granny used to give us tea made outen sage roots, mullen, pine tops and horehound."[104] Fannie Moore remembers well the cures of her grandmother:

> My ole granny uster make tea out o' dogwood bark an' give it to us chillun when we have a cold, else she make a tea outen wild cherry bark, pennyroil, or hoarhound. My goodness but dey was bitter. We do mos' anythin' to get out a takin' de tea, but twarn't no use. Granny jes git you by de collar, hol' yo' nose and you jes swallow it or git strangled. When de baby hab de colic she git rats vein and make a syrup an' put a little sugar in it an' boil it. Den soon as it cold she give it to de baby. For stomach ache she give us snake root. Sometime she make tea, other time she jes cut it up in little pieces an' make you eat one or two ob dem. When you hab fever she wrap you up in cabbage leaves or ginsang leaves, dis made de fever go. When de fever got too bad she take the hoofs offen de hog dat had been killed and parch 'em in de ashes and den she beat 'em up and make a tea. Dis was de most tubble of all.[105]

Respected for their age and for their position as head of the family, grandparents often enjoyed a venerated authority in the family. In most quarter families, children learned that when their family gathered together, it was the commands of grandparents that were to be obeyed first. Often one or more grandparents assumed the role of the arbiter in family disputes and quarrels.

Grandparents also played an important educational role in transmitting the songs and stories of Africa and of plantation history. One of childhood's chief diversions was to listen to the songs and tales of grandparents. Eli Boyd remembers how his grandmother "used to hold up her hand and look at it and sing out of her hand. She'd make them up as she would look at her hand. She sang in Geechee and also made rhymes and songs in English."[106] Charles Davenport's grandmother sang a song which reinforced the role of father:

> Kink head, wherefor you skeered?
> Old snake crawled off, 'cause he's a-feared.
> Pappy will smite on de back
> With a great big club—Ker whack! Ker whack![107]

Phil Towns recalls that his grandmother's and grandfather's descriptions of their capture in Africa and their subsequent cruel treatment was "his most vivid recollection."[108] A former slave named Uncle Andrew says that his chief diversion "was to listen to tales told by his Gran'pap, who was brought over from Africa and who was learned in the lore of his native jungle."[109] As a child Charles Ball passed many long nights with his grandfather "listening to his narratives of the scenes through which he had passed in Africa" and hearing of his grandpa's religion with its strong injunction of "tenderness to wives and children."[110]

Whatever their other functions most grandparents were ready to step into the roles of father and mother if needed. Though Douglass's mother lived close enough to visit him on occasion, it was his "grandmother, whose kindness and love stood in place of my mother's. . . ."[111] Ellen Thompson's father was sold and her mother died when Ellen was still young and she was brought up by her grandmother with the aid of Ellen's uncles.[112] When Dosia Harris' mother, Mary, died when Dosia was still an infant, her Grandma Crecy took her in and raised her.[113] It is the rare black narrative that does not recall fondly the teaching, the songs and stories, the discipline, and the care and little attentions of at least one grandparent.

The education of most quarter children was also affected by the family role played by one or more older siblings. Shortly after mother returned to work, a month or so after giving birth, the care and protection provided by an older sibling became crucial to the child's health and contentment. In those cases where mother took her baby to the fields, it was the responsibility of an older sibling to watch over him and protect him from

The Family

sun, insects, and wild animals. On those plantations where the quarter infants were tended by a woman who was not a family member and who had proven that she was unable to give all needed care to the family's youngest members, it was the duty of the older sibling to make sure that younger brother or sister got enough to eat, was not bullied, and was attended to if hurt.[114]

As the children of the quarters grew older, they learned from their older brothers and sisters the games, riddles, songs and stories of the quarter community. They also learned to share in family responsibilities and to care in turn for their younger siblings. They learned the manners expected when sharing a common bowl at mealtime. They learned to work a single row in the fields, to steal together, to sleep in the same bed together, and to take turns doing the family chores.[115] One ex-slave recounts that in his cabin at night "de boys had one big bed ter sleep in an' me er pallet on de flo'. But when de wind blow, an' de weather git cool, we build er fire in de sleepin' room. I'd stan' up close an' dey make me turn roun' an' roun' so I git warm all over. Den I'd git in bed, crossways et de end. De boys pile in quick an' warm dey feet on me! Dat way, we all slep' warm."[116] In Charlie King's family, "Charlie and all his ten brothers and sisters helped to card and spin the cotton for the looms. . . . Each child had a night for carding and spinning, so they all would get a chance to sleep."[117]

Most young children learned that during those times that an adult family member was not present, it was an older brother or sister to whom they must look for protection, advice, and special favors. Booker T. Washington remembers one such special favor performed to protect a sensitive skin. "In connection with the flax shirt, my brother John, who is several years older than I am, performed one of the most generous acts that I ever heard of one slave relative doing for another. On several occasions when I was being forced to wear a new flax shirt, he generously agreed to put it on in my stead and wear it for several days, till it was 'broken in.' "[118] James Pennington and his older brother "were much attached" and James was in "the habit of looking to him for counsel."[119]

Sometimes it fell upon the shoulders of an older sibling to step into the role of father or mother. After his mother was sold, Henri Necaise was cared for by his sister.[120] In the absence of a father, J. W. Loguen taught his younger brother and sister "to walk and sing and play."[121] Though Mack Brantley's mother died when he was only six months old, his older brother, Green, took care of him. "Green was good and so strong, I never could forget it. Green was my standby."[122] Robert Anderson's sister, Silva, the oldest of the children at fourteen, took over the role and responsibilities of mother when the family's first mother was sold away.

> Silva would sit up until the late hours of the night, working, and then would have to be up early in the morning to do the cooking for the family. Not only did she work, herself, but she made me work, too. Although I was six years old when mother was taken away, she had taught me a number of things. My sister continued this education. She taught me how to patch my own clothes (such as I had), to piece quilts, and to make horse collars stuffed with corn shucks.[123]

So strong were the bonds by which siblings became attached to each other during childhood that in most cases these bonds only strengthened with age. The narratives are full of examples of brothers and sisters of adult age plotting together to escape, preparing or sharing food and clothing, protecting each other, and discussing together their beliefs, their fears and their hopes.[124] If they were fortunate enough to grow up and live their adult lives without being separated, sisters and brothers commonly maintained their mutual responsibilities towards each other as family members and extended this responsibility to each other's children. The frequent appearance in the narratives of uncles and aunts, particularly the mother's brother, caring for, protecting, and educating their sisters' and brothers' children can perhaps best be explained by the familial ties and reciprocal duties which siblings internalized during their childhoods and which continued through their adult lives.[125]

The impression that the children of the quarters had a multitude of family members all vying with one another to nurture, protect, and educate them is neither intended nor accurate.

The Family

However, the black sources do depict a common extended pattern of family relationships in which most quarter children associated closely with many other individuals filling several different kinds of educational roles. Although the realities of slavery meant that the individual membership of given families sometimes changed drastically and suddenly, what stands out is that such change over time did not greatly affect the quarter family's ability to educate its children. For most quarter families were composed of a number of individuals who felt a responsibility to step in and fill roles that were vacated through death or sale. Thus, although many a grandparent, uncle, or older sister played an important educational role in the presence of mother and father, they were ready to fill the roles of father and mother as well. It was this willingness and ability on the part of an extended number of family members to play the primary educational roles of father and mother that made the family not only an effective but a stable educational instrument of the quarter community.

⫷ 14 ⫸

The Peer Group

For much of the happiness, or absence of misery, with which I passed this year, I am indebted to the genial temper and ardent friendship of my brother slaves. . . . They were as true as steel, and no band of brothers could be more loving.

Frederick Douglass

From the time the children of the quarters first began to crawl and toddle about, they came into contact with other slave children. As they learned to talk, walk, and take care of themselves, these occasional contacts became more frequent until much of their waking time was spent in conversing, playing, singing, fighting, and eating with their peer group companions. The nature of the educational impact which the peer group had upon its members is suggested by the large quantity of time which peer group members spent in each other's company. For six days a week the children of the quarters passed most of the time their parents were in the fields, some ten to fourteen hours a day, in close association with the other members of their peer group.

The educational role of the peer group began at play. As with most children, the play of quarter children consisted both of games improvised on the spot and those handed down, with infinite variations, from generation to generation. Davenport says that he and the other children of the quarters, when not busy with light chores such as gathering wood and sweeping the yard, "played together in the street what run de length of the quarters. Us throwed horseshoes, jumped poles, walked on stilts, and played marbles. Sometimes us made bows and arrows. Us could shoot 'em, too, jus' like little Injuns."[1] "De best game us had was marbles," recalls Tom Hawkins of his slave days in South Caro-

The Peer Group

lina, "and us played wid homemade clay marbles most of the time."[2] Sally Murphy reports that her peer group had all the fun they wanted. "Us played jump rope and swung in de grapevine swings mostly."[3] As a child an old Fisk informant and his friends "used to play a game we called 'smut,' but we would play it with corn spots instead of cards. We played it just like you would with cards only we would have grains of corn and call them hearts and spades, and so forth, and go by the spots on the corn."[4]

Bert Mayfield and his companions played a game called "sheep-meat," which appears to have been a version of what is now known as dodge ball. "Sheep-meat was a game played with a yarn ball and when one of the players was hit by the ball that counted him out."[5] "Once over" was another ball game played by the quarter children. It involved throwing a ball over one of the cabins. If the ball was caught by one of the players on the other side, that player would run around to the other side of the cabin and attempt to hit one of the other team with the ball, thus knocking him out of the game. "We'd have to make a ball out of yarn and put a sock around it for a cover. Six of us would stay on one side of a house and six on the other."[6]

Hide and seek in many varieties was also popular. "When us played our hidin' game," remembers Callie Elder, "us sung somepin' lak dis:

> Mollie, Mollie Bright
> Three score and ten,
> Can I get dere by candlelight?
> Yes, if your laigs is long enough!"[7]

Anna Parkes recounts that in playing "Old Hundred" she and her playmates "would choose one, and dat one would hide his face agin' a tree whilst he counted to a hundud. Den he would hunt for all de others. Dey done been hidin' whilst he wuz countin'. Us larned to count a-playin' 'Ole Hundud.' "[8]

Of those games which required a group, some of the most widely played appear to have been several different ring game extrapolations played to the rhythm of a variety of tunes. "When

181

Deep Like the Rivers

us was chillun in de quarters we did a mighty lot of playin',"
recalls Katherine Eppes. "Us useta play 'Sail away Rauley' a
whole lot. Us would hol' han's an' go 'roun' in a ring, gittin'
faster an' faster an' demn what fell down was outa de game."[9]
Martha Colquitt and her peer group "used to play lots, but us
never did have no special name for our playin'. 'Swingin' in de
corner,' was when us all joined hand in a long row, and de leader
would begin to run around in circles, and at de other end of the
line dey would soon be runnin' so fast dey was most flyin'."[10]

Sometimes the play of the children involved singing, storytelling, and the asking of riddles. According to William Henry
Towns, "Dere was a whole lot of games an' riddles to be played
dem days. . . . De riddles was like dis:

  Slick as a mole, black as a coal,
  Got a great long tail like a thunder hole. (skillet)

  Crooked as a rainbow, teeth lak a cat,
  Guess all of your life but you can't guess dat. (blackberry
    bush)[11]

Sometimes the slave children were allowed by their parents to
continue their play at night. Josephine Hamilton says that she
and her friends often "played in the moonlight."[12] Frank Gill
remembers how he and the other little children "played ball, and
marbles, 'specially marbles, hit was our big game. Even after
night, dey had a big light out in de backyard, an' us would
play."[13] On Jane Simpson's plantation "De white folks didn't
want to let de slaves have no time for deir self, so de old folks
used to let us chillun run and play at night, while de folks sleep
and dey watch de stars to tell about what time to call us in and
put us to bed, before de white folks know we was out."[14]

In some quarters a special brand of fireworks marked
Christmas as a highpoint for the children. Pauline Grice remembers the Christmases of her childhood as a slave on a plantation near Atlanta, Georgia:

182

The Peer Group

Us have singing and 'joyment all day. Then at night, the big fire builded, and all us sot round it. There am 'bout hundred hog bladders save from hog killing. So, on Christmas night, the children takes them and puts them on the stick. First they is all blowed full of air and tied tight and dry. Then the children holds the bladder in the fire and pretty soon, "BANG!" they goes. That am the fireworks.[15]

Often the games played by quarter children were highly suggestive of situations similar to those experienced by slaves. While visiting one of her father's large cotton plantations Mary Banks encountered a group of slave children playing a game in which a circle was formed about one child in the middle who tries to break out while all sing:

> Oh, do let me out! I'z in dis lady's gyarden,
> Oh, do let me out! I'z in dis lady's gyarden.

> De gate iz lockt, an' de wall iz high,
> Roun' dis lady's gyarden. Chorus.

> De gate iz lockt, an' de key iz lo',
> Un dis lady's gyarden. Chorus.

> I mus', I will, git out er here,
> Out er dis lady's gyarden. Chorus.

> I'll break my neck but I'll get out er here,
> Out er dis lady's gyarden. Chorus.

While the singing continued, they danced around keeping time to the music, the imprisoned one making efforts all the while to escape, by trying to creep under, jump over, or break down, the wall of the lady's garden.

Finally, effecting her escape, they all attempt to elude her grasp, as the one caught takes her place in the "gyarden" and the play is thus continued, mid the shouts and laughter from all.[16]

A former slave from Arkansas recalls a game which must have hit even closer to home called "Chick-Chick":

183

You'd ketch 'hold a hands and ring up. Had one outside was the hawk and some inside was the hen and chickens. The old mother hen would say—

'Chick-a-ma, chick-a-ma, craney crow, Went to the well to wash my toe; When I come back my chicken was gone, What time is it, old witch?'

One chicken was s'posed to get out and then the hawk would try to ketch him.[17]

Two games which appeared frequently in the narratives were probably means through which slave children helped themselves to cope with two of their greatest fears—whippings and evil spirits. "Hide the Switch," in which a switch was hidden and the child who found it ran after the others in an attempt to strike them, was but one of the many forms of a game which involved slave children whipping each other.[18] Versions of "No Bogey-man Tonight," in which one slave child pretended to be an evil spirit or the Devil and attempted to catch the others, appeared throughout the quarters of the slaveholding South.

The older children were often allowed to roam about within the confines of their home plantation, and the fields, forests, and streams provided them with hours of fun and adventure. A former slave interviewed by the Fisk project remembers that as a slave child his peer group's "biggest amusement was running through the woods, climbing trees, hunting grapes and berries and so forth."[19] Robert Shepherd and his companions used to take to the woods in order to escape the tasks assigned by Aunt Viney, their nursery guardian. "Dere was a big sand bar down on de crick what made a fine place to play, and wadin' in de branches was lots of fun. Us frolicked up and down dem woods and had all sorts of good times—anything to keep away from Aunt Viney 'cause she was sho' to have us fetchin' in wood or sweepin' de yards if us was handy whar she could find us."[20]

As a child Acie Thomas spent much of his time "roaming over the broad acres" of his master's Florida plantation. He and his friends "waded in the streams, fished, chased rabbits and always knew where the choicest wild berries and nuts grew."[21] In addition to small game, berries, and nuts, the woods also produced eggs, which could be traded to the plantation cook or to the white mistress for a sweet. Julia Cole recalls that she and her friends "loved to hunt for turkey nests 'cause dey give us a tea-cake for evvy turkey egg us fotched in."[22] Besides playing marbles, cat ball, base, blindfold, and tag, George Rogers and the other children of his North Carolina quarters "fished a lot in Briar Creek. We caught a lot of fish. Sometimes we used pin hooks we made ourselves. We would trade our fish to missus for molasses to make candy of."[23] Tom Hawkins and his friends used to "catch a heap of fish wid hook and line. De river and crick hole run thoo' Miss Annie's plantation so us didn't have to ax for a pass evvy time us went a fishin'."[24]

After his master moved his slaves from Virginia to Missouri, H. C. Bruce recalls living on a large farm of about thirty-five slaves.

> I was too young to be put to work, and there being on the farm four or five boys about my age, spent my time with them hunting and fishing. There was a creek near by in which we caught plenty of fish. We made lines of hemp grown on the farm and hooks of bent pins. When we got a bite, up went the pole and quite often the fish, eight or ten feet in the air. We never waited for what is called a good bite, for if we did the fish would get the bait and escape capture, or get off when hooked if not thrown quickly upon the land. But fish then were very plentiful and not as scary as now. The hardest job with us was digging bait. We often brought home as much as five pounds of fish in a day.[25]

Sometimes slaves took the opportunity of their childhood leisure to acquaint themselves with the children of neighboring quarter communities. "The patteroles never bothered the children any," reports Allen Johnson. "The children couldn't go anywhere without the consent of the mother and father. And there wasn't any danger of them running off. If they caught a little child between plantations, they would probably just run them home. It was all right for a child to go in the different quarters and play with one another during daytime just so they got back before night."[26] Silas Jackson, who grew up on a plantation of over one hundred slaves near Ashbie Gap, Virginia, says,

"We boys used to take the horns of a dead cow or bull, cut the end off of it, we could blow it, some having different notes. We could tell who was blowing and from what plantation."[27]

Association with peer group members also allowed the children of the quarters to practice roles which they would assume more fully later in life. A favorite pastime, for instance, was "playing grown-ups." Dolls were made with old rags and doll houses (sometimes elaborate play houses) were made with wood, bark, stones, and leaves. The girls would dress up in their mothers' handkerchiefs and aprons and would make necklaces from corn beads and earrings from peanuts split opened at one end. Besides hunting and fishing, the boys refined their singing and storytelling abilities, and practiced their whittling and basket weaving skills.

Both boys and girls played at conjuration and religion. One informant in the Federal Writers' Project study recalls that on his plantation he and the other children "used to play preachin' and baptisin'. We'd put 'em down in the water and souse 'em and we'd shout just like the old folks."[28] Benny Dilliard recalls his life as a slave child in Georgia:

Us would have make-believe preachin' and baptizin' and de way us would sing was a sight. One of dem songs us chillun loved de best went lak dis:

"Why does you thirst
By de livin' stream?
And den pine away
And den go to die.

Why does you search
For all dese earthy things?
When you all can
Drink at de livin' spring,
And den can live."

When us started playin' lak us was baptizin' 'em, us th'owed all us could ketch right in de crick, clothes and all, and ducked 'em. Whilst us was singin':

"Git on board, git on board
For de land of many mansions,

The Peer Group

Same old train dat carried
My Mammy to de Promised Land."[29]

Within the peer group most slave children began to experiment with their courting techniques and to experience their first post-pubescent sexual encounters. Henry Lewis remembers clearly the "well-game" played among the boys and girls of his peer group. "De gal or boy set in de chair and lean way back and pretend like dey in de well. Dey say dey so many feet down and say, 'Who you want pull you out?' And de one you want pull you out, dey s'posed to kiss you."[30] Lucindy Jurdon recounts that when she and her girl friends went courting "us went to walk an' hunted chestnuts. Us would string dem an' put 'em 'round our necks an' smile at our fellers."[31]

When nothing more exciting occurred to them, the children would watch the old folks at work. As a child Randel Lee "delighted in stopping around the tanning yard and watching the men salt the hide."[32]

It was often in the company of peer group members that the children of the quarters had their first experiences in dealing with whites. Henry Watson recalls how, upon the arrival of a strange white, he and the other slave children would run "and hide ourselves until the man had gone."[33] Other former slaves recall how they were spanked with their heads between their masters' knees or forced to sing and dance for master and his company. Others remember how in the company of their peer group members they first heard the tenets of slaveholding priestcraft. It was also in the peer group, given courage by the company of their friends, that children first began to steal eggs, tobacco, and other desired goods.[34] "Us children," confesses Tom Hawkins, "used to tie up de 'bacco, what us stole fum Miss Annie, in de under-arm part of de long loose sleeves of our shirts."[35] David Gullins tells how he and his associates learned together as children to outwit their mistress:

> Some days Mistress was good and kind to us little niggers, and she
> would save us the cold biscuits to give us when we brought in the
> eggs. Sometimes, she would go two or three days without giving
> us any biscuits then she didn't get no eggs. We rascals would get

up the eggs and go off and have a rock battle with them. Every effect has a cause—then Miss would wonder why she didn't get any
eggs and call us all in for cold biscuits, then the eggs would come
again. Of course we had our game of "tell." If one of the gang
threatened to tell, then we all would threaten to tell all we knew
on him, and somehow we managed to get by with it all.[36]

Sometimes peer group members were able to acquire a skill
which they could share with each other. Whether the teaching
was deliberate or not, peer group members learned from each
other how to sing, dance, whittle, hunt, play musical instruments, and sometimes, even, read. Acie Thomas claims to
have known "all the wood lore common to children of his time.
This he learned mostly from 'cousin Ed' who was several years
older than he and quite willing to enlighten a small boy in these
matters."[37] Sam Aleckson had two special friends, Joe and Hector. "These boys were somewhat older than myself. They were
skilled in woodcraft, and taught me how to make bird traps and
soon had me out hunting."[38]

As they grew older and reached the time when they were
forced to join the plantation work force, it was with peer group
brothers and sisters that slave children first discovered the reality of their slave status and began to discuss among themselves
what it meant to live under slavery. The shock of ending what
for many had been a relatively carefree childhood and beginning field work in earnest was eased by the continued companionship of the peer group. Though their leisure time was
now drastically curtailed, even in the fields they could talk, sing,
and help each other bear the burdens of slavery.

This is not to say that all the children of a given quarter community necessarily thought of each other as brothers and sisters,
but to suggest that each child had his or her own special friend,
or group of friends, who became an extension of that child's
family and played an important role in his education. Though
unrelated by blood, peer brothers and sisters often shared a
common grandparent. A child whose father was absent often
adopted the father of a peer brother as his role model. And,
whatever the outlook of the adult world around them, the children of the quarters made no distinction between "biological"

The Peer Group

and "peer" and often took more seriously their felt and assumed responsibility to peer brothers and sisters than that felt for actual siblings. Campbell and two of his friends agreed to help each other even to the point of stopping the overseer from whipping any one of them.[39] When Isaac Mason attempted to escape with two other slaves, they "knelt down and prayed and then took an oath that we would fight for each other till we died."[40]

Sometimes the peer group was even forced to assume almost all of the functions of the family. George Kye, who was born on a large farm in Arkansas, did not sleep at his mother's cabin and was unsure whether or not he had any blood-line brothers or sisters. "My mammy was named Jenny and I don't think I had any brothers or sisters, but they was a whole lot of children at the quarters that I played with. I didn't live with Mammy because she worked all the time, and us children all stayed in one house. It was a little one room log cabin, chinked and daubed, and you couldn't stir us with a stick."[41]

In most quarter communities there was only one group of children of approximately the same age. Thus, although the slave child could choose, theoretically, to remain aloof from her peer group, she could not choose from among different groups. The children of the quarters could no more choose with whom they wished to associate than they could choose their biological parents. The slave child either ran with the other children of her age group or she ran with no one. For most children no such conscious choice ever occurred to them. The bonds of love and mutual need formed between peer group members were molded too early and too strongly to ever suggest themselves to the slave child as anything else than the way things naturally were. The important role which peer group brothers and sisters played in each others' lives well into the adulthood is described in the following passage by Frederick Douglass:

> For much of the happiness, or absence of misery, with which I passed this year, I am indebted to the genial temper and ardent friendship of my brother slaves. They were every one of them manly, generous, and brave. Yes, I say they were brave, and I will add, fine-looking. It is seldom the lot of any one to have truer

friends than were the slaves of their farm. It was not uncommon to charge slaves with treachery towards each other, but I must say that I never loved, esteemed, or confided in men more than I did these. They were as true as steel, and no band of brothers could be more loving. There were no mean advantages taken of each other, no tattling, no giving each other bad names to Mr. Freedland, and no elevating one at the expense of the others. We never undertook anything of any importance which was likely to affect each other without mutual consultation. We were generally a unit, and moved together. Thoughts and sentiments were exchanged between us which might well have been considered incendiary had they been known by our masters.[42]

As slaves grew old enough to work, to marry, and to raise a family of their own, the amount of time which they were able to spend with other peer group members diminished. The roles, friendships, values, attitudes, and understandings formed within the peer group, however, continued, and served as an important foundation upon which slaves acted as adult members of the quarter community.

15

The Clandestine Congregation

As I went down in de valley to pray,
Studying about dat good old way,
When you shall wear de starry crown,
Good Lord, show me de way.

O mourner, let's go down,
O mourner, let's go down, let's go down,
O mourner, let's go down,
Down in de valley to pray.

Allen, *Slave Songs*

Wid a clappin' o' de hands
An' a pattin' o' de feet
De love o' Gawd does run so sweet.

R. Emmet Kennedy,
More Mellows

Despite the fact that many slaves who lived on large plantations were forced to attend church services organized and supervised by whites, nearly all quarter communities organized their
own clandestine congregation without the sanction or participation of plantation authorities. This congregation of the religious faithful was an important instrument in the quarter community's ability to transmit and perpetuate not just its own
religious ideals and beliefs but crucial secular understandings,
values, and attitudes.

In many quarter communities the organization of the clandestine congregation centered upon an individual preacher or re-

ligious leader. Sometimes this individual was the same man who was officially appointed to be the preacher in the white church. His status in the white church, however, did not guarantee his leadership in the secret black church. The narratives make clear that most members of the quarter community realized that the white-appointed preacher "must always act as a peacemaker and mouthpiece for the master. . . ."[1] Although they did not necessarily hold this against him personally, few quarter members followed a religious leader who proved unwilling or unable to expound, in secret, tenets other than those he was forced to proclaim while under the watchful eyes of master, mistress, or their hirelings.[2]

In most quarter communities the religious leader was a man, sometimes a woman, who had achieved a position of influence and respect among his fellow quarter members through his strong faith, his knowledge of the Bible and true Christianity, his demonstrated commitment to the welfare of the quarter community, and, most important, his ability to preach as his congregation wanted him to preach. On the large plantation where Litt Young lived, near Vicksburg, Mississippi, his mistress "built a nice church with glass windows and a brass cupola for the blacks. A yellow man preached to us. She had him preach how we was to obey our master and missy if we want to go to heaven, but when she wasn't there, he come out with straight preachin' from the Bible."[3] Anderson Edwards remembers how he was baptized as a slave child of ten in the "spring branch close to where I finds the Lord." A few years later he started preaching. "When I starts preaching I couldn't read or write and had to preach what Master told me, and he say to tell them niggers iffen they obeys the master they goes to Heaven; but I knows there's something better for them, but daren't tell them 'cept on the sly. That I done lots. I tell 'em iffen they keeps praying, the Lord will set 'em free."[4] Pet Frank, who had been a slave in Mississippi, recounts that "Old Daddy Young was 'bout de bes' preacher us ever had."[5] Clara Young recalls that the most fun she and her companions had under slavery was at their meetings, which usually lasted way into the night on Sundays.

The Clandestine Congregation

De preacher I liked de best was named Matthew Ewing. He was a comely nigger, black as night, and he sure could read out of his hand. He never learned no real readin' and writin' but he sure knowed his Bible and would hold his hand out and make like he was readin' and preach de purties' preachin' you ever heard. De meetin's last from early in de mornin' till late at night. When dark come, de men folks would hang up a wash pot, bottom upwards, in de little brush church us had, so's it would catch de noise and de overseer wouldn't hear us singin' and shoutin'. Dey didn't mind us meetin' in de daytime, but dey thought iffen we stayed up half de night we wouldn't work so hard de next day—and dat was de truth.[6]

Often the leader of the clandestine congregation assumed his position, in part, due to his ability to read. "If there chanced to be among the slaves a man of their own race who could read and write, he generally preached and would at times and places unknown to the master, call his fellow slaves together and hold religious services with them. It was to such leaders as these that the slaves owed much of their religious instruction."[7]

More important even than his preaching skills was the preacher's ability to identify with what W. E. B. Dubois has called "the longing and disappointment and resentment of a stolen people."[8] Unless his congregation felt that their preacher was one of them, had experienced their sorrows and joys and internalized their values and attitudes, they would turn from him. Although his chief concern is with contemporary black preachers, Henry Mitchell might well have been describing the preachers of the clandestine congregation when he wrote: "The black preacher must be up to his ears in the condition of his people, and out of this comes the easy dialogue between people whose lives are intimately close together—so close together that the themes which invade the consciousness of the one also invade the other."[9]

Often the preacher became the most powerful figure in the quarters. He was, in the words of W. E. B. DuBois, "A leader, a politician, an orator, a 'boss,' an intriguer, an idealist . . . and ever, too, the center of a group of men, now twenty, now a thousand in number. The combination of a certain adroitness

193

with deep-seated earnestness, of tact with consummate ability, gave him his preeminence, and helps him maintain it."[10]

In some quarters where no single individual was able to establish his superior religious authority and leadership, a group of elders would share the leadership of the clandestine congregation. Whether held by one person or several, the first responsibility of the religious leadership was to call and to lead clandestine worship services. These meetings were convened from one to two or three times a week and were generally held in the woods or in some other predesignated, hidden, outdoor location. Elizabeth Sparks, who had been a slave in Virginia, recalls that the slaves "used to go way off in quarters and slip and have meetin's. They called it stealin' the meetin'."[11] The members of Joseph Young's quarter community "held their meetings in the under bush arbors made by them."[12] Amanda McCray and her religious brethren held services on a "praying ground where the grass never had a chance ter grow fer the troubled knees that kept it crushed down."[13]

Though the meetings were usually held by the light of the moon or with no light at all, the worshippers were sometimes bold enough to hold them by firelight. Richard Carruthers remembers that he and his sisters and brothers in the Lord "used to have a prayin' ground down in the hollow and sometime we come out of the field, between eleven and twelve at night, scorchin' and burnin' up with nothin' to eat, and we wants to ask the good Lord to have mercy. We puts grease in a snuff pan or bottle and make a lamp. We takes a pine torch, too, and goes down in the hollow to pray."[14] Often when meetings were held in the woods, those attending would "form a circle on their knees around the speaker, who would also be on his knees. He would bend forward and speak into or over a vessel of water to drown the sound."[15]

In cold or rainy weather the congregation would be compelled to take the risk of holding their meetings in the cabin of one of their members. On these occasions some device would be used in order to smother the sounds of their religious expression. Calvin Woods remembers that when he held meetings "the women slaves would take old quilts and rags and wet them thoroughly;

The Clandestine Congregation

then hang them up in the form of a little room and the slaves who were interested about it would huddle up behind these quilts to do their praying, preaching and singing. . . . Many a happy meeting was carried on behind these quilts and rags."[16] In L. Alexander's quarter community, where there was a prayer meeting once or twice a week, the slaves simply sang and prayed in a whisper.[17]

The most common way of absorbing the sound was that of "turning down" the large pots used for cooking or washing. One ex-slave recalls how "we would take pots and put them right in the middle of the floor to keep the sound in the room; yeah, keep the white folks from meddling. Yes'm the sound will stay right in the room after you do that. Well, we allus used these old house wash pots like you boil clothes in, you know. Just turn one down in the middle of the floor, that was sufficient."[18] John Hunter, who lived as a slave on an Arkansas plantation, says that when "the spirit would come on them" to have a service by themselves slaves would "go down to the house at night and turn up those big iron pots and master never would hear. They wouldn't put the washpot flat on the ground. They'd put sticks under it and raise it up about a foot from the ground. If they'd put it flat on the ground the ground would carry the sound."[19]

Occasionally the black congregation was not so secret as it intended, although the knowledge that they were under suspicion rarely deterred the membership from gathering together. James Reeves, whose parents were slaves in Arkansas, says that some slaves would "steal out" every Sunday and "slip off in the woods" where they would hold meetings. Invariably the master found out and had each of them whipped on Monday morning. "Next Sundy they would do the same thing again and get another whipping. And it went on like that every week."[20] "Whipping," agrees another former slave, "did not stop them from having their meetings. When one place was located they would find another."[21] Susan Merritt, in remembering the times when she and her friends, despite their fear of the white folks, would "gather round the fireplace and pray and sing and cry," is grateful that no such stealth is now necessary. "Thank the Lord us can worship where us wants nowadays."[22]

On those nights that a meeting was to be held, instructions as to time and place would be circulated among the membership by the preacher or elders. Often the time and place were traditionally set and the message of a meeting was passed on through a song:

> I take my text in Matthew, and by de Revelation,
> I know you by your garment, Dere's a meeting here tonight.
> Dere's a meeting here tonight, (Brudder Tony,)
> Dere's a meeting here tonight, (Sister Rina,)
> Dere's a meeting here tonight, I hope to meet again.[23]

> Join Brethren, join us O,
> Join us, join us O.
> We meet tonight to sing and pray;
> In Jesus name we'll sing and pray.[24]

Often songs with a more ambiguous message had to be used to call meetings. "Steal away, steal away, steal away to Jesus," was one sometimes used for this purpose. Even songs without an obvious or symbolic message in their texts could be used, however, as long as the membership understood the significance of their being sung.[25]

The meetings themselves would usually start around eleven o'clock at night, or at whatever time coincided with an hour or so after the overseer's last round of the quarter cabins. In general, the meeting consisted of three parts: an exhortation by the preacher or one of the leadership, prayers and songs, and "testifications" as to faith and feeling the Spirit by any and all members. The purpose of the exhortation, or sermon, was both to instruct the membership and to stir their faith and raise their religious spirit. Whether the emphasis of a given exhortation was upon instruction or conversion and ecstasy depended greatly upon the personality and the ability of the preacher. Most quarter congregations desired both from their sermons. While creating with his passionate eloquence an atmosphere of religious fervor, the preacher was also expected to comment upon the trials and tribulations of life under slavery, to draw parallels between the sorrows and sufferings of his congregation and those of Jesus and the people of Israel, and to outline the path to salvation and proclaim the certainty of eventual Freedom. "Black preaching at its best," writes Mitchell, "has stuck to problems which people confront daily and feel needs in meeting. Black people are always preoccupied with problems, and the Black preacher has had to give strength for the current day's journey, and guidance and vision for extended survival in a brutally oppressed and absurd existence."[26]

Sometimes an especially fervent and well-spoken exhorter's reputation would travel from quarter community to quarter community, and arrangements would be made for him to hold services with the congregations of neighboring quarters. Such an exhorter was not necessarily a religious leader. He might be merely a man who had perfected the art "of filling a meeting with the Holy Spirit." In such cases he was expected to preach only. Instruction would be left to others.[27]

During the exhortation all of the members were expected to express their feelings of faith and their agreement with the words of the preacher with a heartfelt "Amen," a "so glad brother," or a "thank-ya Jesus." Just as the preacher stirred the religious joy of the congregation, so the congregation encouraged the preacher and let him know when he had moved them and helped to ignite them with the Spirit. To be merely an observer was to deprive oneself of the soul satisfaction which accompanied a heartfelt shout of supplication and belief and to deprive the congregation of one more soul happy in the Lord. Indeed, one's fellowship with the other members made it a right and a duty to give enthusiastic testimony to the fact that the Spirit had descended and filled the heart with the power and joy of its uplifting grace.[28]

In the absence of any member graced with the gift of preaching, the members of the clandestine congregation knew full well how to conduct their services by themselves. In such cases the testimonies of each member took the place of the sermon. As brother William, or sister Mary, spoke, sang, or shouted his sufferings, his personal experiences with God and Lord Jesus, and his wrestlings with the devil, the other members would stand around him and encourage him with their shouts just as they did a regular preacher.

Some congregations, in fact, seemed to feel that they were better off without a preacher because each member would then have more attention given to his own particular religious needs and feelings. Isaac Williams remembers that: "There would seldom be silence in our meetings, waiting for each other to speak, as I am told there is often in a white man's prayer meeting. We were always ready, that is the religious ones, to testify, and felt much better for doing so."[29] One ex-slave recalls that at the meetings he attended "everyone was so anxious to have a word to say that the preacher did not have a chance."[30]

Like the sermon, testimonies, and prayers, the songs also required the active participation of the entire membership— their bodies as well as their voices. Anderson recounts that every quarter community meeting involved singing. "While singing these songs, the singers and the entire congregation kept time to the music by swaying of their bodies or by patting of the foot or hand. Practically all of their songs were accompanied by motion of some kind."[31] James Smith, who grew up in the quarters of a Virginia plantation, writes: "The singing was accompanied by a certain ecstasy of motion, clapping of hands, tossing of heads, which would continue without cessation about half an hour; one would lead off in a recitative style, others joining in the chorus. The old house partook of the ecstasy; it rang with their jubilant shouts, and shook all its joints."[32]

> I really believe Christ is comin' again
> He's comin' in de mornin'
> He's comin' in de mornin'
> He's comin' wid a rainbow on his shoulder
> He's comin' again bye and bye.[33]

Often dancing around in a circle holding hands accompanied this singing, although when white missionaries expressed disapproval of such practice in the sanctioned services, blacks were quick to make "the distinction that dancing was innocent if the legs were not crossed, because the devil crossed his legs when he

The Clandestine Congregation

danced."[34] Henry Spaulding, a white Unitarian minister, writes about the "religious dance of the Negroes" which he observed at Port Royal, South Carolina, during the Civil War:

> Three or four, standing still, clapping their hands and beating time with their feet, commence singing in unison one of the peculiar shout melodies, while the others walk round in a ring, in single file, joining also in the song. Soon those in the ring leave off their singing, the others keeping it up the while with increased vigor, and strike into the shout step, observing most accurate time with the music. This step is something halfway between a shuffle and a dance, as difficult for an uninitiated person to describe as to imitate. At the end of each stanza of the song the dancers stop short with a slight stamp on the last note, and then, putting the other foot forward, proceed through the next verse. . . . They will often dance to the same song for twenty or thirty minutes. . . .[35]

The shaking of hands all around as a sign of the close of the meeting and of the brotherhood of the membership was a common practice. Alice Sewell gives the following description of a typical meeting and its close:

> We used to slip off in de woods in de old slave days on Sunday evening way down in de swamps to sing and pray to our own liking. We prayed for dis day of freedom. We come from four and five miles to pray together to God dat if we don't live to see it, to please let our children live to see a better day and be free, so dat dey can give honest and fair service to de Lord and all mankind everywhere. And we'd sing "Our little meetin's about to break, chillen, and we must part. We got to part in body, but hope not in mind. Our little meetin's bound to break." Den we used to sing "We walk about and shake hands, fare you well my sisters, I am going home."[36]

Often the name of the brother or sister whose hand was being clasped was added into the parting song:

Good-bye, my brudder, good-bye, Hallelujah!
Good-bye, sister Sally, good-bye, Hallelujah!
Going home, Hallelujah! Jesus call me, Hallelujah!
Linger no longer, Hallelujah! Tarry no longer, Hallelujah![37]

199

Deep Like the Rivers

Besides secret prayer and preaching meetings the clandestine congregation also organized special services, in particular baptisms and funerals, whenever such ceremonies were not permitted by the plantation authorities or were carried on by them to the dissatisfaction of the membership.

Henry Box Brown tells of the activities on a neighboring plantation where the slaves "managed their religious affairs in their own way. An old slave, whom they called Uncle John, decided upon their piety, and would baptize them during the silent watches of the night, while their master was 'taking his rest in sleep.' Thus is the slave under the necessity of even 'saving his soul' in the hours when the eye of his master, who usurps the place of God over him, is turned from him."[38] Most quarter congregations practiced total immersion at baptisms and believed that the water symbolized both purification from sin and rebirth in Christ Jesus. No matter how cold the water, those experiencing the joy of baptism should not mind it.

> Sister, if your heart is warm,
> Snow and ice will do you no harm.
>
> I done been down, and I done been tried,
> I been through the water, and I been baptized.[39]

On most plantations the authorities allowed their slaves to hold their own funeral services, although the day appointed had to coincide with a break in the plantation work schedule. For this reason official funeral services for the deceased were sometimes not held until months after his death. In Isaac Williams' neighborhood, when slaves died their bodies were "quietly disposed of in the burial ground set apart for colored people, their graves marked, and then on different Sundays in the months of July and August, a sort of wholesale funeral service was held over all who had died in the few months previous."[40]

At the gravesite prayers and perhaps a sermon would be said for the deceased and almost always songs would be sung:

> Hark from de tomb a doleful sound.
> My ears hear a tender cry.

The Clandestine Congregation

A livin' man come through the ground
Where we may shortly lie.
Here in dis clay may be your bed
In spite of all your toil
Let all de wise bow reverent head
Must lie as low as ours.[41]

Who gwine to lay dis body,
Member, O, shout glory.
And-a who gwine lay dis body,
Oh ring Jerusalem.

O call all de member to de graveyard.
O graveyard, out to know me.
O grass grow in de graveyard.
O I reel and I rock in de graveyard.[42]

Sometimes part of the funeral service was markedly African in nature. Elige Davidson says that the slaves of his community would march around the grave three times after the body was lowered into the ground.[43] "We had all our funerals at the graveyard," recalls Harriet Robinson. "Everybody, chillen and all, picked up a clod of dirt and throwed it on top the coffin to help fill up the grave."[44] Thomas Higginson recalled helping to arrange a black funeral during the war. "Just before the coffins were lowered an old man whispered to me that I must have their positions altered—the heads must be towards the west."[45]

Ball gives this description of the funeral of a slave child whose father was captured in Africa:

. . . [I]ts father buried with it, a small bow and several arrows; a little bag of parched meal; a miniature canoe, about a foot long, and a little paddle, (with which he said it would cross the ocean to his own country) a small stick, with an iron nail, sharpened, and fastened into one end of it; and a piece of white muslin, with several curious and strange figures painted on it in blue and red, by which, he said, his relations and countrymen would know the infant to be his son, and would receive it accordingly, on its arrival amongst them.[46]

Whatever the time or form of the funeral service, however, the quarter congregation usually visited the family of the deceased on the day of his death and sat up with them long into the night praying and singing. According to Bill Crump, when a slave died on his North Carolina plantation the other slaves would "mo'n, an' shout, an' sing all de night long, while de co'pse laid out on de coolin' board. . . ."[47] Captain J. S. Rogers relates that at the death of one of their number the blacks would get together in groups of six or eight around a small fire, and sing and pray alternately from nine o'clock till three the next morning.

> Good-bye, brother, good-bye, brother,
> If I don't see you more;
> Now God bless you, now God bless you,
> If I don't see you more.
>
> We part in de body but we meet in de spirit,
> We'll meet in de heben in de blessed kingdom.[48]

According to Peter Randolph: "If the slave who died was a Christian, the rest of the Christians among them feel very glad, and thank God that brother Charles, or brother Ned, or sister Betsey, is at last free, and gone home to heaven—where bondage is never known."[49]

When a 'pater-familias dies, his family assemble in the room where the coffin is, and, ranging themselves round the body in order of age and relationship, sing this hymn, marching round and round.

Dese all my fader's children,
Dese all my fader's children,
Dese all my fader's children,
Outshine de sun.

My fader's done wid de trouble o' de world,
Wid de trouble o' de world, wid de trouble o' de world,
My fader's done wid de trouble o' de world,
Outshine de sun.

The Clandestine Congregation

Dey also take the youngest and pass him first over and then under the coffin. Then two men take the coffin on their shoulders and carry it on the run to the grave.[50]

At the death of an infant slaves might sing:

> Little baby gone to heaven
> To try on his robe
> Oh, Lord, I'm most done toiling here
> Little baby, m-m-m-m-m-m.[51]

Although many slaves were listed as official members of white-controlled churches of many different religious sects, the members of the clandestine congregation "were not," in the words of a former slave, "much on denomination. They just preached the Bible as well as they knew."[52] Lucretia Alexander, who used to slip off to the secret services with her father, says that "You couldn't tell the difference between Baptists and Methodists then. They were all Christians."[53]

Unfortunately, there is little data with which to estimate the percentage of the overall slave population which attended the secret meetings or the special services of the clandestine congregation. A few generalizations, nonetheless, can be proffered about the composition of the typical congregation. Only persons who could be trusted to guard the secrecy of the meetings and the identity of the worshippers were invited to attend. Younger members of the community, though zealously pressed by the membership, did not seem to worship as regularly as did the older folks. From the narratives it seems that those old enough to court yet still unmarried were the least likely to be among the participants of a secret meeting. Children sometimes attended, although perhaps more often they were left at home due to the lateness of the hour and the necessity of insuring the secrecy of the meeting. House servants, even those trusted and respected by the members of the quarter community, were also less likely to attend, as their absence was far more apt to be detected by whites who might call on them at any time during the day or night.

Holding meetings was not, however, the sole function of the quarter congregation, or the only means by which it acted as an educational instrument. Most of the membership took on the responsibility to struggle with the unconverted, to help uphold the faith of the believer, to attend to the sick and dying, to administer to the physically abused, and to take an active role in the instruction of their children, grandchildren, and fellow quarter members as to the ways of the Lord and the nature of true Christianity. In the fields, on the way to and from work, in the quarters, and in their cabins, the members of the quarter congregation were constantly expressing their religious feelings and convictions and, if only by example, passing them on to others.

Often the membership used songs in an attempt to convert those who had not yet found religion:

> You'd better be praying while you're young,
> You'd better be praying while you're young,
> You'd better be praying without waiting any longer,
> You'd better be praying while you're young.

> You'd better seek religion while you're young,
> You'd better seek religion while you're young,
> You'd better seek religion without waiting any longer,
> You'd better seek religion while you're young.[54]

and to bolster the spiritual fortitude of those tiring under the yoke of slavery:

> Breddren, don' get weary, breddren don' get weary,
> Breddren don't get weary, Fo' de work is mos' done.
> Keep yo' lamp trim an' a burnin', Keep yo' lamp trim an' a burnin',
> Keep yo' lamp trim an' a burnin', Fo' de work is mos' done.[55]

The educational role of the quarter congregation was not limited, however, to purely religious matters. Seldom did the congregation, or any small part of it, gather together without some discourse or prayers for freedom from the abuse of whites and the other evils of slavery. Mingo White says that "when de day's wuk was done de slaves would be foun' lock in dere cabins prayin' for de Lawd to free dem lack he did de chillun of Is'ael."[56] It was in the woods back of the barn that W. L. Bost often heard his mother and her fellowship secretly singing and praying "to the Lord to deliver us out o' bondage."[57]

The meetings of the clandestine congregation, especially when they were participated in by members of more than one quarter community, were also places where slaves could pass along information. Amanda McCray relates that she first heard of the Civil War from a black preacher who "held whispered prayers for the success of the Union soldiers. . . ."[58] Mary Gladdy says that "it was customary among slaves during the Civil War period to secretly gather together in their cabins two or three nights a week and hold prayer and experience meetings. . . . Then, the slaves would sing, pray, and relate experiences all night long. Their great, soul-hungering desire was freedom— not that they loved the Yankees and hated their masters, but merely longed to be free and hated the institution of slavery."[59]

Not only were members taught to provide for the less fortunate—that it was their duty to care for, protect, and instruct other blacks—but also to regard and address each other as sisters and brothers, united by the grace of Jesus and the fatherhood of God. The white minister C. C. Jones recognized full well the cohesive effect which the black church had upon its membership, although he uses it to illustrate what he believed to be the slaves' general moral turpitude: "The members of the same church are sacredly bound by their religion not to reveal each other's sins, for that would be backbiting and injuring to the brotherhood."[60]

The very fact that the meetings so often had to be held in secret reinforced the quarter community's belief in the hypocrisy of whites. Most slaves interpreted their owners' reluctance to allow them to hold their own services without supervision as a means of keeping hidden the full, true message of Christianity. Furthermore, as we have seen, what slaves viewed as the sterile sobriety of white churches, in contrast with their own dancing, shouting, and rejoicing in the Spirit, gave most blacks a happy confidence in the superiority of their services and their religion. Only at their own private religious gatherings, organized and controlled by their own black leaders, surrounded only by their own black brothers and sisters, did blacks feel they could practice religion as God meant it to be practiced.

Finally, the meetings of the clandestine congregation undoubtedly helped blacks to survive under slavery by providing them with a vehicle of momentary escape from the trials and tribulations of slave life on the ante-bellum plantation. Within the arms of the black church, surrounded by trusted friends and relatives, black people, while still legally slaves under the white man's political system, were able to experience moments of peace, ecstasy, fellowship, and Freedom. For a few hours they were free to express themselves as they saw fit. They could testify to their religious feelings, pour out their troubles, and express their fears, joys, and hopes to listeners who shared their sufferings and longings, participated in their joys, and supported and loved them.

In this manner the sustaining and uplifting effect of the black church under slavery blended with its role as an educational instrument of the quarter community. In the fellowship of the clandestine congregation, the people of the quarter community certainly did have "a balm the white man didn't know. He had a religion and a religious tradition which gave him a motive for living and the freedom to live. No matter what the externals of his existence, in his church he was safe in the context of love. God's love and the love of his people."[61]

❧ 16 ☙

Songs and Stories

O I'm goin' to sing,
Goin' to sing,
Goin' to sing,
Goin' to sing all along my way.
O I'm goin' to sing,
Goin' to sing,
Goin' to sing,
Goin' to sing all along my way.

Slave Spiritual

This study of the quarter community has used the songs and stories of black people under slavery to help determine and understand the values, attitudes, and beliefs with which slaves viewed the world and struggled to survive in it. In so doing, the book has followed the lead of such sociologists and folklorists as Sterling Stuckey, Alan Lomax, Howard Thurmond, Sterling Brown, Orlando Patterson, and others, who, in the words of Stuckey, generally concur that: "Folklore in its natural setting is of, by and for those who create and respond to it, depending for its survival upon the accuracy with which it speaks to needs and reflects sentiments."[1] Both the narratives and the numerous compilations of slave songs and stories lend weight to the conclusion that, though they differed from region to region, the songs and stories of the quarter community expressed similar values, beliefs, and attitudes throughout the ante-bellum South.

In addition to giving voice to the themes of the quarter community, songs and stories were also an essential medium by which those themes were evoked, supported, and transmitted from generation to generation. At play, at work, in their cabins, at church, or outdoors in the quarters, the words, rhythms, and melodies of their community's songs and stories surrounded slaves of the quarters everywhere.

Although the debate concerning African survivals in, and white influence on, slave music still rages, contemporary observers, both white and black, seem to agree that slaves made the songs they sang uniquely their own. Thomas Wentworth Higginson, who professes to having been "a faithful student of Scottish ballads" before he had an opportunity to study the songs of newly freed slaves in South Carolina during the Civil War, writes:

> As they learned all their songs by ear, they often strayed into wholly new versions, which sometimes became popular, and entirely banished the others. This was amusingly the case, for instance, with one phrase in the popular camp-song of "Marching Along," which was entirely new to them until our quartermaster taught it to them at my request. The words, "Gird on the armor," were to them a stumblingblock, and no wonder, until some ingenious ear substituted, "Guide on de army," which was at once accepted and became universal.[2]

Two white travelers noted the slave penchant for creating songs about their masters. "Nicholas Cresswell declared in 1774 that in the songs of slaves of Maryland, 'they generally relate the usage they have received from their Masters and Mistresses in a very satirical style and manner.' William Faux wrote from Charleston in 1819 of the songs of the slaves: 'Some were plaintive love songs. The verse was their own abounding either in praise or satire intended for kind and unkind masters.' "[3]

The slaves themselves provide numerous instances in which it is clear that the inspiration of many of their songs was the crucible of their own experience under slavery. One former slave reports that when she attended the religious meetings of the quarter community, "I'd jump up dar and den holler and shout and sing and pat, and dey would all cotch de words and I'd sing it to some old shout song I'd heard 'em sing from Africa, and dey'd all take it up and keep at it, and keep a-addin' to it, and den it would be a spiritual."[4] Another former slave, upon being asked how the slave songs originated, responded: "I'll tell you; it's dis way. My master call me up and order me a short peck of corn and a hundred lash. My friends see it and is sorry for me. When dey come to de praise meeting dat night dey sing about it. Some's very good singers and know how; and dey work it in, work it in, you know; till dey get it right; and dat's de way."[5] Lorenzo Ezell, who grew up on a small plantation in South Carolina, recalls how the slaves recorded the running off of their master when Sherman's men approached the plantation. "Dey a funny song us make up about him runnin' off in de woods. I know it was make up, 'cause my uncle have a hand in it. It went like dis:

> White folks, have you seed old massa
> Up de road, with he mustache on?
> He pick up he hat and he leave real sudden
> And I believe he's up and gone.
>
> Old massa run away
> And us darkies stay at home.
> It must be now dat Kingdom's comin'
> And de year of Jubilee.[6]

In his search for the origins of the spirituals Higginson was largely unsuccessful until one day a former fieldhand explained how "I been a-raise a sing, myself once."

"Once we boys," he said, "went for tote some rice, and de nigger-driver, he keep a-callin' on us; and I say, 'O, de ole nigger-driver!' Den anudder said, 'Fust ting my mammy tole me was, notin' so bad as nigger-driver.' Den I made a sing, just puttin' a word, and den anudder word."

Then he began singing, and the men, after listening a moment, joined in the chorus as if it were an old acquaintance, though they evidently had never heard it before. I saw how easily a new "sing" took root among them.

"O, de ole nigger-driver!
    O, gwine away!
Fust ting my mammy tell me,

Deep Like the Rivers

O, gwine away!
Tell me 'bout de nigger-driver,
O, gwine away!
Nigger-driver second devil,
O, gwine away!
Best ting for do he driver,
O, gwine away!
Knock he down and spoil he labor,
O, gwine away!"[7]

The speed with which slaves fashioned songs to express their joy over their newfound freedom gives ample evidence that they were old hands at creating their own songs. Louis Hughes recalls that during the war the slaves "would laugh and chat about freedom in their cabins; and many a little rhyme about it originated among them, and was softly sung over their work."[8]

We'll soon be free,
We'll soon be free,
We'll soon be free,
    When de Lord will call us home.
My brudder, how long,
My brudder, how long,
My brudder, how long,
    'Fore we done sufferin' here?
It won't be long (Thrice)
    'Fore de Lord will call us home.
We'll walk de miry road (Thrice)
    Where pleasure never dies.
We'll walk de golden street (Thrice)
    Where pleasure never dies.
My brudder, how long (Thrice)
    'Fore we done sufferin' here?
We'll soon be free (Thrice)
    When Jesus sets me free.
We'll fight for liberty (Thrice)
    When de Lord will call us home.[9]

Songs and Stories

Susie Melton remembers a song she and the other slaves sang as they prepared to leave their Virginia plantation following their emancipation. "Nex' mornin' at daybreak we all started out wid blankets an' clothes an' pots an' pans an' chickens piled on our backs, 'cause Missus said we couldn't take no horses or carts, an' as de sun come up over de trees de niggers all started to singin':

> Sun, you be here an' I'll be gone
> Sun, you be here an' I'll be gone
> Sun, you be here an' I'll be gone
> Bye, bye, don't grieve arter me
> Won't give you my place, not fo' your'n
> Bye, bye, don't grieve arter me
> 'Cause you be here an' I'll be gone.[10]

Ex-slaves from Virginia say they first heard "Slavery Chain Done Broke at Last" on April 3, 1865, the day the Federal forces occupied Richmond. "One story had it that imprisoned slaves in Lumpkin's Jail started the song when Negro soldiers marched before their barred windows and that Negroes on the street took it up spontaneously:

> Slavery chain done broke at last!
> Broke at last! Broke at last!
> Slavery chain done broke at last!
> Gonna praise God till I die![11]

Whatever their origins, songs could be sung anytime, anywhere, and for many different purposes. Previous chapters have told how songs were used at baptisms and funerals, to call meetings, to lull a baby to sleep, to accompany games, and to warn of the approach of master or overseer. Many slaves also sang at work:

> A cold frosty morning,
> The niggers feeling good,

211

Deep Like the Rivers

> Take your ax upon you shoulder,
> Nigger, talk to the wood.[12]

to commemorate an opossum hunt and feast:

> 'Possum meat is good an' sweet,
> I always finds it good to eat.
> My dog tree, I went to see.
> A great big 'possom up dat tree.
> I retch up an' pull him in,
> Den dat ole 'possum 'gin to grin.
>
> I tuck him hom' an' dressed him off,
> Dat night I laid him in de fros'.
> De way I cooked dat 'possum sound,
> I fust parboiled, den baked him brown,
> I put sweet taters in de pan,
> 'Twus de bigges' eatin' in de lan'.[13]

at corn shuckings:

> Five can't ketch me and ten can't hold me,
> Ho, . . . round the corn, Sally!
> Round the corn, round the corn, round the corn, Sally!
> Ho, ho, ho, round the corn, Sally![14]

for courting purposes:

> O Jane! love me lak you useter,
> O Jane! chew me lak you useter,
> Ev'y time I figger, my heart gits bigger,
> Sorry, sorry, can't be yo' piper any mo.[15]

to initiate lovemaking:

> Sleepy creature, sleepy creature,
> There's something to do sides sleeping.[16]

Songs and Stories

to cajole presents from master at Christmas:

> Poor massa, so dey say;
> Down in de heel, so dey say
> Got no money, so dey say;
> Not one shillin', so dey say;
> God A'mighty bless you,
> So dey say.[17]

to warn a runaway:

> Go 'way from dat window, "My Honey, My Love!"
> Go 'way from dat window! I say.
> De baby's in de bed, an' his mammy's lyin' by,
> But you cain't git yo' lodgin' here.
>
> Go 'way from dat window, "My Honey, My Love!"
> Go 'way from dat window! I say;
> Fer ole Mosser's got 'is gun, and to Miss'ip'
>   youse been sol';
> So you cain't git yo' lodgin' here.[18]

when contemplating escape:

> O Canaan, sweet Canaan,
> I am bound for the land of Canaan,
> I thought I heard them say
> There was lions in the way;
> I don't expect to stay
>   Much longer here.
> Run to Jesus, shun the danger.
>   I don't expect to stay
>   Much longer here.[19]

and as a signal that an escape was in progress:

> When dat ar ole chariot comes,
>   I'm gwine to lebe you,

Deep Like the Rivers

I'm boun' for de promised land,
    Frien's, I'm gwine to lebe you.

I'm sorry, frien's, to lebe you,
    Farewell! Oh, farewell!
But I'll meet you in de mornin',
    Farewell! oh, farewell!

I'll meet you in de mornin',
    When you reach de promised land;
On de oder side of Jordan,
    For I'm boun' for de promised land.[20]

Although many of the songs were meant to be sung between individual slaves, as in the lullabies and love songs, singing often took on the air of a community event. Clara Young recalls laboring in the fields under a mean overseer near Aberdeen, Mississippi. "We worked hard in de field all day, but when dark come we would all go to de quarters and after supper we would set around and sing and talk."[21] "At night, especially in the summertime," remembers an ex-slave interviewed by the Fisk project, "after everybody had eaten supper, it was a common thing for us to sit outside. The old folks would get together and talk until bedtime. Sometimes somebody would start singing an old hymn and then the next door neighbor would pick it up. In this way it would finally get around to every house and then the music started. Soon everybody would be gathered together, and such singing."[22] Gug Feaster lived on a plantation in South Carolina where the slaves were allowed to attend Methodist camp meetings in the summer.

At night when the meeting done busted up till next day was when the darkies really did have they freedom of the spirit. As the wagon be creeping along in the late hours of moonlight, the darkies would raise a tune. Then the air soon be filled with the sweetest tune as us rid on home and sing all the old hymns that us loved. It was always some big black nigger with a deep bass voice like a frog that'd start up the tune. Then the other mens jine in, followed up by the fine little voices of the gals and the cracked voices of the old women and the grannies. When us reach near

Songs and Stories

the big house us soften down to a deep hum that the missus like! Sometimes she hist up the window and tell us sing "Swing Low, Sweet Chariot" for her and the visiting guests. That all us want to hear. Us open up, and the niggers near the big house that hadn't been to church would wake up and come out to the cabin door and jine in the refrain. From that we'd swing on into all the old spirituals that us love so well and that us knowed how to sing. Missus often 'low that her darkies could sing with heaven's inspiration. Now and then some old mammy would fall outen the wagon a-shouting Glory! and Hallelujah! and Amen! After that us went off to lay down for the night.[23]

Storytelling also frequently took the form of a community happening. Ball describes the sound-filled atmosphere of his quarter community on the Saturday night before a feast day: "Singing, playing on the banjo, and dancing occupied nearly the whole community, until the break of day. Those who were too old to take part in our active pleasures, beat time with their hands, or recited stories of former times. Most of these stories referred to affairs that had been transacted in Africa, and were sufficiently fraught with demons, miracles and murders, to fix the attention of many hearers."[24]

Although the songs and stories of black life under slavery probably affected the education of individual quarter children in any number of undefinable ways, there are five specific kinds of learnings which most quarter children acquired from their community's songs and stories. First, and most obviously, they learned by rote a vast repertoire of songs and stories which they in turn passed down to their children. By attending the community performances of these songs and stories they learned not only words and melodies but the performing techniques and practices that were considered essential to any inspired rendition of either song or story.

Alan Lomax prepared the following list of required ingredients of a song performance from observations he made in the nineteen forties and fifties. They are in marked agreement with those learned and practiced by the members of the quarter community. Song performances were:

Mainly choral.
The group needs an expert leader to cue them into various points

of a song, when they take over with blending voices, improvised harmony, hand and rhythm, dancing, etc.

The body of the singer moves sinuously or in relaxed easy response to the beat. He dances his song.

The singer's expression changes with the mood of the song, line by line; there is a great deal of smiling and even laughing in many performances.

The voice is based in the singer's normal speaking pitch, is markedly relaxed and resonant. It plays through the entire vocal range, introducing falsetto passages and bass grunts with no self-consciousness.

Tunes are composed of short phrases which tend to wander from song to song. Improvisation is prized. Polyrhythms and a hard driving beat which normally dominates tune and text.

The texts are often fragmentary, consisting of one new line per stanza with extensive refrains. Both verses and refrains wander from song to song. Each singer recreates the song and reorders the words with each performance. No premium on memory; improvisation prized.[25]

And always the performance was evaluated by the extent to which the song infused the listener/participant with its beauty, excited his spirit, and became reality in his mind's eye. "We used to sing, 'Swing low, sweet chariot,' " recalls Hannah Davidson. "When our folks sang that, we could really see the chariot."[26]

Storytelling was often performed in a similar manner, although the participation of the wider group was more limited to expressions of agreement, wonder, outrage, sympathy. Sometimes, as in many sermons, the telling of a story was chanted in a way that resembled singing. "A man telling a story or a yarn, particularly if his rendition is effective, will often stimulate conversational responses such as 'Oh Lord,' 'Yeah,' 'Ain't it so,' and 'It's true' at appropriate places. The interplay of narration and exclamation sometimes sets up a rhythmic, near-musical pattern."[27] As with songs, a vividly realistic dramatization of the story is essential. Emma M. Backus, who spent many years collecting folk tales from blacks in Georgia, states: "I don't know

Songs and Stories

how they do it, but they will say 'lipity clipity, lipity clipity,' so you can almost hear a rabbit coming through the woods. They talk animatedly, especially in the dialogues, and change the voice to represent the different animals, but not in a chanting tone."[28]

Often the songs, and sometimes the stories, were accompanied by musical instruments. Among the instruments most commonly played by the quarter community were banjos, fiddles, quills, and jaw-bones.[29] Because drums were forbidden on many plantations, for fear slaves on adjoining plantations would use them to communicate with each other during revolts, quarter residents often accompanied themselves with sticks, tin pans, or bones. "In de evening," remembers James Southall of his slave days in Tennessee, "when we was through wid our work dey would gather at one of de cabins and visit and sing or dance. We'd pop corn, eat walnuts, peanuts, hickory nuts, and tell ghost stories. We didn't have any music instruments so de music we danced by wasn't so very good. Everybody sang and one or two would beat on tin pans or beat bones together."[30]

Of course, not all quarter children became song leaders or expert storytellers. Most children of the quarter community did learn from the performance of their community's songs and stories, however, what they were allowed and expected to do as a participating audience. Regardless of their own individual skills, or lack of them, most quarter children internalized an understanding, a feeling, of how black music should be sung and played and how stories should be told. They learned to distinguish between a true virtuoso performance and one that did not quite catch fire.

A second kind of learning drawn from the stories and songs of the quarter community was the actual factual content delivered through their texts. Thus, for example, it was possible to learn from the spirituals about the trials and triumphs of any number of Biblical characters.

> The spirituals make an anthology of Biblical heroes and tales, from Genesis where Adam and Eve are in the Garden, picking up leaves, to John's calling the role in Revelations. There are numerous gaps, of course, and many repetitions. Certain figures are

217

seen in an unusual light. Paul, for instance, is generally bound in jail with Silas, to the exclusion of the rest of his busy career. Favored heroes are Noah, chosen of God to ride down the flood; Samson, who tore those buildings down; Joshua, who caused the walls of Jericho to fall (when the rams' lambs' sheephorns began to blow); Jonah, symbol of hard luck changed at last; and Job, the man of tribulation who still would not curse God.[31]

Other Biblical figures mentioned frequently in the songs of blacks under slavery included: Methuselah, "de oldest man"; father Abraham; wrestling Jacob and his ladder; Moses and his freeing of the Hebrew children and his death on the mountain; Ezekiel and his wheel; David and his harp; Daniel in the lions' den; Isaiah, "mounted on de wheel of time"; John, "de Holy Baptist"; Herod, and his slaying of the innocents; Fisherman Peter; Nicodemus, the man among the Pharisees; Lazarus; weeping Mary; mourning Martha; Gabriel and his trumpet; and, always, Satan, Jesus, God, and the Holy Spirit. Because few slaves could read and fewer still had access to a Bible, much of what quarter members knew of Biblical persons and events they learned from the religious songs of the quarter community.

Part of the educational value of many of the stories of the quarter community also lay in their informative content. Through the medium of stories blacks learned of life in Africa, of the nature of slavery in other slave states, of the existence of the North and Canada, of the history of their home plantation and the happenings on neighboring plantations, and of the deeds and daring of black heroes and folk-heroes. Often it was through stories that slave children learned bits of their family history. Richard Jones of South Carolina was told the story of how his grandmother, Granny Judith, was enticed onto the slave ship along with Uncle Tom, Aunt Chany, and Aunt Daphne. "Granny Judith born Millie, and Millie born me."[32] Robert Solomon was told how his father, an African slave, courted his mother, a Cherokee Indian. ". . . my father stole my mother one night. He couldn't understand them and he was afraid of her people. . . . He said he knowed her 'bout two years 'fore they married. They sorter courted by signs. . . . My father said she was just so pretty he couldn't help lovin' her. He kept making

Songs and Stories

signs and she made signs."[33] Adelaide J. Vaughn heard the story of how her mother was sold at the age of four:

> My grandfather was allowed to go a certain distance with her when she was sold away from him. He walked and carried her in his arms. Mamma said that when he had gone as far as they would let him go, he put her in the wagon and turned his head away. She said she wondered why he didn't look at her; but later she understood that he hated so bad to part from her and couldn't do nothing to prevent it that he couldn't bear to look at her.[34]

A third way in which songs and stories were an important educational instrument of the quarter community was through the values, attitudes, and sentiments transmitted through their words or story line. In the case of many songs these values were probably understood similarly by most persons who heard them. The words of the song recorded by Frederick Douglass, "We raise de wheat,/ Dey gib us de corn . . ." (quoted in full on page 77) leaves little doubt of the anger and anti-white hostility being expressed. Other songs were even more concise and direct in the message they imparted:

> Don't know what my mother wants to stay here fuh,
> Dis ole world ain't been no friend to huh.[35]

Many of the songs, including most of the spirituals, transmit values and attitudes more by implication than literal meaning. Take for instance the following song:

> When I get to heaven, gwine be at ease,
> Me and my God gonna do as we please.
>
> Gonna chatter with the Father, argue with the Son,
> Tell um 'bout the world I just come from.[36]

From such a song an individual black child might take in the quarter community's confidence that they will someday live in a heaven where the hardships of slavery are ended—*when* I get to heaven, not if. The words also imply that the world known by

219

slaves is an evil place that the Lord might like to know about in a little more detail. Finally, it picturesquely communicates that the quarter community considered God and Jesus to be rather intimate personal friends.

These attitudes were not, of course, transmitted each time any slave sang or heard this song. Often songs were sung as pure entertainment, and the "message" blended with the memory of the pleasure received. It is probably safe to assume that neither listener nor singer sang the songs of black life under slavery over and over again without internalizing some of the values and attitudes they express—the values and attitudes contained in the themes of the quarter community.[37]

The folktales and stories told in the quarters, though they ranged over many topics and involved plots of infinite variety, also reaffirmed those values and attitudes most strongly held by the quarter community. Buh Rabbit, though smaller and less physically powerful than the other animals, was able through cunning and quick wit to outmaneuver and make fun of the larger animals. He won his victories by telling lies and making up tall tales; studying the weaknesses and strengths of the other animals and using that knowledge against them; telling jokes or making others laugh at moments of crisis when it appeared he was in for a beating or worse; being able to run fast and think quickly; and being able to laugh at himself without impairing his confidence or feeling of supreme self-importance. Buh Rabbit was at once, in the words of Arna Bontemps, "a practical joker, a braggart, a wit, a glutton, a lady's man, and a trickster. But his essential characteristic was his ability to get the better of bigger and stronger animals."[38] Though it is possible to make too much of the obvious parallel between Buh Rabbit and the slave and Buh Bear, Fox, *et al.,* and the master, the animal tales, at the very least, must have suggested to their slave listeners the many ways in which slaves could subvert the power of whites.[39]

Whereas the animal tales more frequently imply attitudes and values, many of the stories of John the Trickster (also called Efram and "High John de Conquer") openly express them.[40] By employing the same strategies as did Buh Rabbit, he outwits whites, runs away, steals, disobeys master and overseer, gets

Songs and Stories

beaten, expresses the desire for revenge, and gains his own freedom and that of fellow slaves. "In one tale John prays 'for God to come git him [master] and take him to Hell right away because Massa is evil.' On another occasion Efram prays: 'I'm tired of staying here and taking all these beatings . . . kill all the white folks and leave all the niggers.' "[41] In other stories John portrays the slave's ability to poke fun at himself and at the pretentiousness of other slaves. At heart, however, he symbolized the slaves' hatred for the institution of slavery while simultaneously demonstrating to them how it was possible to survive within it.

Most quarter communities also generated and told stories which perpetuated the memory of more or less historical quarter figures. By building the legends of these persons through telling their story the quarter community gave great sanction to the deeds of these men and women. The legendary figures most often immortalized in story were of three general types: those who fooled or made fun of whites; those who sacrificed for family or friends; and those who physically confronted plantation authorities.[42]

The best proof that slaves were well aware of the attitudes and values of their songs and stories is that they were careful about which songs and stories reached white ears. Trickster John stories were never told to whites. Songs containing overtly anti-white feelings were, of course, not sung in white hearing. Even many of the spirituals contained ideas that slaves knew would not be pleasing to whites. As one ex-slave recalls: "We chillun would get in the woods and have meetings and sing them spirituals but we wouldn't sing them to the white folks."[43] Attempting to collect black folksongs in the early nineteen hundreds, Howard Odum discovered: "Many of them are sung only when the white man does not hear; they are the folk-songs of the Negro, and the Negro is very secretive. Not only are they not commonly known by the whites but their existence is only recognized in general."[44]

The mode of the performance provided a fourth way in which the children of the quarters were able to learn from the songs and stories of their community. It cannot be stressed too force-

221

fully that the style of expression, the mood or feeling with which a song was sung or a story told, was often crucial to the value which the listener drew from the words. For example, the way in which the famous song "Run, nigger, run" is sung greatly affects whether it transmits a fear of the patrol, a sense of comedy in the hapless plight of a slave caught off the home plantation, a feeling of pride in blacks when compared with whites, or any or all of these.

> Run, nigger, run; de patter-roller catch you;
> Run, nigger, run, it's almost day.
> Run, nigger, run; de patter-roller catch you;
> Run, nigger, run, and try to get away.
>
> Dat nigger run, he run his best,
> Stuck his head in a hornet's nest,
> Jumped de fence and run fru de paster;
> White man run, but nigger run faster.
>
> Dat nigger run, dat nigger flew,
> Dat nigger tore his shirt in two.

Often the importance of the mood transcended the meaning of the words. Thus, by listening to the emotional tone of his mother's voice when she sang, the child of the quarters could tell when she was happy, troubled, peaceful, angry, weary. From the singing and storytelling of larger groups, he learned to sense when his community was tense, feeling good, troubled, expectant, or swept away in the throes of a religious revival.

Finally, most quarter children gained through their participation in the singing and storytelling of their community a sense of communal spirit and camaraderie with their fellows and a feeling of identification with the larger community of American slaves. At the same time these songs and stories set blacks apart from whites, who were not allowed to hear them or did not understand, and who could not adequately sing or tell them.[45]

Whatever their individual personalities, experiences, and degree of political awareness, all quarter children were drawn together by the songs and stories of their childhood within a circle of black security and kinships. "The child," writes Lomax, "begins to learn the musical style of his culture as he acquires the language and the emotional patterns of his people. This style is thus an important link between the individual and his culture, and later in life brings back to the adult unconscious the emotional texture of the world which formed his personality.[46]

In later years, no matter how old they became or how far they traveled from their quarter home, these feelings of communality and kinship would always be rekindled with the soulful singing of a quarter song or the old-time-style-performance of a quarter story. The significance of songs and stories to the black people who lived under slavery was thus not just their entertainment value, or even their educational importance, but that these songs and stories became a part of their individual personalities and their collective consciousness.

❦ 17 ❧

The Community

My army cross over,
My army cross over,
O, Pharaoh's army drowned!
My army cross over.

We'll cross de mighty river,
    My army cross over;
We'll cross de river Jordan,
    My army cross over;
We'll cross de danger water,
    My army cross over;
We'll cross de might Myo,
    My army cross over.
    O, Pharaoh's army drowned!
    My army cross over.

Higginson, *Negro
Spirituals*

In the educational interactions of the family, peer group, clandestine congregation, and songs and stories, many of the ways in which the community itself influenced the education of its members have already been discussed. Indeed in many quarters, especially the smaller ones, the structure and influence of the extended family or the religious brotherhood merged with, and sometimes supplanted, the structure and influence of the community. Even in many of the larger quarters it would be a futile exercise to attempt to determine where the ties and reciprocal obligations of family, peer group, and congregation end and those of community begin. It is possible, however, to isolate

224

The Community

some educative functions which the community seemed to play more often than one of its component institutions.

One of the most important ways in which the community as a whole influenced the education of its members was by providing alternative role models for its children. Among the more prestigious and widespread of these roles—besides those already discussed of family member, preacher, singer, storyteller—were: community leader, doctor, conjuror, reader/writer, skilled athlete, hunter, musician, dancer, and rebel.

A quarter member became a community leader by the common assent of the other members of the community who recognized his or her special skills, wisdom, and dedication to the needs, will, and solidarity of the quarter community. Often the leader, or leaders, played a second role in the community in conjunction with their leadership role: storyteller, trusted house servant, doctor, athlete. Most often, they were also preachers. Even the preacher, however, if he were also a community leader, had responsibilities that went beyond those he assumed as the head of the clandestine congregation. Perhaps the primary function of community leaders was to head the process by which the members of the community made common decisions. It was these men and women who decided when it was time to petition the great house, take action against a cruel master or overseer, organize a work slowdown, or chastise a straying community member. To these leaders the other slaves brought their disputes, their domestic problems, and their suggestions for community initiatives.[1]

Although sometimes these indigenous leaders of the quarter community were given official positions of power by plantation authorities, it is important to distinguish between those blacks given official positions due to the favor they had won in white eyes and those whose position reflected the leadership role they had already achieved within the quarter community. The power accorded the former officials by the slaves of the quarters was limited to those occasions where it would be backed up by the coercive power of whites. The power accorded to the natural leaders of the quarters, on the other hand, was often virtually unlimited.

225

Deep Like the Rivers

The black doctor and the conjuror were figures familiar to most quarter communities. The slave doctor was a self-made expert in diagnosis and herbal cures, ever ready to attend the sick of his home quarters. Depending on his or her reputation for successful cures, he was frequently called to slip out at night to care for neighboring quarter communities. George Rodgers recalls that on the North Carolina plantation where he lived as a young slave "We had an old colored man who doctored on all us chillun. He gave us roots and herbs."[2] Among the slaves on the Virginia plantation where Della Harris grew up, a white doctor was rarely called because Della's mother took care of most complaints. "Mother always said you got to feed sickness 'cause it's in de blood. Said dat rubbin' was bad, 'cause it jus' rub de pain inside. Mother had a tea fo' ev'y which complaint, even one she used to give fo' child birth."[3]

Some of the most frequently prescribed cures of these men and women of medicine included: for fever, may-apple root and boiled mullen weed; for colds, horehound tea, pinttop tea, and lightwood drippings on sugar; for indigestion, holly leaves and roots boiled together; for colic, calamus root; for severe burns, the fried fat of a fresh killed hog mixed with some hog hairs; and for constipation, tea made from sheep droppings. As Josephine Bacchus, an ex-slave from South Carolina, recalls, "de people never didn' put much faith to de doctors [white doctors] in dem days. Mostly, dey would use de herbs in de fields for dey medicine."[4]

The midwife was also an important figure in the quarters. "My grandmammy," remembers Dellie Lewis, "was a midwife an' she useta gib de women cloves an' whiskey to ease de pain. She also gib 'em dried watermelon seeds to get rid of de grabel in de kidneys."[5] Julia Brown, who lived as a slave in Georgia, says that, when it came time, the quarter women "just had our babies and a granny to catch 'em."

> The granny would put a rusty piece of tin or a axe under the mattress and this would ease the pain. The granny put a ax under my mattress once. This was to cut off the after-pain and it sure did, too. We'd set up the fifth day and after the "layin-in" time

226

was up we was allowed to walk outdoors and they told us to walk around the house just once and come in the house. This was to keep us from takin' a 'lapse.[6]

Often slave doctors mixed their medicine with conjuration. Gus Smith, who was born on a large plantation in Missouri in 1845, had a grandfather who used butternut root to cure chills, onion tea with sugar for sore throats, and poke root in whiskey for rheumatism. He also had a secret cure for cases of severe burn. "In 'blowing fire,' my grandfather simply blew on de burn and de fire and pain was gone. It was a secret charm handed down from generation to generation. He said only one could be told. He told my Aunt Harriet and she could 'blow fire' de same as my grandfather."[7] Some of the other charms used by quarter conjurors were: to be successful in love, scratch the bare skin of the courted with the dry bone of a frog or wear a lock of her hair in your shoes; to prevent the separation of husband and wife, wrap a rabbit's forefoot, a piece of lodestone, and nine hairs from the top of the head in red flannel and bury it under the door steps; to prevent white abuse, mix fresh cow manure with red pepper and white people's hair, scorch it until it can be ground into snuff, and sprinkle it about the master's bedroom, in his hat and shoes, etc.; to keep off witches or the jinx of your enemies, fill a red flannel bag with a piece of High John the Conqueror root, magnetic lodestone, five finger grass, controlling powder, and wear it around your neck, sprinkling it every morning for seven mornings with holy oil. Because of the quarter community's widespread belief in the spirit world, those men and women thought able to control and channel spirit forces often became very powerful quarter personalities.[8]

Another of the more important figures which slave children had to look to as patterns for their own behavior, was the trusted house servant upon whom the quarters could rely to keep a close watch in the great house for opportunities to assist the other slaves. Sarah Burke, who was a slave in West Virginia, related to her interviewer how the cook in the master's kitchen used to bake cookies for all the slaves every Sunday morning when the white folks went to church.[9] Bruce writes that the house servants "would listen carefully to what they heard their owners say while talking to each other on political matters, or about the fault of another slave, and as soon as opportunity would admit, go to the quarters and warn the slave of his danger, and tell what they heard the master say about the politics of the country."[10] Henry Gowens, who experienced slavery in Virginia, North Carolina, Tennessee, Albama, and Mississippi, remembers that the plantation nurse of his Alabama slave days was able successfully to petition her mistress to stop the overseer's cruelty towards the female fieldhands.[11]

Besides being able to teach others their skills, the slaves who could read or write often were able to provide the quarters with valuable information. On Sundays Douglass Dorsey and his fellow slaves were ordered to church where they heard a white minister admonish them "to honor their masters and their mistresses, and to have no other God but them, as 'we cannot see the other God, but you can see your master and mistress.' After the services, the driver's wife who could read and write a little would tell them that what the minister said 'was all lies.' "[12] William Johnson recalls the efforts of a slave by the name of Joe Sutherland, who was a coachman in Henrico County, Virginia: "Joe always hung aroun' de courthouse wid Marsa. He went on business trips wid him, an' learned to read and write unbeknownst to Marsa. Joe got so good dat he learned to write passes for de slaves."[13] As a serving girl on another large Virginia plantation, Susan Broaddus used to stand behind the Mistress at the table and pass her whatever she wanted.

> Ole Marsa would spell out real fas' anything he don't want me to know 'bout. One day Marsa was fit to be tied, he was in setch a bad mood. Was ravin' 'bout de crops, an' taxes, an' de triflin' niggers he got to feed. "Gonna sell 'em, I swear before Christ, I gonna sell 'em," he says, Den ole Missus ask which ones he gonna sell an' tell him quick to spell it. Den he spell out G-A-B-E and R-U-F-U-S. 'Course I stood dere without battin' an eye, an' makin' believe I didn't even hear him, but I was packin' dem letters up in my haid all de time. An' soon's I finished dishes I rushed down to my father an' say 'em to him jus' like Marsa say 'em. Father say quiet-like: "Gabe and Rufus," an' tol' me to go on back to de house an' say I ain't been out. De next day Gabe and Rufus was gone—dey

had run away. Marsa nearly died, got to cussin' an' ravin' so he took sick. Missus went to town an' tol' de sheriff, but dey never could fin' dose two slaves.[14]

During the Civil War house servants and readers became especially important sources of information. Rebecca Hooks, who lived as a slave on the Georgia plantation of William Lowe, learned of the reasons behind the war by reading newspapers and confided this information to other slaves.[15] Marrs "would read the newspapers as I would bring them from the post-office, and I kept the colored population of the neighborhood well posted as to the prevailing news."[16] Whenever the slaves wanted to say something to the master of the Louisiana plantation where Victoria McMullen's grandmother worked as a house servant, "they would have my grandma say it because they knew she wouldn't be whipped for it." This same grandmother "used to steal newspapers out of the house and take them down to the quarters and leave them there where there were one or two slaves that could read and tell how the War was goin' on. . . . Later she could slip off and they would tell her the news, and then she could slip the papers back."[17] "How did we get news?" asked Benjamin Russell of South Carolina. "Many plantations were strict about this, but the greater their precaution the alerter became the slaves, the wider they opened their ears and the more eager they became for outside information. The sources were: girls that waited on the tables, the ladies' maids and the drivers; they would pick up everything they heard and pass it on to the other slaves."[18]

On some plantations the black driver who supervised the work of fieldhands and often did the whipping was one of the most hated individuals in the quarters. On other plantations he used his position for the benefit and protection of his fellow slaves. Wes Turner remembers such a driver from his slavery days in Virginia: "Old Gabe didn't like dat whippin' business, but he couldn't help hisself. When Marsa was dere, he would lay it on 'cause he had to. But when ole Marsa wasn't lookin', he never would beat dem slaves. Would tie de slave up to one post an' lash another one. 'Cose de slave would scream an' yell to satisfy

Marsa. . . ."[19] Solomon Northup served time as a driver in Louisiana. "I learned to handle the whip with marvellous dexterity and precision, throwing the lash within a hair's breadth of the back, the ear, the nose, without, however, touching either of them."[20] When forced by the overseer to whip a female field-hand, James Williams waited until the overseer's back was turned and then "struck the tree instead of the woman, who, understanding my object, shrieked as if the whip at every blow was cutting into her flesh. The overseer heard the blows and the woman's cries, and, supposing that all was going according to his mind, left the field."[21]

Many quarter communities also contained individual slaves who were esteemed by their community as skilled musicians, singers, dancers. On one South Carolina plantation there was a slave by the name of John Drayton who played for all the dances on the plantation and who could, according to Ephraim Lawrence, "fair make a fiddle talk. . . . Yes, sir, that man sure could play. When he saw down on the fiddle and pull out that tune, 'Oh, the Monkey Marry to the Baboon' Sister,' he make a parson dance."[22] Georgianna Gibbs retained for many years a clear memory of Charlie Snipes, the lead singer on the Virginia plantation where she was a slave. "We'd all be hoein' potatoes 'long behindst Charlie, an' he would be prancin' an' singin' chunes for us to chop by. Dis de song Charlie used to sing on Saddays:

> Gwine to de ball
> Feet de de diddle
> Whose gwine to de ball?
> Feet de de diddle
> Gwine wear a raid gown
> Feet de de diddle
> Wear a raid gown
> Feet de de diddle
> Gwine wear a velvet coat
> Feet de de diddle. . . .

The Community

An' keep it up, puttin' in words an' kickin' de clods in step. An' sometimes dey take it up all over de fiel', jus' a feet de de diddlin' an' steppin' high an' choppin' right in chune."[23]

Hannah Crasson recalls the impression made upon her as a slave child in Wake County, North Carolina by an aunt who was "a royal slave." "She could dance all over de place wid a tumbler of water on her head, widout spilling it. She sho could tote herself. I always luved to see her come to church. She sho could tote herself."[24] Often word of a slave's skill carried from quarter community to quarter community. On the Texas plantation where James Smith was born there was a slave whose reputation for dancing the jig was known throughout the neighborhood.

> Everyone round tries to git somebody to best him. He could put the glass of water on his head and make his feet go like triphammers and sound like the snaredrum. He could whirl round and such, all the movement from his hips down. Now it get noised round a fellow been found to beat Tom and a contest am 'ranged for Saturday evening. There was a big crowd and money am bet, but Master bets on Tom, of course.
>
> So they starts jigging. Tom starts easy and a little faster and faster. The other fellow doing the same. They gits faster and faster, and that crowd am a-yelling. Gosh! There am 'citement. They just keep a-gwine. It look like Tom done found his match, but there am one thing yet he ain't done—he ain't made a whirl. Now he does it. Everybody holds he breath, and the other fellow starts to make the whirl and he makes it, but just a spoonful of water sloughs out of his cup, so Tom am the winner.[25]

Other slaves acquired prominence in the quarters for their skills as hunters, athletes, cooks, and wood carvers. Such persons served not only as observable role models for slave children but often took an active role in teaching their skills to an interested member of the younger generation.

Many quarter communities also contained slaves who were able consistently to outsmart whites and others who were willing to defy and sometimes physically confront the power and authority of plantation whites.[26] Most slave children either witnessed themselves, or heard about, the deeds of slaves who

231

dared to run off, who refused to be whipped, who intervened in the abuse of spouse, parent, child, or community member, who refused to brutalize another slave, who escaped from slavery only to return for others still in bondage, who stood up to the power and force of white society in order to maintain their personal dignity and group pride. Willis Dukes recalls that when the slaves on his plantation learned of a slave who had successfully escaped to the North, was saving money to buy his family, and was even attending school, it "fired all the slaves with an ambition to go north. . . ."[27] Douglass writes of the impact which the escape of two slaves had upon him as a child. "The success of Aunt Jennie and Uncle Noah in getting away from slavery was, I think, the first fact that made me seriously think of escape for myself. I could not have been more than seven or eight years old at the time of this occurrence, but young as I was, I was already, in spirit and purpose, a fugitive from slavery."[28] J. W. Loguen remembers being inspired by a slave named Jerry, who fought his new buyers in a tremendous fight rather than be separated from his wife and children.[29] When she was a young slave girl Lila Nicholas was deeply impressed by the words a slave spoke in refusing to allow her mistress to whip her: " 'No sir, Missus, I ain't 'lowin' nobody what wa'r de same kind of shirt I does ter whip me.' "[30] Charity Morris tells of an aunt who killed a mean master with a fire poker.[31] On the plantation where Peter Bruner experienced life as a slave there lived a slave named Tandy who was not whipped very often. He had the audacity to assert that he did the best he knew how and that therefore he would not be whipped. They would have to kill him first.[32] On John Thompson's plantation there was a slave with similar sentiments:

> On the plantation was a slave named Ben, who was highly prized by Mr. T., being, as he thought, the best and most faithful servant on the farm. Ben was a resolute and brave man, and did not fear death. Such courage did not suit the overseer, who wanted each slave to tremble with fear when he addressed him. Ben was too high-minded for such humiliation before any insignificant overseer. He had philosophically concluded that death is but death any way, and that one might as well die by hanging as whipping; so he resolved not to submit to be whipped by the overseer.[33]

The Community

Later Ben nearly killed his overseer when the overseer did attempt to whip him, and for this "he was whipped until his entrails could be seen moving within his body." After this episode, however, he was never again struck by either the master or the overseer. "Ben," concludes Thompson, "was a brave fellow, nor did his flogging lessen his bravery in the least. Nor is Ben the only brave slave at the South; there are many there who would rather be shot than whipped by any man."[34]

James Roberts witnessed the hanging of a slave named Joe, accused of using a hoe to kill an overseer who was severely whipping another slave. He had confessed to the crime rather than to allow the other slaves "be whipped around." Addressing his friends Joe's last words before hanging were: "Don't one of you grieve for me; I die an honorable death. Do not grieve for me, my friends. I bid you all adieu. Here is an end to Joe in this life. Though I die with a sore back, I die a man's death. Let no white man kill you, but you kill him."[35]

Most quarter communities also influenced the education of its membership through heavy sanctions against individual slaves who gave evidence they could not be relied upon to live by the norms of communal support and protection. Although physical chastisement and even the execution of traitors were not unknown, the community as a whole most frequently employed the weapons of shame and ostracism. At the very least, unreliable slaves were excluded from clandestine meetings and unsanctioned social events. One former slave tells how his master forced him to disclose the names of those blacks who had attended an unauthorized moonlit dance or be "whipped all daylight." After his betrayal he was not allowed to attend any of the quarter community parties. "The niggers would kick me out if they saw me; they wouldn't have me there."[36] Another slave remembers the time when, as a young boy, fear of punishment made him tell his white mistress the names of those slaves who had not deemed him too young to be trusted to attend a private dance. "I knew it was wrong but I did it to save my hide. Nobody got any whipping though, but it was the last time I got to go along with them to a frolic."[37]

Perhaps the best example of how the quarter community used

233

ostracism as both a controlling and a protective device can be seen in the way quarter slaves acted towards those blacks whose special relationship to or with whites made their loyalty to the quarter community suspect. Any slave given a favored position by the white authorities was tested and, if found not primarily committed to the quarter community, made persona non grata in the quarters. The effectiveness of such ostracism is proved by the relative ignorance of quarter life shown by those ostracised. Isaac Adams, when a child, was the personal companion and slave of a young mistress in Louisiana. "She never did go around the quarters, so I don't know nothing much about the negroes Mr. Sask had for the fields."[38] Easter Brown, sold from her parents and brought up by the white family, admitted that she didn't "know much 'bout slave quarters, or what dey had in 'em, 'cause I wuz raised in de house wid de white folkses."[39] Recalling his life in the great house, another former house servant informed his interviewer that the slaves of the quarters "wouldn't say anything before me, 'cause I stayed in the house, and et in there, and slept in there."[40]

The organization of special events and joint actions provided for the pleasure and entertainment of quarter community members while at the same time instilling and maintaining a sense of group solidarity and communal spirit. In past chapters we have discussed how the songs, stories, and secret religious meetings helped to affect a feeling of communality among quarter members. Many quarters also organized dances, feasts, hunting and stealing expeditions, and athletic events. Mary Reynolds says that in her Louisiana quarter community on Saturday evenings the slave musicians would bring "fiddles and guitars and come out and play. The others clap they hands and stomp they feet and we young-uns cut a step round."[41] Saturday nights were also big occasions for James Bolton and the other slaves of his Georgia quarters.

> Sadday nights we played and danced. Sometimes in the cabins, sometimes in the yards. Effen we didn't have a big stack of fat kindling wood lit up to dance by, sometimes the mens and 'omans would carry torches of kindling wood whilst they danced and it sho' was a sight to see! We danced the "Turkey Trot" and "Buz-

zard Lope," and how we did love to dance the "Mary Jane!" We would git in a ring and when the music started we would begin walkin' our footses while we sang "You steal my true love and I steal your'n!"

Atter supper we used to gather round and knock tin buckets and pans, we beat 'em like drums. Some used they fingers and some used sticks for to make the drum sounds and somebody allus blowed on quills.[42]

Sarah Byrd was so glad when Saturday night came she couldn't eat. "Yes sir we would frolic all night long sometimes when the sun rise on Sunday morning us would all be layin' round or set-tin' on the floor."[43]

The dances done on such evenings, according to Robert Anderson, "were individual dances, consisting of shuffling of the feet, swinging of the arms and shoulders in a peculiar rhythm of time developed into what is known today as the Double Shuffle, Heel and Toe, Buck and Wing, Juba, etc. The slaves became proficient in such dances, and could play a tune with their feet, dancing largely to an inward music, a music that was felt, but not heard."[44] If no musical instruments were available the slaves would dance the juba. By Solomon Northup's account this involved "striking the hands on the knees, then striking the hands together, then striking the right shoulder with one hand, the left with the other—all the while keeping time with the feet, and singing. . . ."[45]

Sundays and holidays were also times used for special events. Speaking of slaves generally, Campbell asserts that Sunday was "a great day for sports. The slaves would all get together and wrestle and box and play, and pass a jovial day, and we all passed the time very pleasantly."[46] Though masters often encouraged these events, they occurred frequently without official sanction. In either case the impetus and the style of the event came from the quarter community. One Fisk respondent remembers that she and the other slaves "had dances often in the summer, down in the woods. They would have lanterns hanging out in the trees all around."[47] According to Charlie Grandy the best times were had by the slaves when they gathered in some quarter cabin without permission.

235

Marsa ain't sayed we cain't have no dance, an' he ain't sayed we can. But sometimes we felt like raisin' a ruckus—make plenty noise wid de winders wide open, shout, clap, and sing. 'Course Marsa don't take de trouble to get outer bed an' come down 'cause he know he gonna fin' e'vy slave in bed an' a-snorin'. Might whip us de nex day, but we done had our dance. Stay as late as we want—don't care if we is got to be in de field at sunrise. When de dance break up we go out, slam de do' if we wants, an' shout back at de man what had de party:

Eat yo' meat an' show yo' bone,
Goodbye, Charlie, I'se gwine home.[48]

In many quarters, individual members shared the responsibility of providing extra food and comforts for the community as a whole. An ex-slave of the Fisk project recalls that when her father and uncle killed a great big mutton, "They invited company in to help eat it up."[49] Steward says that stolen food, especially animals, was cooked in the woods at night.[50] M. E. Abrams of South Carolina asserts that her uncle and the other slaves "used to steal our hog every Saturday night and take off to the gully where us'd git him dressed and barbecued."[51]

In some quarter communities the slaves shared the food they grew in their garden patches. Ball relates how different families would agree to raise different vegetables and then trade them. On feast days "every family made some preparation of vegetables, from their own garden, to enlarge the quantity, if not heighten the flavour of the dinner of this day."[52] Those who were skilled at the intricacies of making baskets and other artifacts traded their handcrafts for the eggs of chicken raisers, and both of them traded with the skilled distiller. Often housebuilding, sewing, spinning, and washing were done communally. Mary Colbert remembers how the slave women in her Georgia quarters at the onset of winter "went from one house to another and quilted as many as twelve quilts in one night sometimes."[53]

Most quarter communities occasionally acted in concert in order to protect individual members and the community as a whole from overwork and white abuse. The study has shown already how slaves maneuvered to protect themselves from a work overload.[54] Most quarter members felt a responsibility to care for each other's wounds, to warn each other of punishments, and to care for each other in sickness and old age. Moses Grandy relates that when slaves received whippings "their fellow-slaves rub their backs with part of their little allowance of fat meat."[55] Jordan Smith remembers how the slaves of his Georgia quarters would slip bread and meat to slaves locked up in the log house.[56] On those plantations where old slaves were put off the grounds when they could no longer work, they were able to survive through the care of the other slaves.

> No care is taken of them, except, perhaps, that a little ground is cleared about the hut, on which the old slave, if able, may raise a little corn. As far as the owner is concerned, they live or die, as it happens: it is just the same thing as turning out an old horse. Their children, or other near relations, if living in the neighborhood, take it by turns to go at night with a supply saved of their own scanty allowance of food, as well as to cut wood and fetch water for them: this is done entirely through the good feelings of the slaves, and not through the masters' taking care that it is done.[57]

Most quarters also pitched in to protect those of their number who were forced to take to the woods to prevent punishment or sale. "When the slaves would run away out in the woods," relates one ex-slave, they would "come around and get something to eat and hide out. They would fix something to eat and send it by one of the children. They wouldn't send but one, 'cause the white folks might suspicion."[58] Another Fisk informant reports how he and the other slaves would steal "butter and stuff" from their master's spring house and give it to the runaways.[59] Julia Brown says that some of the slaves she remembers from her childhood in Georgia would hide out in forest caves when their masters were mean to them. "They get along all right—what with other people slippin' things to 'em."[60] Leah Garret, who was also a slave in Georgia, recounts the story of a slave couple who lived for seven years in a cave where they had three children. During this time "diffunt folks helped keep 'em in food."[61]

If a quarter slave decided to attempt to escape from slavery altogether, it was usually with the blessing and often with the assistance of his community. A fellow servant of George Johnson's, about to be sold away from his home near Harper's Ferry, made an effective appeal for help. "We made up a purse," recollects Johnson, "and sent him on his way."[62] Andrew Jackson, who was born a slave in Kentucky in 1814, affirms that liberty was "the theme of almost every meeting among them, and one of the most happy events whenever one escapes. And it is a very rare thing that one slave ever becomes informer against his brother who intends to take the long walk. When one is ready to start, those who remain will often help him in every way in their power."[63]

Sometimes quarter slaves, especially those in the larger communities, organized to settle disputes among themselves. Ulrich Phillips cites the case of the plantation of the Jefferson brothers in Warren County, Mississippi, where "the discipline of the plantation was vested in courts composed wholly of slaves, proceeding formally and imposing penalties to be inflicted by slave constables except when the master intervened with his power of pardon."[64] More often slaves preferred to organize in their own way. The slaves of Jacob Stroyer's community, as already shown, used the slaves' fear of the spirit world to bring to justice those slaves who stole from other quarter members.[65] When two young slaves started to feud while courting Aunt Ella, the other slaves supervised a fair fight held on "a smooth grassy plot near a clump of trees below the quarters, well out of sound of the Big House."[66]

One of the most important roles which the community as a whole played in the education of its members was that of encouraging and sustaining the family. Quarter communities were careful to nurture and protect the integrity of the family unit. In many quarters, the community insisted that young slaves who wished to marry get the consent of their parents before taking up the proposition with plantation authorities.[67] Although some kind of marriage ceremony was often performed by whites, the quarters usually attempted to impress upon the bride and the groom the solemnity of the union into which they were entering. Caroline Harris of Virginia states that if two slaves in her quarters wanted to get married they were sent to talk it over with Aunt Sue.

She tell us to think 'bout it hard fo' two days, 'cause marryin' was sacred in de eyes of Jesus. After two days Mose an' I went back an' say we done thought 'bout it an' still want to git married. Den she called all de slaves arter tasks to pray fo' de union dat God was gonna make. Pray we stay together an' have lots of chillun an' none of 'em git sol' 'way from de parents. Den she lay a broomstick 'cross de sill of de house we gonna live in an' jine our hands together. Fo' we step over it she ask us once mo' if we was sho' we wanted to git married. 'course we said yes. Den she say, "in de eyes of Jesus step into de Holy land of mat-de-money." When we step 'cross de broomstick, we was married.[68]

When a slave baby was born the other members of the community visited his family to offer their congratulations. When a slave died "the quarter became mourners' row. Every one came quietly to pay his respects to the bereaved family. All night long friends would 'set' with the family and sing and chant over the body."[69] One of the surest ways of gaining the disrespect of the quarter community was by proving oneself, man or woman, too lazy or too promiscuous to take care of one's family. Only the highest respect, on the other hand, was accorded to those who stood by their families and worked hard to protect them and raise them according to the principles of the quarter community. The man who cared and provided for his family became, according to William Green, "a great man amongst them."[70] Charles Ball writes that, if a community member had a family on a neighboring plantation, the other slaves were willing "to work a little harder to permit him to enjoy the pleasure of seeing his family."[71] Joint community action was taken to help families protect their members from the sexual coercion of whites or other slaves.

Members of the quarter community knew that in the absence of family members, the community expected them to share in the nurture, protection, and discipline of quarter children. In the event a family was torn apart by death or sale the community made certain that the children were placed with a family able and willing to provide for them. Sometimes an orphaned quarter child was cared for not by one specific family but by a communal effort. After the Yankees took her mother away with them, Mandy Lewis was raised jointly by the other slaves of her quarter community.[72] When Charles Davenport's mother died in childbirth, the suckling mothers of the quarters took turns wet nursing him and he "growed up in the quarters and was as well and as happy as any other chile."[73]

Many quarter communities built a network of mutual aid and communication with neighboring quarter communities. Slaves from different plantations often got together for both authorized and secret dances, barbecues, funerals, and religious meetings. "During the slack times," relates Robert Anderson, "the people from one plantation could visit another, by getting permission and sometimes they would slip away and make visits anyway."[74] Often quarters within walking distance of each other shared common leaders. Many preachers, doctors, and conjurors took seriously obligations to quarter communities at several miles distance from their homes. Slave musicians were sometimes paid, or came voluntarily, to play at dances. Interplantation dancing and athletic contests were held frequently. Paine writes that the law forbidding visiting without a pass had little or no effect upon the slaves' nocturnal activities:

> . . .[F]or as the patrol grows more vigilant, they grow more cautious and by taking the woods, and cutting across the fields, and going along the by-paths, they accomplish their ends, without having been caught. As the night season is their only time for wandering about, they have to adopt some plan to keep from getting lost. They make the stars their guide, and by practice are soon able to determine the location of all the surrounding plantations, to tell the principal points of the compass, and to designate the situation of any place they have been to, though probably they could not tell the North Star from one of the pointers. Men and women like to stroll about at night. It seems one of their greatest pleasures; and with the exceptions of Sunday, it is probably their greatest. They will travel a long way, and be with but little sleep, that they may indulge in this propensity.[75]

Often the well fed slaves of one plantation would help feed the hungry slaves of another.[76] Runaways from whatever plantation were aided without question.

Most importantly, slaves relayed to each other information which whites did not care to provide. Often family members miles apart were able to keep informed of each other's whereabouts and circumstances. After Robert Glenn had been sold to a North Carolina slave merchant who traded him to a man about to move to Kentucky, his "mother found out by 'grapevine telegraph' that I was going to be carried to Kentucky. She got permission to see me before they carried me off."[77] John Wise, the white son of a wealthy Virginia planter, relates that at slave auctions, whenever a successful bidder was named, "the announcement was greeted by the darkies themselves with broad grins, and such expressions as 'Thank Gord,' or 'Bless de Lord,' if it went as they wished, or in uncomplaining silence if otherwise. It was surprising to see how thoroughly they all seemed to be informed concerning the men who were bidding for them."[78] According to Daniel Dowdy, who had been a slave in Georgia, the grapevine telegraph consisted of slaves who "carried news from one plantation to another by whut they call relay."[79] Hal Hutson recollects that when the slaves in the Tennessee neighborhood where he lived as a slave needed to "git each other word" they would avoid the patrol "by sending a man round way late at night. Always take news by night."[80]

This interplantation communication system worked so well in some localities that slaves were able to keep abreast of political events. Lewis Clarke asserts that the slaves of Kentucky learned of the emancipation of West Indian slaves "in a very short time after it took place. It was the occasion of great joy. They expected they would be free next. This event has done much to keep up the hopes of the slave to the present hour."[81] Bruce reports that during the election of 1856 the slaves in his district were all Fremont supporters. "Slave holders never talked politics in the presence of slaves, but by some means they learned the news, kept posted as to what was going on, and expected to be set free if Fremont was elected."[82] In Wake County, North Carolina, the slaves known to Mary Anderson sent the news of the Civil War from plantation to plantation.[83] Once he had made known to them his abolitionist sentiments, Conway discovered that the slaves of his father's plantation "had a complete knowledge of all the stages through which the United States Government had gone towards the recognition of their rights."[84]

Booker T. Washington writes that he never fully understood

"how the slaves throughout the South, completely ignorant as were the masses so far as books and newspapers were concerned, were able to keep themselves so accurately and completely informed about the great National questions which were agitating the country.

> From the time that Garrison, Lovejoy, and others began to agitate for freedom, the slaves throughout the South kept in close touch with the progress of the movement. Though I was a mere child during the preparation for the Civil War and during the War itself, I now recall the many late-at-night whispered discussions that I heard my mother and the other slaves on the plantation indulge in. These discussions showed that they understood the situation, and that they kept themselves informed of events by what was termed the "grape-vine" telegraph.
>
> During the campaign when Lincoln was first a candidate for the Presidency, the slaves on our far-off plantation, miles from any railroad or large city or daily newspaper, knew what the issues involved were. . . . Often the slaves got knowledge of the results of great battles before the white people received it. This news was usually gotten from the coloured man who was sent to the post-office for the mail. In our case the post-office was about three miles from the plantation and the mail came once or twice a week. The man who was sent to the office would linger about the place long enough to get the drift of the conversation from the group of white people who naturally congregated there, after receiving their mail, to discuss the latest news. The mail-carrier on his way back to our master's house would as naturally retail the news that he had secured among the slaves, and in this way they often heard of important events before the white people at the "big house," as the master's house was called.[85]

In many ways, the educational impact of the community can be understood in terms similar to that of the family. Like the family, the community provided early significant others, numerous and diverse role models, strong negative sanctions and positive rewards, a unique language, and constant reinforcement of family-like obligations and relationships. Indeed, the community was able to provide quarter members with a security and a continuity of experience that the slave family could not always guarantee. When the parents of a slave died or were sold away he would be cared for by the members of his home community. If a slave were sold, the potential trauma of separation from home and family was cushioned by entry into a new, but familiar, quarter community. Though quarters differed in size, organization, and relationship to plantation authorities, most were similar enough to provide a sense of home to those who had grown up within any quarters. With some regional variation, the preparation of food, the songs and stories, the language, and most important, the themes of quarter communities throughout the South were similar. A slave could move from quarter to quarter with little discontinuity in the way he was expected to understand the world and interact with plantation whites and other slaves. It is in this sense that the members of each quarter community partook in the wider fellowship of the total slave quarter community.

Conclusion

Despite the obvious implications which the preceding chapters hold concerning the efficacy of the attempt to have plantation blacks internalize the values and behavioral norms of the perfect slave, some of white teaching was successful. Nearly all slaves learned a job skill which made them, potentially at least, a productive part of the plantation economy. Most blacks also learned how whites wished them to behave, the injunctions of plantation etiquette and regulation, and what their masters wanted them to believe about the world and the black's relationship to it. Furthermore, the sources indicate that white teaching was often successful in those areas, usually factual, where a given quarter community had no information with which to contradict this teaching, or where slave experience corroborated it. Thus, for example, many slaves did believe that being "sold down river" to the deep South was a fate worse than death. "Such is the terror," writes Campbell, "among all the more intelligent slaves of going South (meaning Mississippi, Alabama, Louisiana, etc.) that they had rather suffer death."[1]

Many slaves, especially those in the deep South who had little or no contact with blacks who had been to the free states, believed that life in the North or in Canada was worse for blacks than was life under slavery. Even many of those slaves who knew that a Union victory might mean their freedom from slavery were confused as to what would happen to them if they fell into Yankee hands.

White teaching, coupled with their own experience, also prompted many slaves to believe that the life of the free black in the South was no better, and sometimes worse, than the life of the slave. Douglass, speaking from direct observation, states that, "No colored man was really free while residing in a slave state. He was ever more or less subject to the condition of his slave brother. In his color was his badge of bondage."[2] In a similar vein H. C. Bruce observes that free blacks "had to choose guardians to transact all their business, even to writing them a pass to go from one township to another in the same county. They could not own real estate in their own right, except through their guardian, neither could they sell their crop without his written consent. Of course, he made a charge for everything he did for them, which was quite a drain upon their resources."[3]

Most slaves believed in the great determination and power of white authorities to maintain and perpetuate slavery. Many slaves had no confidence that an armed rebellion could be successful, that permanent escape was very probable, or that the chance of openly resisting white authority and remaining physically unchastised was very likely.

The primary conclusion which grows from the study of education in the slave quarter community, however, is that most of the values, attitudes, and understandings that whites taught their slaves were rejected by the members of the slave quarter community. The question arises—where did whites go wrong as potential educators of slaves? One reason for the failure of white teaching may have been simply that plantation authorities did not try hard enough. Considering the fact that the fundamental goal of the plantation was to raise salable crops, it is more than likely that some planters did not have a deep personal stake in seriously affecting black values, attitudes, and sensibilities as long as their slaves did the work assigned to them and seemed to act in accordance with plantation rules. Though many large plantation owners spent Sundays providing for the religious instruction of their slaves, many did not care what their quarter population did with its time after work during the week. One South Carolina planter, for instance, told Hall and his companions that he "interfered as little as possible with their domestic habits, except in matters of police. 'We don't care what they do when their tasks are over—we lose sight of them till next day. Their morals and manners are their own business.' "[4] Robert Anderson remembers that the slaves of his community "could get together almost any time they felt like it, for little social affairs, so long as it did not interfere with the work on the plantation."[5] Marrs says that his master "allowed us generally to do as we pleased after his own work was done, and we enjoyed the privilege granted to us."[6]

It must also be remembered that whatever the determination of a given planter to instill in his slaves a certain set of values and attitudes, he was unable to interact with any more than a small number of slaves, usually house servants and skilled craftsmen, on more than an infrequent and superficial basis. This meant that, except on a small number of plantations where the master himself supervised the work in the fields, the extent of white surveillance and the nature of white teaching that reached field-hands between Sundays depended largely upon the personality and disposition of the overseers. Most of these men held their jobs for reasons of pecuniary reward and were skeptical at best about their ability, or anyone else's, to greatly affect the values and understandings of slaves. Most overseers believed that the only sure way of making slaves do a decent day's work was close supervision and fear of the whip. Few overseers cared what slaves thought or believed as long as they kept it to themselves and did their work. At night and during holidays only the rare overseer had either the desire or the energy to snoop around the quarters making sure that slaves were not holding secret meetings, visiting other plantations, trafficking with free blacks or poor whites, or stealing. Most overseers preferred to tend to their own nocturnal business.

A second possible reason for the failure of white teaching is that most whites made the mistake of assuming, unless they were faced with clear evidence to the contrary, that what they taught their slaves was what their slaves learned. All but a few whites failed to realize that slaves were persons able to interpret, disregard, adapt for their own purposes, and turn white teaching around and use it in their ideological struggle against white oppression.[7] On the ante-bellum plantation both white and black children were taught by whites that God, "as demonstrated by His Holy Writ," had ordained that the "Negroid race" was meant to be the servants of whites. From such teaching white children seem to have learned not only Southern society's scrip-

tural defense of slavery but also a belief in their own moral superiority to blacks and position of favor in the eyes of God. Black
children, too, learned how whites rationalized slavery. From the
same teaching, however, slaves also gleaned an understanding
of what whites wanted them to believe and through this knowledge became convinced of the destitution of the white man's
religion. Those blacks with a knowledge of what slaves termed
"true Christianity," seem to have gained from this white teaching a belief that whites were reading from a fake Bible or making up their lessons altogether, and that, in either case, whites
were cunningly untrustworthy and their instruction hypocriti-
cally self-serving. Most whites, however, were completely un-
aware of the unintended conclusions which blacks drew from
white teaching.*

Another reason for the failure of white teaching was that
white plantation owners and their missionary hirelings employed teaching methods which would have failed no matter
how often and diligently they were used. Quarter residents were
not comfortable in solemn church services or Sabbath Schools
where they were required to maintain the "strictest order" and
were prohibited from shouting, moaning, or dancing. They
were seldom enlightened by sermons or oral instruction given
only in "the purest Saxon" and certainly were not inspired by the
storytelling and singing style promoted by the planter class. If
whites had allowed heartfelt religion in their churches, encouraged shouting, dancing, and other expressions of religious
ecstasy, used the language of the quarters in their sermons, and
incorporated the singing and storytelling style of the quarters,
they might have had more success in transmitting those attitudes
and understandings which they wished slaves to learn. Indeed,
many of the earlier narratives suggest that the revival meetings
of the eighteenth and early nineteenth centuries (which many
slaves were allowed to attend before 1831) which were more similar to the slaves' own religious services, had a greater impact

---

*To be sure, the inability of whites to realize the ineffectiveness of their teach-
ing can be traced in large part to the unceasing efforts of slaves to keep whites
uninformed as to the true nature of quarter beliefs, values, and attitudes.

Conclusion

upon slaves than did the decorous church services of the rich planters.*

A fourth reason why many slaves rejected white teaching was that so few whites were able to establish a relationship of trust with the quarter community. Under slavery the successful teachers of the quarter community were largely those quarter slaves trusted to protect the interests of the community as understood by quarter slaves. On the plantation the establishment of such trust necessitated a personal and a political commitment impossible for any pro-slavery white to make. Throughout the black sources contempt is expressed towards those erstwhile educators who, in the words of the black informants, "preached one thing Sunday and practiced the contrary Monday." The slaves' consciousness of the moral and political inequity of slavery placed an insurmountable barrier before persons who, in order to achieve teaching positions, had to go along with the slave system. Slaves, no matter how much they liked individual masters, preachers, overseers, or officially sanctioned black exhorters, took the preaching of anyone supported by the slave regime with a large grain of salt, believing that ultimately it must seek to support and perpetuate their servitude.

The conclusion suggested most strongly by this study, however, is that white teaching failed because most whites saw blacks as people without a culture, without themes and educational instruments of their own. Whites saw blacks as savages to be civilized; as children at best and animals at worst. As such, slaves were assumed to be without strong values or beliefs and certainly without a coherent culture or social organization of their own. For this reason, white teaching reflected an unstated attitude of filling up empty brains, of scratching white understandings upon the tabula rasa of a limited black intelligence. That the content of white teaching directly contradicted understandings, attitudes, values, and feelings which slaves had learned from birth in an educational process created and con-

---

*Of course, it may be more to the point that these meetings were also less guarded about the message they taught than were the carefully planned, assiduously supervised plantation services of the late years of slavery.

trolled by slaves themselves, was a notion too incredible and too dangerous to entertain. To suggest that slaves were capable of molding their own culture, of fashioning and maintaining their own educational instruments, would be to undermine the most fundamental arguments with which whites rationalized their enslavement of other human beings.

18

The Slave Quarter and the Indian Reservation

One of the major intentions of this study has been to demonstrate that new and important insights into the nature of slave life arise from the asking of the slave literature fundamental educational questions. It has concluded that by creating and controlling their own educational instruments the slave quarter community was able to reject most of white teaching and to pass on to their children a set of unique cultural themes. This final chapter tries to explain and enlighten this conclusion through the use of enculturation/acculturation theory and the application of a new sociological model. In so doing it hopes to underscore the inadequacies and potential distortions of viewing slavery through the lens provided by total institution theory.[1]

Because this book believes that the fundamental social dynamics of the slave quarter are best understood as a community within a community, it presents the American Indian Reservation as a more fruitful comparison with the slave quarter. Unlike concentration camps, prisons, or asylums, but like the slave quarter, the Indian Reservation was able to maintain agencies, like the family, of cross-generational enculturation. Like the quarters, the Indian Reservation also existed within a larger white society which largely circumscribed Indian political and economic organization but did not actively attempt to influence Indian attitudes, understandings, and values until young Indians reached the age of six, eight, or even older.* Finally, Indian Reservations, unlike the quarters, but like many total institutions, have been largely accessible to anthropologists and other social scientists who have been able to study closely the dy-

* The past tense is used here because all of the Indian data referred to here was gathered more than twenty years ago.

251

namics of enculturation, acculturation, and assimilation within the Reservation. The Navaho data compiled by Clyde Kluckhohn and Dorthea Leighton and the research done on the Mandan-Hidatsa by Edward Bruner are but two of many Indian studies which offer strong support to the contention that many useful insights into slave life and education can be gained by comparing the education of slaves within the quarter community with data drawn from the study of Indian culture within the reservation.

In the early 1940's, Clyde Kluckhohn and Dorthea Leighton studied the Navaho Indians living on reservation lands which included parts of Arizona, New Mexico, and Utah.[2] In brief, their findings were that although the bulk of the material objects which the Navaho used in the 1940's were of white derivation or influence, their way of life and especially their religion were much less affected. "The really astonishing thing is the degree to which the People have taken over parts of white technology with so little alteration in the distinctive flavor of their own way of life."[3] Their explanation for this "astounding" conclusion is that most Navahos grew up within small groups in which most of the individuals depended upon each other "for help with the various tasks, and for companionship and advice. . . . They share very intimately each other's good and bad fortune and emotional ups and downs."[4] Furthermore, those Navahos with whom the child interacted were related by clan, though not necessarily blood lines, and were designated as sisters, mothers, uncles, fathers, etc., by those within the group. "In an extended family group the child may well have not merely three or four but fifteen or more persons whom he calls 'my older brother.' And the Navaho child calls not one but a number of women 'my mother.' "[5]

Within such a group Kluckhohn and Leighton observed that ambivalent feelings seemed not to be centered upon one or two individuals but filtered out among group members.[6] Deviant attitudes and opinions were largely repressed. "It is hard to live so closely and interdependently if opinions and attitudes vary greatly; so their differences are rarely expressed. The children, even more than the adults, are limited in their nonfamily contacts; unless they go to school their only companions are the other children in the group of close relatives, for whom they develop as strong feelings as if they were all real brothers and sisters."[7] For these reasons Navaho social controls are extremely effective for those who remain within their group. "Thus the major threat which restrains the potential offender is the withdrawal of the support and the good will of his neighbors, most of whom are 'family' to the Navaho."[8] One of the most frequently enunciated behavioral norms of the Navaho leaders, or "headmen," was: "Act as if everybody were related to you."[9]

According to Kluckhohn and Leighton, the child in such a society, probably within the first six years of life, internalizes an intuitive understanding not only of what is, and is not, acceptable behavior, but also an understanding and acceptance of "the system of values by which life events take on meaning for those around him. Probably by the time the Navaho child is six months old, typical Navaho conceptions of life have begun to permeate and to attain a sway which will last forever."[10] While noting that exactly when the child learns different aspects of the Navaho view of life remains "rather mysterious," the authors assert that the tests which they administered to Navaho school children "make it very plain that these conceptions have somehow become deeply engrained by the time the child goes to school."[11]

Thus, although Kluckhohn and Leighton were well aware of the changes in attitudes and values that could occur when Navaho children, or adults, were separated for long periods from their community (as when they attended boarding school or served in the armed forces), the general conclusion of their study was that, given a life within the Navaho reservation community, the conceptions of adult Navahos would remain those imparted and learned while children. In such circumstances the teachers and missionaries of the white-controlled mission schools had a difficult, largely impossible, job in their attempt to change the larger, thematic values and attitudes of Navaho children.

> For six or eight or more years before the children came to the missionaries, they had heard the myths and seen and participated

in the small rites of daily life. They had been patients in the curing chants. They had gone with their families to all-night public exhibitions, where dancers, masked to imitate the Navaho divinities, sang, danced, and shouted in the light of large fires. This imagery and the excitements and fears accompanying it were stored away in the unconscious long before the youngsters could reason or objectify what they saw. All this conditioned them fundamentally, so that subsequent Christian imagery could not supplant or alter it.[12]

Edward Bruner's study of reservation life takes an even closer look at the dynamics of enculturation and acculturation in a society within a society. In 1951 and 1952–53, Bruner lived among the Mandan-Hidatsa Indians of the Lone Hill Reservation in North Dakota.[13] The central purpose of his observations was an attempt to explain why some Lone Hill villagers became more acculturated than others. Using as his criteria of acculturation, non-participation in the Mandan-Hidatsa ceremonial "give-away dance," Bruner determined that of the forty-eight families he studied, thirty-four families, the unacculturated, regularly participated in the dance and fourteen families, the acculturated, did not.[14] Comparing this information with the census data, Indian Bureau records, village genealogies, informal interviews and extensive life histories, Bruner was able to determine that each of the fourteen acculturated families had contained at least one white parent, grandparent, or great-grandparent, or functional substitute for such, who had actually lived with the nuclear family long enough to "provide a model for the children."[15] Of the thirty-four unacculturated families, three had had such a white model and the other thirty-one had not had one. In terms similar to those used by Kluckhohn and Leighton, Bruner argues that the apparent prerequisite of a white model for acculturation can be explained by the fact that on the Lone Hill Reservation other "acculturative influences are operative primarily in the adult years."[16]

During his early, formative years, according to Bruner, the Lone Hill child internalizes the way of life of an intimate group of close relatives. Before he attends school he "eats Indian food, attends the ceremonial dances, and hears about the daring exploits of the Stone Hammer Society from his old grandfather." Although he attends an occasional movie and listens to the radio, his contact with whites is so infrequent, and his concept of the outside world so vague that he has "no context within his own experience with which to relate these impersonal mass media." When whites do come to Lone Hill their business is with adults and they rarely interact with the children. Life for the unacculturated child revolves around his family, peer, and residential groups. Within such a world, "the unacculturated Indian child soon learns that his emotional security and his very identity are dependent upon his maintaining good relationships with his kinsmen."

By the time the unacculturated child becomes an adult, he has been so effectively socialized to Indian ways that white contact has very little influence. But the adult reality is such that he must live in a superordinate white world. This is the sharp discontinuity in his life career. Every Indian must deal with members of white society in order to perform necessary economic and educational activities. The unacculturated Indian does not change himself to become like a white person; instead he learns how to adjust to white people. One informant described the technique as follows: "We Indians are just like those lizards that change their colors. When we are with whites we act one way and when with Indians we act another way." I think this kind of compartmentalized behavior is called "situational role specificity"—but possibly the analogy of the chameleon has a virtue of its own. In a sense, the unacculturated people of Lone Hill came to learn two cultures, but it is a case of differential learning with different points of origin. The unacculturated Indian character is incorporated into the child in his formative years, while superficial knowledge of white culture and of the techniques of adjustment to white people are learned primarily in adulthood. The unacculturated people of Lone Hill are not torn with inner conflict between two worlds; they just internalize the Indian way as children and learn aspects of the white way as a necessary accessory when they become adults. . . .

The unacculturated Indian does not internalize white ways as an adult, not because all learning stops in childhood, but because of the vast cultural differences between members of the two groups, the nature of the situations in which adult Indian-white interaction occurs, and the attitude of white people towards Indians. Indian relationships to whites are made difficult by the many points of incompatibility between their respective value systems.[17]

Having reached this conclusion, Bruner turns to a consideration of the social interaction between the unacculturated and acculturated families themselves. He is aware that the presense of the acculturated group could provide a channel through which white ways are spread to the entire population. That this, in fact, does not happen, Bruner demonstrates by first making a further distinction among the fourteen acculturated families. Of the fourteen acculturated families, seven virtually never attended the dances and the remaining seven, which Bruner labeled the "marginal," did participate in the ceremonies during those six to eight months a year they lived at Lone Hill. Through his observations Bruner determined that while in residence at Lone Hill the marginal families interacted primarily with the unacculturated Indians, were very active in community affairs, seemed to uphold Indian beliefs and values, and at times were among the staunchest defenders of traditional Indian ways.[18] The relationship between the seven acculturated families and the thirty-four unacculturated families, on the other hand, were of a low frequency and often of a hostile nature.

> The acculturated people rarely visit at unacculturated homes, do not participate in the dances or other community activities, and make special efforts to keep their children isolated from the unacculturated children. White "middle class" values are the criteria by which the acculturated Indian appraises his worth and evaluates himself, even though he is not a member of any white social group. Some acculturated individuals actually over-react to those white standards which form the basis for white disapproval of indian behavior. . . . The unacculturated majority feel that the acculturated families have taken for themselves what belongs to everyone, have violated the primary Indian values of generosity and emphasis on group welfare, and are "in cahoots" with the Indian Bureau against the best interests of the Indian people. They see the acculturated Indians as traitors and collaborationists.[19]

The Slave Quarter and the Indian Reservation

Thus, far from acting as a catalyst for cultural change, the acculturated families, because of the mutual hostility and mistrust between themselves and the remainder of the community, have helped to make Lone Hill into "a community divided into two conflicting and relatively noninteracting social groups."[20]

Summing up his research findings, Bruner concludes that although the presence of a white model in the nuclear family may have been a necessary condition, it was not in itself a sufficient condition, for acculturation in Lone Hill. Three of the seventeen families who had a white role model through intermarriage remained unacculturated and of the remaining fourteen, seven were acculturated and seven marginal. Noting that cultural transmission is not an automatic process in which adults "mechanistically stamp their culture into the child," Bruner concludes that there are two processes which must take place for a Lone Hill resident to become acculturated. First, at least one of the parents must have been a white model, or obtained a fundamental understanding of American culture from a white model. Second, the child's parents must have "consciously, deliberately, and actively" trained their children to become like whites. Although their culture is mixed and continually changing, the thirty-one unacculturated families who train their children to reject white ways and to live among the people of Lone Hill "have relatively clear-cut identifications with and adjustment to contemporary reservation culture."[21]

The conclusions of these two Reservation studies reinforce and expand our understanding of the nature of education in the slave quarter community. As in the cases of the Navaho and the Mandan-Hidatsa, the emotional security and very identity of the young quarter slave depended on his relationship with other quarter members. The world experienced and internalized by the quarter child in his first years of life was a world largely controlled and certainly mediated by the members of his community. It is for this reason that the most crucial elements of slave thought and social organization, and of the interaction between slaves and whites and among slaves, can be understood only in the context of the slave child's primary enculturation within the quarter community and of his or her continuing participation in, and reference to, the persons and primary groups of that community in adult life.*

From the time of the quarter child's birth until the time he became an integral part of the plantation work force, some eight, ten, fourteen years later, he spent the great majority of his time, and formed most, if not all, of his close personal relationships with other quarter members. In most cases he was born into a family which provided him with his food, shelter, and all of his sensual and psychological comforts. The breasts that nourished him and the hands that soothed as well as slapped him, were black. The children he played with, ate with, slept with, and fought with were black. The world beyond the plantation and the world of the great house were usually unexperienced by him, except as pictured and explained by his elders. The rare visits of the white mistress, the Sunday lessons of the white missionary, the occasional orders or heavy hand of the overseer, the times of singing for master and his company were frequent enough, and sometimes anxiety-filled enough, to make a strong impression but, in most instances, were not of the sustained and intimate nature necessary for the transmission of lasting values and attitudes.

To be sure, quarter children lived in a larger world created for, and controlled by, whites who had the power to profoundly disrupt the security, comfort, and relationships of quarter children and their families. At the same time, however, it was their parents, older siblings, and other members of the quarter community who, on a day to day basis, provided the behavioral standards and controlled the negative and positive sanctions most crucial to the happiness and positive self-image of quarter children, and who became the child's most profound significant others.

Due to their close association in the quarters and their reliance upon each other for psychological sustenance and protection from whites, the ambivalency of quarter members toward

---

* Primary enculturation is used here in the same way that the symbolic interactionist school of George Herbert Mead, Charles Horton Cooley, and others employ the term primary socialization: "The first socialization an individual undergoes in childhood through which he becomes a member of society." [22]

quarter norms (though not necessarily toward quarter individuals) was probably repressed in early childhood. This is not to suggest that all members adhered constantly to community norms or to deny that some were even openly deviant. The individual's introjection of his society's culture is, as psychoanalytic theory reminds us, never complete.[23] In the quarters deviance took several forms. Some slaves kept to themselves, openly asserting they wanted nothing to do either with quarter affairs or with the society of house servants. Other slaves, while generally disdainful of white society, were hell raisers within the quarters. Still others openly campaigned to win the confidence and approbation of plantation whites. These slaves were sometimes openly contemptuous of quarter values and life-style and desired to become house servants so they could live among whites and learn white ways.

For the most part, however, the threat of the withdrawal of community support and good will restrained many a would-be offender. Deviancy most often took forms which did not radically alter the deviant's relationship with other quarter members. Some slaves occasionally fought, drank, or made love to the marriage partners of other quarter members. Others feigned sickness or "lazied off" in the fields despite their knowledge that if they did so the other slaves would have to work harder. All slaves undoubtedly acted when alone in ways they would not in public, or had private thoughts which they would not admit to even within the confines of the quarter. Some slaves also attempted to retain their complete African identity, ridiculing any acceptance of white ways, or terminology, no matter how superficial. And finally, some slaves internalized and identified with one or more quarter themes to such an extent that they were not balanced by other themes.* Whatever the nature of their indi-

---

* Thus, the behavior of the family man who protects and provides for his family to the exclusion and hurt of other community members, the slave who strikes out for freedom no matter what the cost to family and friends, and even the behavior of the slave consumed with the fear of white power, or conversely, with a great hatred of all things white (Sambo and Nat) should be seen not so much as deviant behavior but as behavior intimately related to the themes of the quarter community.

vidual attempts to proclaim and affirm their individual identity within their group, however, they acted within a definite black cultural context. Only the rare slave dared, or thought to dare, to step beyond the bounds laid down by quarter beliefs and community sanctions. To risk losing membership in the quarter community was to most slaves the unthinkable; their primary enculturation within that community had made it so.

Bruner's analysis of the interaction between the unacculturated, the marginal, and the acculturated Mandan-Hidatsa has a meaningful correlation with the interaction between quarter members, house servants who maintained quarter affiliation, and acculturated house servants who did not participate in quarter social relationships and ceremonies. On many plantations, especially the larger ones, the interaction of house servants with the members of the quarter community was drastically curtailed if not effectively cut off altogether. Often whites chose their house servants while they were very young (frequently from among the children of house servants) and had them live within the great house or in cabins near the great house separated from the quarters. These slaves lived intimately with whites, sometimes sleeping in the same rooms and often becoming their personal servants, constant playmates, and adult companions. Furthermore, the duties of house servants were such that they were on call at all times, night and day and even Sundays. In such circumstances, it is safe to assume that while no slaves were allowed membership in the larger white society, these house servants had white models during the period of their primary enculturation and adopted many of the values and attitudes of their "white family." Indeed, the sources suggest that some house servants consciously patterned themselves after white ways and looked down upon the life-style of quarter slaves. Such servants attempted to dress as their masters, speak as their masters, and even believe and practice religion as their masters. They did not participate in the activities of the quarter community, like the clandestine worship services, which ceremonialized some of the deepest quarter values and attitudes. In addition, they made special efforts to keep their children away from quarter children.[24]

The Slave Quarter and the Indian Reservation

Many house servants, however, did not internalize the values and attitudes of Sambo, the virtuous and trustworthy servant. Many, as we have seen, attended the secret services of the clandestine congregation, used their position in the great house to the advantage of quarter slaves, and often became the leading supporters of quarter themes and the most loyal and respected of quarter members.[25] Thus, those acculturated slaves who had adopted white values and could have been a source of the infusion of white values into the quarters by and large chose not to interact with quarter members. The quarter community, for its part, ostracized them and cautioned its members against associating with them. Those house servants who participated in quarter ceremonies whenever possible, like the marginal Mandan-Hidatsa, did not act as catalysts of cultural change because they did not espouse white ways and values. Instead they often became the most influential of spokesmen in the quarters against white values, attitudes, and behavioral norms and the staunchest defenders of the themes and traditions of the quarter community.

By the time plantation authorities seriously began their attempts to influence the beliefs and values of their slaves, most slave children had already internalized the themes and behavioral modes of the quarter community.[26] They had learned the language, sung the songs, eaten the food, attended the secret ceremonies, and stored away in their unconscious the imagery, the hopes and fears of their people. During their interaction with whites they were able to adopt the roles required by plantation etiquette without an identification with the reality suggested by the role.[27] Like adult Indians they could "play the chameleon," maintaining basic quarter values while superficially adjusting to white expectations. Thus quarter slaves, like the Mandan-Hidatsa, came to learn two cultures. Instead of being torn with inner conflict between two worlds, the people of the slave quarter community internalized the themes of quarter life as children and, while rejecting white values and attitudes, learned as adults how to adapt their behavior to white norms and expectations when dealing with whites.

Thus, to understand the nature of education in the slave

261

quarter community is to come to grips with the paradox of the "free slave." Though the chains with which whites controlled black bodies were very real, try as they might, whites could not control black minds. These were molded from birth in an educational process created and managed by the quarter community. By passing their unique set of cultural themes from generation to generation, the members of the quarter community were able to resist most of white teaching, set themselves apart from white society, and mold their own cultural norms and group identity. While still legally slaves, the black men, women, and children of the quarter community successfully protected their psychological freedom and celebrated their human dignity.

Appendix

Methodology and Sources

This study is both anthropological and historical. It is perhaps best understood as "culture history," an extension of what Margaret Mead and others have termed "the study of culture at a distance."[1] Historically it is the study of a past era and of a community which no longer exists and whose characters are dead. Anthropologically it is an analysis of a society which was, with notable exceptions, non-literate, and it has based its understandings primarily upon sources elicited from informants who experienced life as slaves and from oral literature.[2] Its very definition of education follows the direction pointed to by such scholars as Margaret Mead in anthropology and Bernard Bailyn in history. Mead writes: "In its broadest sense, education is the cultural process, the way in which each newborn infant, born with a potentiality for learning greater than that of any other mammal, is transformed into a full member of a specific human culture."[3] Bailyn defines education simply as "the entire process by which a culture transmits itself across the generations."[4]

The study assumes, as do most cultural anthropologists and some historians, that the primary understanding of how a group views the world and operates within it must be reached, as nearly as possible, from that group's perspective. Only through the members of a given social system, through the attempt to see the world as they see it, can we hope to understand the subjective meaning with which that group and its individual members understand themselves and the world in which they live.[5]

In order to get at this subjective meaning Morris Opler's theory of "themes in culture" has been applied to the slave data in Part II.[6] Basic to Opler's theory is the proposition that it is possible to identify within every society a "limited number of dynamic affirmations," or themes, which by their nature, expression, and interrelationship provide a key to the understanding of that society and its culture.[7] A theme is defined as: "a postulate or position, declared or implied, and usually controlling behavior or stimulating activity, which is tacitly approved or openly promoted in a society."[8] The "expressions" of a theme are the "translations of a theme into conduct or belief," or, more specifically, "the activ-

Appendix: Methodology and Sources

ities, prohibitions of activities, or references which result from the acceptance or affirmation of a theme in society."[9]

Opler sees several types of thematic expressions. There are "formalized" expressions which have become "fixed in time or place and to which everyone to whom they apply must respond without significant variation," and there are "unformalized" expressions "whose precise character, time or place are not carefully defined by the culture."[10] Expressions can also be considered "primary" (those which are "directly and obviously related to the theme") or "symbolic" (in which case they are defined as "substances, gestures, ideas, or figures of speech not necessarily logically related to themes but which have become recognized vehicles for their representation").[11] In Opler's framework, the expressions of themes are the anthropologist's chief aids in searching for and identifying the themes of a society or smaller social system.

In a paper written more than twenty years after that in which he first outlined his general approach to the search for themes, Opler sums up his approach to finding themes and determining their importance.

> Before I name something a theme in a culture, I would hope to know approximately how often it is expressed in behavior and precept, how pervasive it is, and how many aspects of the culture are touched and influenced by it. Significant, too, in making a judgment about the reality and force of a theme are questions of the number of persons involved in its implementation and perpetuation, the sectors of the population enlisted in its functioning, the tendency to the repetitions of its forms, the degree to which it is projected to every recess of conscious and unconscious life by the symbols it commands, and the protection afforded it by sanctions and attitudes that penalize those who flout or deny it.[12]

Once a theme has been identified it is still necessary to determine its importance to the society under study and its place in comparison with the other themes. Opler suggests four approaches to the problem of determining the significance and the comparative importance and mutual influence of themes.

The simplest way to evaluate the importance of a theme, Opler argues, is to count the number of its expressions. Although Opler admits to a certain crudeness in this approach due to its avoidance of qualitative considerations, he argues that: "In general, a theme which is expressed many times in a culture, especially in a variety of contexts, is

Appendix: Methodology and Sources

likely to be more fundamental and to exert more influence than one which is expressed infrequently."[13]

In addition to the frequency of its expression the importance of a theme can also be gauged by the intensity of the group reaction to a violation of the theme's terms and by the character of the sanctions against such violations.

Third, the assessment of a theme's relative importance in a given culture can be aided by analyzing whether or not the theme appears in more than one facet of the culture's total system of ideas and practices. Most important themes, Opler implies, are represented in more than one branch (ritualistic as well as economic for example) of the group's thought and endeavor.

Finally, Opler argues that the most important step "in judging the place of a theme in the cultural whole is the recognition of the restraints which exist to its extreme and unimpeded expression." "These are the *limiting factors,* the circumstances (often the existence of other opposed or circumscribing themes and their extensions) which control the number, force and variety of a theme's expression. Unless I am mistaken, the concept of limiting factors is the key to understanding of the integration of equilibrium that is achieved or approximated in the structure of most cultures."[14]

Although themes are often formulated in philosophical abstractions generalized from many different actions and statements, they should not be viewed as "ideal rather than actualized or expected patterns of behavior." Crucial to Opler's theory is that themes "are distilled from the details of the culture as it is alleged to have functioned and therefore represent requirements and guides to action and not merely pious hopes."[15]

People do, however, deviate from these requirements and guides. Nonconformity to cultural themes is found in every society. "It must not be thought," cautions Opler, "that the behavior of any individual conforms neatly and completely to the themes of a culture. . . . Themes set the course and current of thought and action, but they do not eliminate the ripples and agitations of the waters. Nor do they guarantee that the river will not change its course sometime in the future."[16]

This book's application of Opler's anthropological methodology, however, should not obscure the fact that the study was forced to proceed without the primary tool of the cultural anthropologist, the field study. For obvious reasons the author was not able to enter the physical world of the slave quarters and to observe firsthand their childrearing practices, their daily interactions, their familial relationships, and their

Appendix: Methodology and Sources

secret and sanctioned ceremonies. Nor has the author had access to living persons whose personalities were formed in the quarter community. The study's understandings and conclusions were drawn primarily from the examination of a variety of personal documents left by persons who experienced life in the quarter community but who are no longer living. This absense of living informants placed a heavy burden upon the available source material. It has had to serve as both the data from which the original understandings and conclusions were drawn and as the primary data against which these conclusions were finally tested.

There exist today, according to Marion Starling, over six thousand "narratives" which purport to contain the comments regarding their lives under slavery of black men and women who lived at least a part of their lives in the American South.[17] Although some of these documents were written, or dictated, by persons who lived in the eighteenth and early nineteenth centuries, or by persons who, by living in towns or on small plantations, had little contact with quarter slaves, the vast majority were left by persons who experienced life in the quarter community at some time during the years 1831–1865. These sources are found in abolitionist publications, in court files, church records (particularly those of Quaker meetings), in regularly published and in self-published editions, in diaries, in letters, and in the vast collected material of special projects such as those conducted at Fisk University and the University of Louisiana, as well as in the massive files of the Federal Writers' Project. They range in length from two or three sentence testimonies, such as that of James M. Williams who recorded simply, "I came from bondage in Norfolk, Virginia. Slavery is horrible! horrible! horrible!"[18] to the full-length autobiographies of several hundred pages of men like Charles Ball, William Wells Brown, Frederick Douglass, and nearly one hundred others.

In addition, insights into the values and attitudes of the quarter community were sought through an exploration of the themes and sentiments of slave folklore: the songs, spirituals, and folktales, which the quarter community made such an important part of their daily lives.

The contention that the understanding of the world of the quarter community must come primarily through the sources left by those who experienced life in the quarters as slaves has obvious advantages for the student who would probe for the truth of what it was like to be a slave, as well as several disadvantages which we will discuss shortly. In the first place, the sheer quantity of the sources dictate against the kind of distortions to which the social scientist is liable when he is forced to select a

Appendix: Methodology and Sources

given number of informants for the study of a given social system. The author has not had to decide if one, twelve, or a hundred life histories would be sufficient for his purposes. The number of women, drivers, conjurors, to be included in the sample is, quite simply, dictated by the sources already collected by hundreds of interviewers, folklorists, and self-appointed autobiographers. If some of these documents are marred by the foggy or distorted memories of old men and women, the biases of abolitionists, the editorializing or outright doctoring of over-zealous interviewers, they can be weighed against hundreds of others which were written or dictated by men and women with keen memories and a desire to "tell it like it was," years after the issue of slavery was a dead one, and by interviewers who made an honest effort to reproduce a verbatim record of what they were told.

Admittedly, if one applies the seven criteria suggested by John Dol-lard in his *Criteria for the Life History,* all but a few of the slave sources fall far short of the standards which Dollard has set for "an adequate view of the individual life."[19] On the other hand, the sources stand up well when Dollard's criteria are applied to them as a group. Thus, although it would be extremely difficult to make an adequate analysis of the life or character of any individual slave, a satisfactory analysis of the education of the quarter community as a whole can be achieved when the sources are studied in their entirety.[20]

Furthermore, the oral literature presents a wealth of material against which the narratives can be questioned and compared. And, as Sterling Stucky has pointed out, ". . . folklore in its natural setting is of, by, and for those who create and respond to it, depending for its survival upon the accuracy with which it speaks to needs and reflects sentiments" and it is therefore "safe to assume that the attitudes of a very large number of slaves are represented by the themes of folklore."[21] The conclusion that most of the narratives and the oral literature portray a similar set of broad themes can be checked by any researcher who desires to study these sources, which are now readily available.

What is of perhaps even greater importance, the central questions addressed herein are those which these materials are best suited to handle. In an article exploring the potential uses of the personal document in anthropology Clyde Kluckhohn writes:

> Personal documents are probably the closest approximations we can obtain to the cultural structure as actually experienced as op-posed to being viewed in the light of abstract models which the anthropologist constructs. . . . Personal documents will prove the

Appendix: Methodology and Sources

primary sources for the dissection out of covert or implicit culture. If we are to infer inductively the tacit principles, the unstated assumptions which pervade the act, decisions, and "mental processes" of those acculturated by a given tradition, we must have recourse to materials where the thinking of individuals may be studied and checked in not a few but thousands of instances. If ever we are truly to learn—on other than metaphysical or preconceived bases—"how natives think," personal documents must be ransacked with exhaustive analyses. . . . While by no means a completely adequate substitute for sustained direct observation, autobiographies are probably the next best means of learning how a culture is acquired. To be sure, there will be little (and that little likely to be stereotyped culturally) on the period before five years of age. Still, the analyst can tabulate from whom and at what periods various skills were acquired; when, where, and by whom aspects of the value system are said to have been verbally imparted; the culturally standardized inducements for absorbing the cultural heritage.[22]

The pertinency of our particular set of documents to questions of cultural transmission is underscored by the fact that in recalling slavery most of the informants from the Fisk, Louisiana University, and WPA interviews were recalling events which occurred exclusively during their childhoods.

That these sources exist in great volume and contain material that is essential to any understanding of the education of the quarter community is not to absolve them of several problems regarding their reliability as primary sources. The first problem in handling many of them is to establish their external legitimacy. Not only is there some legitimate skepticism over whether some of the larger narratives were actually written by persons who were once slaves but there can be no doubt that most of the narratives were written with the assistance of second persons or recorded completely by interviewers. It is often impossible to determine where the words and thoughts of the black actor, himself, end and the words and extrapolations of his assistant, or interviewer, begin. This problem of authenticity is doubly acute with regard to the folklore sources. It is extremely difficult to be sure which songs and folktales were actually sung or told by a significant number of slaves and which were embellished or created in toto by those who recorded, or claim they recorded, them.

Furthermore, many of the longer autobiographies were written and published with the financial support of militant abolitionists and de-

Appendix: Methodology and Sources

signed for, and directed to, a mostly white, antislavery audience. They tend to place a heavy emphasis upon the brutality and "sinfulness" of slavery, often to the point of excluding more culturally relevant information. They were written by and large by men who experienced slavery in the border states, and who not only attempted to escape but who were successful in doing so.[23]

The question of "typicalness" is one which can be raised about all personal documents no matter what scheme is devised for their creation and collection. The average man or woman, especially in a predominantly nonliterate society, usually does not think about recording his life history, much less actually writing his autobiography. Even with regard to the WPA narratives "there is very little about the sample that is random, and it would be unwise to make statistically precise calculation about the material. The method of selection of the ex-slaves interviewed was by pure happenstance, which not only does not assure randomness, but introduces self-selection as a factor. It is clear from the interviews themselves that very often the ex-slaves being interviewed were either volunteers or were known previously by the interviewer."[24] A similar concern is raised by the question: what kind of black person would want to tell his life history, his deepest understandings and feelings, to a white interviewer, or to a black representative of the white-controlled government?

Many of the narratives were collected years after the Civil War by untrained, or barely trained, interviewers. In describing the problems of the WPA narratives, Benjamin Botkin, folklore editor of the project, wrote:

> Many are damaged or weakened by internal contradictions and inconsistencies; obvious errors of historical fact; vague, confused, or ambiguous statements; lapses of memory; and reliance on hearsay rather than firsthand experience. . . . In spite of instructions against editing or censorship, some of the narratives show signs of having been retouched. And, in spite of instructions against taking sides, the interviewer, in his editorial introductions and asides, his notes and leading questions, often betrays his personal prejudices and sympathies.
> The informant himself is often guilty of flattery and exaggeration, of telling only what he wants to tell or what he thinks the interviewer wants to hear. . . .[25]

Although the collections of the Fisk projects and interviews conducted under the direction of John Cade at the University of Louisiana were

Appendix: Methodology and Sources

carried out by persons trained and skilled in the process of the expressive interview, even these cannot escape the limitations of aged informants recalling events and thoughts of some sixty to seventy years past.

Because of these concerns over the validity of its primary source material, and because of the great amount of research still to be done on the external verification of specific sources, a careful effort has been made to draw most heavily upon those narratives which appear to be internally clear, consistent, and to have a ring of truth. Though this is undeniably a somewhat subjective criterion, it becomes easier and easier, after reading thousands of interviews to sense which interviewers have added their own thoughts and opinions, which are adhering strictly to a predetermined set of questions, and which are allowing the informant to ramble without interference. Similarly, one grows able to distinguish between passages in which the informant is speaking of events he or she actually witnessed or participated in, and those in which he or she is repeating stories heard secondhand or simply creating, or greatly embellishing, events.

The concern over the atypicalness of all personal documents, and of autobiographies in particular, is balanced, on the other hand, by the sheer bulk of the material and by the inherently typical nature of folklore. It is a fact that the themes of the narratives and those of the folklore do not vary significantly. Furthermore, there is much merit to the argument that the best of the larger autobiographies are important and useful for the very reason that they were written by persons whose intellect and sensibility made them perceptive and empathetic commentators not only about their own experience but also about the experiences of the other slaves with whom they associated.

> The great slave narrative, like all great autobiography, is the work of the especially perceptive viewer and writer. In describing his personal life, the sensitive and creative writer touches a deeper reality that transcends his individuality. Frederick Douglass, for example, was certainly an exceptional man, but his autobiography has much to teach us about the slaves around him, his friends and enemies on the plantation and in the city, and many other typical aspects of American slavery. . . . To exclude the "exceptional" is to eliminate all strong autobiography as a distortion of the events of its time. Yet it is these writers whose books are most likely to interpret reality with insight and clarity.[26]

The antislavery polemics contained in many of the works published before the Civil War can also be balanced against the often nostalgically

Appendix: Methodology and Sources

wistful remembrances of elderly former slaves.[27] They can be evaluated, as can all the slave sources, against the facts, figures, and descriptions contained within, or gathered from, the white sources. These sources include both the memoirs, diaries, letters, and plantation records of slaveholders, their families and employees, and the accounts of persons traveling through the South or visiting friends and relatives upon the plantation.[28] With careful attention to the advantages and limitations of the sources and the constant testing of the material both internally and against each other, it seems possible to construct a sound study of education in the slave quarter community.

Acknowledgments

This book began in 1970 as an eleven-page paper in Lawrence A. Cremin's course, the History of American Education, at Teachers College, Columbia University. Five years later it emerged as a doctoral dissertation; and now in a somewhat revised form as a book. During these years Lawrence Cremin has remained steadfastly its most vocal supporter, insightful critic, and greatest obstacle to its completion before it had satisfied his high standards of scholarship. On all these counts, and as someone who as a great teacher challenged and inspired me, I am truly in his debt.

For three of the years of my graduate study, I was supported by a grant from the Ford Foundation under the Program for Educational Leadership. I am grateful to the staff of the Foundation and of PEL for encouraging the kind of cross-disciplinary study of which this book is a product.

Earlier versions were read, edited, and commented upon by Roger Sherman, Fran Blake Smith, and John Strand. I thank them for their labor of friendship as well as for their suggestions. Stephen Sunderland also read an earlier version and through several long discussions helped me see the mistake of adopting too romantic and simplistic a notion of the process of enculturation. His encouragement and praise helped me through a period when I was becoming uncertain about the worth of my project.

In the end the book was a family affair. From the first my wife, Andrea, has helped refine my prose and labored with me rewriting several crucial chapters. My father-in-law, Angelo P. Bertocci, filled three blue books with literary criticism and very usable editorial comments. Discussions with my brother-in-law, Phillip Bertocci, were invaluable in helping me decide how to turn a dissertation into a book. My mother, Helen Webber, kept me mindful of why I was writing and whom I was writing for. After reading the book my grandmother, Edith Webber, sup-

Acknowledgments

ported and promoted its publication by putting me in contact with the man she trusts most in the publishing business, Elliot Graham. Finally, I am grateful to my children, Aili and Matthew, the fourth generation of my family to aid in the book's completion, for allowing me to experience the mixed joys and fears of parenthood and thus to appreciate more humanly the terrible anguish of slave parents.

Notes

Preface

1. James W. C. Pennington, *The Fugitive Blacksmith; or Events in the History of James W. C. Pennington, Pastor of a Presbyterian Church, New York, Formerly a Slave in the State of Maryland, United States.* (Westport, Conn.: Negro Universities Press, 3rd ed., 1971), pp. iv–v. First published in 1850.

2. Ben Brown in George P. Rawick, ed., *The American Slave: A Composite Autobiography.* (Westport, Conn.: Greenwood Publishing Company, 1972); Ohio Narratives, Vol. XVI, p. 14.

3. William Francis Allen, *Slave Songs of the United States.* (New York: A. Simpson and Company, 1867), p. 48.

4. Stephen McCray in Rawick, ed., Oklahoma, VII, p. 209.

5. Harriet Robinson in Rawick, ed., Oklahoma, VII, pp. 270–71.

6. This definition of education—inspired by that of Lawrence Cremin—"the deliberate, systematic, and sustained effort to transmit or evoke knowledge, attitudes, values, skills, and sensibilities" (*American Education: The Colonial Experience* [New York: Harper and Row, 1970], p. xiii)—has the apparent weakness of being too all inclusive, or, as Cremin has suggested, "overly latitudinarian (*Tradition of American Education* [New York: Basic Books, 1977], p. 154)." Admittedly the study's definition of education closely resembles what social scientists would call culture. The author would argue, however, that the study of education should include learning processes which are deliberate, systematic, and sustained and well as processes not nearly so intentional. To limit the study of education to less than the entire learning proesss is to risk excluding many of those processes and dynamics which most profoundly influence how individuals and groups learn, think, feel, and act.

7. Kenneth M. Stampp, *The Peculiar Institution: Slavery in the Ante-Bellum South.* (New York: Vintage Books, 1956), p. 364. Eugene D. Genovese, *Roll, Jordan, Roll: The World the Slaves Made.* (New York: Pantheon Books, 1974), pp. 3, 147, 658.

8. Fisk Collection, *Unwritten History of Slavery: Autobiographical Accounts of Negro Ex-Slaves.* (Nashville: Social Science Institute, Fisk University, 1945), pp. 45–46.

Chapter 1

1. Frederick Law Olmsted, *A Journey in the Seaboard Slave States, with Remarks on Their Economy* (New York: Dix and Edwards, 1856), p. 111.

2. Julia E. Harn, "Old Canoochee-Ogeechee Chronicles," Georgia Historical Chronicles, XVI (June, 1932), 149. This desire on the part of the slaves often fitted right in with the desires of their owners who did not wish to have the noise and structures of the quarters spoil the peace and beauty of the great house. The houses of the house servants were often whitewashed and closer to the great house, "so the white folks," according to one ex-slave, "could get to them easy if they wanted them; and they had to have it that way to keep from spoiling the looks of the big house." Fisk Collection, *Unwritten History of Slavery; Autobiographical Account of Negro Ex-Slaves* (Nashville: Social Science Institute, Fisk University, 1945). (Hereafter noted as Fisk, *Unwritten . . . .*)

3. Genovese says that by the 1850's the great majority of slave cabins were at least sixteen by eighteen feet and housed on the average five to six slaves. Eugene D. Genovese, *Roll, Jordan, Roll: The World the Slaves Made* (New York: Pantheon Books, 1974), p. 524.

4. James Battle Avirett, *The Old Plantation: How We Lived in Great House and Cabin Before the War* (New York: F. Tennyson Neeley, 1901), p. 46. Avirett, an Episcopalian minister, grew up on his father's large North Carolina plantation.

5. Fisk, *Unwritten . . . ,* p. 10.

6. Ralph Betts Flanders, *Plantation Slavery in Georgia* (Chapel Hill: The University of North Carolina Press, 1933), p. 152.

7. Louis Hughes, *Thirty Years a Slave; From Bondage to Freedom. The Institution of Slavery as Seen on the Plantation and in the House of the Planter.* (Milwaukee: M. E. Haferkorn, 1897), pp. 25–26.

8. Charley Williams in Rawick, ed., Oklahoma, VII(1), p. 334.

9. Austen Steward, *Twenty-Two Years a Slave and Forty Years a Freeman, Embracing a Correspondence of Several Years While President of the Wilberforce Colony.* (Rochester, New York: W. Alling, 1857), p. 13.

10. Margaret Nillin in Rawick, ed., Texas, V(3), p. 152.

11. Austin Penn Parnell in Rawick, ed., Arkansas, X(5), pp. 263–64.

12. Norman R. Yetman, ed., *Life Under the "Peculiar Institution": Selections from the Slave Narrative Collection* (New York: Holt, Rinehart and Winston, 1970), p. 52.

13. Fisk, *Unwritten . . . ,* p. 13.

14. Jaspar Battle in Rawick, ed., Georgia, XII(1), p. 63.

15. Alec Pope in Rawick, ed., Georgia, XIII(3), p. 172.

16. Georgia Baker in Rawick, ed., Georgia, XII(1), p. 39.

17. Olmsted, p. 111.

18. Jacob Stroyer, *Sketches of My Life in the South* (Salem: Newcombe and Gauss, 1898), pp. 44–45.

19. William Brown in Rawick, ed., Arkansas, VIII(1), p. 320. See also Hattie Ann Nettles in Rawick, ed., Alabama, VI, p. 297.

20. Celeste Avery in Rawick, ed., Georgia, XII(1), p. 22.

21. Cull Taylor in Rawick, ed., Alabama, VI, p. 364.

22. Addie Vinson in Rawick, ed., Georgia, XIII(4), p. 99.

23. Fisk, *Unwritten . . . ,* p. 33.

24. Willis Dukes in Rawick, ed., Florida, XVII, p. 121. Also, Isaam Morgan in Rawick, ed., Alabama, VI, p. 283.

25. Julia E. Haney in Rawick, ed., Arkansas, IX(3), p. 152.

26. Yetman, p. 267.

27. Benny Dillard in Rawick, ed., Georgia, XII(1), p. 289.

28. Ulrich B. Phillips, *American Negro Slavery: A Survey of the Supply, Employment and Control of Negro Labor as Determined by the Plantation Regime* (Baton Rouge: Louisiana State University Press, 1966), p. 267.

29. Captain Basil Hall, *Travels in North America, in the Years 1827 and 1828*, Vol. 3, Third edition (Edinburgh: Robert Cadell, 1830), p. 181.

30. Frances Anne Kemble, *Journal of a Residence on a Georgia Plantation in 1838–1839* (New York: Alfred A. Knopf, 1961), p. 69. (Originally published in 1863.)

31. See, for example, Victoria Clayton, *White and Black under the Old Regime* (Milwaukee: The Young Churchman company, 1899), p. 22.

32. Ivan E. McDougle, *Slavery in Kentucky 1792–1865* (Westport Connecticut: Negro Universities Press, 1970), p. 73. (Originally published in 1918.)

33. See Phillips, *American Negro Slavery . . .* , p. 253.

34. Sarah Katherine Stone Holmes, *Brokenburn: The Journal of Kate Stone 1861–1868*, ed. John Q. Anderson (Baton Rouge: Louisiana State University Press, 1955), p. 6.

35. See Genovese, *Roll, Jordan, Roll . . .* , p. 488.

36. Shade Richards in Rawick, ed., Georgia, XIII(3), p. 203.

37. Sam Aleckson, *Before the War and after the Union. An Autobiography* (Boston: Gold Mind Publishing Company, 1929), p. 28. See also Kemp Plummer Battle, *Memories of an Old-Time Tar Heel* (Chapel Hill: The University of North Carolina Press, 1945), p. 121. Henry James Trentham in Rawick, ed., N. Carolina, XIV, p. 364.

38. Ben Brown in Rawick, ed., Ohio, XVI, p. 11.

39. Clayton Holbert in Rawick, ed., Kansas, XVI, p. 2.

40. B. A. Botkin, ed., *Lay My Burden Down: A Folk History of Slavery* (Chicago: University of Chicago Press, 1945), pp. xi–xii.

41. John Brown, *Slave Life in Georgia: A Narrative of the Life, Sufferings, and Escape of John Brown, a Fugitive Slave, Now in England* (London: W. M. Watts, 1855), p. 2. Brown's father lived on a neighboring plantation.

42. Phillips, *American Negro Slavery . . .* , p. 264. A high mortality rate for both whites and blacks was a fact of life, although the slave rate does seem to have been significantly higher than that of whites. See Kenneth M. Stampp, *The Peculiar Institution: Slavery in the Ante-Bellum South* (New York: Vintage Books, 1956), pp. 318–21.

43. Work Projects Administration, *Drums and Shadows: Survival Studies among the Georgia Coastal Negroes* (Athens: University of Georgia Press, 1940), p. 29. (Hereafter noted WPA, *Drums and Shadows. . . .*)

44. Duncan Gaines in Rawick, ed., Florida, XVII, p. 136.

45. See Herbert G. Gutman, *The Black Family in Slavery and Freedom*

1750–1925. (New York: Pantheon Books, 1976)) pp. 185–201. From his study of the slave family Gutman concludes that slaves named their children most frequently after father, dead siblings, grandparents, aunts and uncles, and sometimes great-aunts and great-uncles, in that order. Whereas sons, especially first or second born, frequently had their father's name, daughters almost never had the name of their mother. Gutman also suggests, on admittedly inconclusive data, that grandparents may have played a prominent role in the naming process.

For a discussion of how slaves blended names of African origins with anglicized versions, see Genovese, *Roll, Jordan, Roll,* pp. 449–50.

46. Henry Watson, *Narrative of Henry Watson, a Fugitive Slave. Written By Himself* (Boston: Bela Marsh, 1848), p. 5. See also, H. C. Bruce, *The New Man: Twenty-Nine Years a Slave, Twenty-Nine Years a Free Man. Recollections of H. C. Bruce* (York, Pa.: P. Anstadt and Sons, 1895), p. 11.

47. Yetman, p. 104. Sometimes, though infrequently, the children would be tended by an older man as in Harry Smith's quarters where the little slaves were "raised and nursed by an old colored negro, named Uncle Paul." Harry Smith, *Fifty Years of Slavery in the United States of America.* (Grand Rapids, Michigan: Western Michigan Printing Company, 1891), p. 34.

48. For a description of typical nurse houses see: Estella Jones in Rawick, ed., Georgia, XII(2), p. 346; and Hughes, p. 44.

49. This estimate has been made from statistics of particular plantations given in the following sources: Phillips, *American Negro Slavery . . . ,* pp. 230, 244; Ulrich Bonnell Phillips and James David Glunt, eds., *Florida Plantation Records From the Papers of George Noble Jones* (St. Louis: Missouri Historical Society, 1927), pp. 538, 547–49, 556–71; Hall, Vol 3, p. 218; Olmsted, *Seaboard . . . ,* pp. 57–58; and Mary Ross Banks, *Bright Days in the Old Plantation Time* (Boston: Lee and Shepard, 1882), pp. 143–44. Fogel and Engerman, using more comprehensive data, concur in this estimate at least for cotton plantations. See Robert William Fogel and Stanley Engerman, *Time on the Cross. The Economics of American Negro Slavery* (Boston: Little, Brown and Company, 1974), p. 42.

50. Dicey Thomas in Rawick, ed., Arkansas, X(6), pp. 290–92. Phillips reports that Hammond's rules allowed mothers "forty-five minutes at each nursing to be with their children. They return three times a day until their children are eight months old—in the middle of the forenoon, at noon, and in the middle of the afternoon; till the twelfth month but twice a day, missing at noon; during the twelfth month at noon only. . . ." Phillips, *American Negro Slavery . . . ,* p. 264.

51. Amanda McCray in Rawick, ed., Florida XVII, p. 213. See also, Genovese, *Roll, Jordan, Roll . . . ,* pp. 498–99.

52. Charles Ball, *Fifty Years in Chains* (New York: Dover Publications, 1970), p. 151. (Originally published in 1837.) John Thompson, *The Life of John Thompson, a Fugitive Slave: Containing His History of Twenty-Five Years in Bondage, and His Providential Escape. Written by Himself* (Worcester: By the author, 1856), p. 17. Sara Colquitt in Rawick, ed., Alabama, VI, p. 87.

53. Jeff Bailey in Rawick, ed., Arkansas, VIII(1), p. 87.

54. Hughes, p. 43. Cornelia Robinson in Rawick, ed., Alabama, VI, p. 332.

55. On Hammond's plantation they were to have "hominy and milk and corn bread," for breakfast; "for dinner, vegetable soup and dumplings or bread; and cold bread or potatoes were kept on hand for demands between meals. They were also to have molasses once or twice a week. Each child was provided with a pan and spoon in charge of the nurse." Phillips, *American Negro Slavery . . .* , p. 226.

56. Yetman, p. 104. Ben Brown recalls the bread of his slave days: "Sometimes we got wheat bread, we call dat 'seldom bread' an' cohn bread was called 'common' becos we had it ev'ry day." Brown in Rawick, ed., Ohio, XVI, p. 11.

57. Lunsford Lane, *The Narrative of Lunsford Lane, Formerly of Raleigh, North Carolina* (Boston: by the author, 1842), p. 13.

58. Mahalia Shores in Rawick, ed., Arkansas, X(6), p. 155.

59. George Strickland in Rawick, ed., Alabama, VI, p. 359; Frank Cannon in Rawick, ed., Arkansas, VIII(2), p. 1; Estella Jones in Rawick, ed., Georgia, XII (2), p. 346.

60. Kemble, p. 64.

61. Charlie King in Rawick, ed., Georgia, XIII(3), p. 19.

62. For some description of these adornments see page 121.

63. Fisk, *Unwritten . . .* , p. 56.

64. Robert Anderson, *From Slavery to Affluence. Memoirs of Robert Anderson, Ex-Slave* (Steamboat Springs, Colorado: The Steamboat Pilot, 1927), p. 56.

65. Benjamin Drew, ed., *A North-Side View of Slavery, The Refugee: or the Narratives of Fugitive Slaves in Canada* (Boston: John P. Jewett, 1856), p. 105.

66. Yetman, p. 105.

67. Will Sheets in Rawick, ed., Georgia, XIII(3), p. 239. Often children wrapped their feet in bagging sacks to help keep warm. See Lewis Favor in Rawick, ed., Georgia, XII(2), p. 320.

68. Elisha Doc Garey in Rawick, ed., Georgia, XII(2), p. 4. John Cade, "Out of the Mouths of Ex-Slaves," *Journal of Negro History*, Vol. XX (1935), p. 298.

69. Fisk, *Unwritten . . .* , p. 255. For a notable exception to this general rule see Susan Smedes, *Memorials of a Southern Planter* (Baltimore: Cushings and Bailey, 1887).

70. Yetman, pp. 312–13.

71. Waters McIntosh in Rawick, ed., Arkansas, X(5), p. 20.

72. Olmsted, *Seaboard . . .* , pp. 424–25.

73. Susan Bradford Eppes, *The Negro of the Old South: A Bit of Period History* (Mason, Georgia: J. W. Burke, revised copyright, 1941), pp. 67–68.

74. For a fuller description of the games and other activities of the older quarter children, see Chapter 14.

75. Sam Aleckson, p. 77. A "piggin" was a wooden bucket.

76. Fisk, *Unwritten . . .* , p. 298.

77. Yetman, p. 227.

78. Henry Cheatam in Rawick, ed., Alabama, VI, p. 67.

79 Randel Lee in Rawick, ed., Florida, XVII, p. 199.

80. Fisk, *Unwritten . . .* , pp. 110, 115.

81. Georgia Baker in Rawick, ed., Georgia, XII(1), p. 46.

82. Frank Gill in Rawick, ed., Alabama, VI, p. 150.

83. For a discussion of the songs and stories of the quarter community see Chapter 16.

84. For more material on community events see all of Part III.

85. See Chapters 13 and 16.

86. Uncle Jack Island in Rawick, ed., Arkansas, IX(3), p. 380.

87. Yetman, p. 71.

88. Botkin, p. 121.

89. Frederick Law Olmstead, *A Journey In The Back Country* (London: Sampson Law, Son and Company, 1860). p. 142.

90. Charles Davis in Rawick, ed., South Carolina, II(1), p. 250.

91. Lewis W. Paine, *Six Years in a Georgia Prision. Narrative of Lewis W. Paine, Who Suffered Imprisonment Six Years in Georgia, for the Crime of Aiding the Escape of a Fellow-man from that State after He Had Fled from Slavery* (New York: For the Author, 1851), p. 128. The feeling that the head was the most important part of the body to keep warm was also noticed by Fanny Kemble, who observed that even on warm nights the babies were wrapped in swarthing with one or more caps on their heads but nothing on their feet. Kemble, pp. 69, 128.

92. Minnie Davis, in Rawick, ed., Georgia, XII (1), p. 254.

93. Dosia Harris in Rawick, ed., Georgia, XII (2), p. 105.

94. Allen Sims in Rawick, ed., Alabama, VI, p. 343; Malindy Maxwell in Rawick, ed., Arkansas, X (5), p. 59.

95. C. C. Jones, *The Religious Instruction of the Negroes in the United States* (New York: Negro University Press, 1969), pp. 114–15. (Originally published in 1842.) Charlie Smith's explanation for this occurrence on his plantation was that the older children needed to take care of the babies when the old folks were at church. Charlie Smith in Rawick, ed., Georgia, XIII (3), pp. 275–76.

96. Douglass, *Life and Times . . .* , p. 33.

97. Sam Aleckson, p. 113.

98. J. Vance Lewis, *Out of the Ditch: A True Story of an Ex-Slave, by J. Vance Lewis* (Houston: Rein and Company, 1910), p. 8.

99. Lane, pp. 2–3.

100. A. J. Mitchell in Rawick, ed., Arkansas, X(5), p. 104.

101. James W. C. Pennington, *The Fugitive Blacksmith; or, Events in the Life of James W. C. Pennington, Pastor of a Presbyterian Church, New York, Formerly a Slave in the State of Maryland, United States.* Third Edition (Westport, Conn.: Negro University Press, 1971), p. 2. (Reprint of the 1850 edition.)

102. *Ibid.,* pp. 2–3.

103. Douglass, *Life and Times . . .* , pp. 30–33.

104. Charlotte Martin in Rawick, ed., Florida, XVII, p. 166.

105. Josiah Henson, *The Life of Josiah Henson, Formerly a Slave, Now an Inhabitant of Canada* (Boston: Arthur D. Phelps, 1849), p. 1.

106. William Wells Brown, *Narrative of William Wells Brown, a Fugitive Slave, Written by Himself* (Boston: Anti-Slavery Office, 1847), p. 16.

107. Bruce, p. 24.

108. Yetman, p. 58.

109. Aunt Sally, *Aunt Sally; or, the Cross the Way to Freedom. A Narrative of the Slave-Life and Purchase of the Mother of Reverend Isaac Williams, of Detroit, Michigan* (Cincinnati: American Reform Tract and Book Society, 1858), p. 27.

110. Yetman, p. 182.

111. Tom Baker in Rawick, ed., Alabama, VI, p. 17.

112. Yetman, p. 40.

113. Booker T. Washington, *Up From Slavery* (New York: Dell, 1965), pp. 17–18. (Originally published in 1900.)

114. Hughes, p. 31.

115. John Brown, p. 12. James Davis in Rawick, ed., Arkansas, XIII(2), p. 109.

116. Olmsted, *Seaboard . . . ,* p. 433.

117. Henry Waldon in Rawick, ed., Arkansas, XI (7), p. 16.

118. Clayton Holbert in Rawick, ed., Kansas, XVI, p. 1.

119. Yetman, p. 232.

120. Botkin, p. 120.

121. Lane, pp. 7–8.

122. Douglass, *Life and Times . . . ,* p. 50.

Introduction to Part I

1. Booker T. Washington was perhaps one of the earliest and most prominent perpetuators of the idea of the plantation as a vocational school. See Henry Allen Bullock, *A History of Negro Education in the South* (New York: Praeger Publishers, 1967) pp. 5–7. Among historians, Ulrich Phillips was for many years the chief proponent of the idea. In *American Negro Slavery* he writes: "On the whole the plantations were the best schools yet invented for the mass training of the sort of inert and backward people which the bulk of the American negroes represented." See page 243. Recently Robert Fogel and Stanley Engerman have attempted to give fresh impetus to Phillips's arguments. See Robert William Fogel and Stanley L. Engerman, *Time on the Cross . . . ,* pp. 40, 43.

Chapter 2

2. The childlike character of the plantation slave is, as Stanley Elkins has amply demonstrated, a motif that runs through the writings of many Southern whites of the ante-bellum period. "The Negro was to be a child forever. 'The Negro . . . in his true nature, is always a boy, let him be ever so old. . . .' 'He is . . . a dependent upon the white race; dependent for guidance and direction even to the procurement of his most indispensable necessities. Apart from this protec-

tion he had the helplessness of a child—without thrift of any kind.' Not only was he a child; he was a happy child. Few Southern writers failed to describe with obvious fondness the bubbling gaiety of a plantation holiday or the perpetual good humor that seemed to mark the Negro character, the good humor of everlasting childhood." Stanley Elkins, *Slavery: A Problem in American Institutional and Intellectual Life*. Second Edition (Chicago: University of Chicago Press, 1959, 1968), p. 132. Edward A. Pollard, *Black Diamonds Gathered in the Darkey Homes of the South* (New York: Pudney & Russel, 1859), p. viii, and John Pendleton Kennedy, *Swallow Barn: or, A Sojourn in the Old Dominion*. Revised Edition (New York: G. P. Putnam's Sons, 1906), p. 453.

3. As Robert Fogel and Stanley Engerman have pointed out, " 'Perfect' submission was the rhetorical position of the master class, not its practical objective." Robert William Fogel and Stanley L. Engerman, *Time on the Cross* . . . , p. 232. It was the strategy of the planters, nonetheless, to urge the struggle for "perfect" submission so that, in the end, "optimal" submission might be attained.

4. In a brilliant synthesis of the historical conceptions of the years 1831–1861, Eugene Genovese concludes: "Historians have correctly viewed the period from 1831 to 1861 as one of reaction. Yet they have also correctly viewed it as one in which the treatment of slaves became progressively better. Both views have been correct in that they refer to different aspects of the same process. The condition of the slaves worsened with respect to access to freedom and the promise of eventual emancipation; it got better with respect to material conditions of life. The same men who fought for the one more often than not fought for the other. Their position made perfect sense: Make the South safe for slaveholders by confirming the blacks in perpetual slavery and by making it possible for them to accept their fate." Genovese, *Roll, Jordan, Roll* . . . , pp. 50–51.

5. Stampp, p. 150.

6. See Phillips, p. 269.

7. Olmsted, *Seaboard* . . . , p. 674.

8. Yetman, pp. 275–76.

9. Fisk University, *Unwritten History* . . . , p. 21.

10. Stampp, p. 208.

11. Genovese, *Roll, Jordan, Roll* . . . , p. 208.

12. Stampp, p. 208.

13. Carter Woodson, *The Education of the Negro Prior to 1861,* Second Edition (Washington, D.C.: The Associated Publishers, 1919), p. 177.

14. John Thompson, *The Life of John Thompson, A Fugitive Slave; Containing His History of 25 Years in Bondage, and His Providential Escape* (Worcester, Mass.: published by the author, 1856), p. 67. See also Henry Bibb, *Narrative of the Life and Adventures of Henry Bibb, An American Slave* (New York: Published by the author, 1849), pp. 101–2.

15. Titus T. Byrnes in Rawick, ed., Florida, XVII, p. 53, and Douglass Dorsey in Rawick, ed., Florida, XVII, pp. 95–96. Abran Harris, who lived as a slave for approximately twenty years on a plantation in South Carolina, reports: "Dere weren't none of de white folks in dem slavery times what would let dey niggers

have any learnin'. You sure better not be cotch a-tryin' to learn no readin' or wri-tin'. Our marster even never allowed dat. Iffen a nigger was to be found what could write, den right straight dey would chop his forefinger offen dat hand that he write with." Yetman, p. 161.

16. Jamie Parker, *Jamie Parker, the Fugitive. Related to Mrs. Emily Pierson* (Hartford: Brockett, Fuller, and Company, 1851), pp. 20–22.

17. M. D. Conway, *Testimonies Concerning Slavery* (London: Chapman and Hall, 1864), p. 112.

18. John Spencer Bassett, *The Southern Plantation Overseer as Revealed in His Let-ters* (New York: Negro Universities Press, 1968, copyright 1925), pp. 53–54.

19. Frederick Douglass, *Life and Times of Frederick Douglass* (New York: Collier Books, 1962). Reprinted from the revised edition of 1892, p. 161.

20. See, for example, Rebecca Hooks in Rawick, ed., Florida, XVII, p. 175. Also, pp. 49–50 of present study.

21. These stories were often well founded in fact. The situation of the free black man in the South, especially as the Civil War approached, was a precarious one. One example of their plight is the case of William Bass, who petitioned the South Carolina General Assembly in 1859 to be made the slave of Philip Pledger stating "That as a free negro he is preyed upon by every sharper with whom he comes in contact, and that he is very poor though an able-bodied man, and is charged with and punished for every offence, guilty or not, committed in his neighborhood; that he is without house or home and lives a thousand times harder and in more destitution than the slaves of many planters in his district." Phillips, *American Negro Slavery*, p. 446.

22. James Williams, *Life and Adventures of James Williams, a Fugitive Slave, with a Full Description of the Underground Railroad*. Fifth Edition. (Philadelphia: A. H. Sickler, 1893, originally published 1873), p. 11.

23. Conway, p. 112.

24. William Craft, *Running a Thousand Miles for Freedom; or, the Escape of Wil-liam and Ellen Craft from Slavery* (London: W. Tweedie, 1860), p. 45.

25. Lewis Clarke, *Narrative of the Sufferings of Lewis Clarke, during a Captivity of More than Twenty-Five Years, Among the Algerines of Kentucky, One of the So-Called Christian States of North America* (Boston: D. H. Ela, 1845), p. 39.

26. See Guion Griffic Johnson, *A Social History of the Sea Islands with Special Reference to St. Helena Island, South Carolina* (Chapel Hill: The University of North Carolina Press, 1930), p. 157.

27. Yetman, pp. 131, 34.

28. Stampp, p. 207.

29. Stampp, p. 193. This entire paragraph concerning the slave code is drawn principally from Stampp, pp. 192–236.

30. Charles H. Nichols, *Many Thousand Gone: The Ex-Slaves' Account of Their Bondage and Freedom* (Bloomington: Indiana University Press, 1963), p. 70.

31. Yetman, p. 16.

32. Stroyer, pp. 44–45.

33. Lewis W. Paine, p. 128.

34. Jermain Wesley Loguen, *The Rev. J. W. Loguen, as a Slave and as a Freeman. A Narrative of Real Life* (Syracuse, New York: Office of the *Daily Journal*, 1859), p. 165.

35. Genovese, *Roll, Jordan, Roll . . .* , p. 119 citing "The Southern Cultivator," IV (March, 1846), p. 44.

36. John Dixon Long, *Pictures of Slavery in Church and State, Including Personal Reminiscences, Biographical Sketches, Ancedotes, Etc., Etc.* (New York: Negro Universities Press, 1969), p. 15. (Originally published in 1857.) Gutman concludes, however, that less than one percent of the slaves carried Greek or Roman names. Gutman, *The Black Family . . .* , p. 186.

37. Eppes, p. 81.

38. Craft, p. 77.

39. William Grimes, *Life of William Grimes, the Runaway Slave* (New York: Published by the author, 1825), p. 13.

40. Charles Ball, *Fifty Years in Chains* (New York: Dover Publications, 1970), p. 58. This is an unabridged and unaltered republication of *Slavery in the United States: A Narrative of the Life and Adventures of Charles Ball, a Black Man* (New York: John S. Taylor, 1837).

41. Solomon Northup, *Twelve Years a Slave, Narrative of Solomon Northup, a Citizen of New York, Kidnapped in Washington City in 1841, and Rescued in 1853, from a Cotton Plantation near the Red River in Louisiana* (Buffalo: Derby, Orton and Mulligan, 1853), p. 183.

42. Yetman, p. 252.

43. Fisk, *Unwritten . . .* , p. 80.

44. Stampp, pp. 144–45.

45. Benjamin Drew, *A North-Side View of Slavery. The Refugee: or the Narratives of Fugitive Slaves in Canada* (New York: Negro Universities Press, 1968), p. 73. (Originally published by John P. Jewett and Company, 1856.)

46. Watson, p. 32.

47. Frederick Douglass, *Narrative of the Life of Frederick Douglass, an American Slave* (Boston: Anti-Slavery Office, 1845), pp. 87–88.

48. Rev. W. B. Allen in Rawick, ed., Georgia, XII (1), pp. 14–15.

49. See Harry Smith, p. 11. Also Pierce Cody in Rawick, ed., Georgia, XII (1), p. 196, and Fisk Collection, *God Struck Me Dead: Religious Conversion Experiences and Autobiographies of Negro Ex-Slaves* (Nashville, Tennessee: Social Science Institute, Fisk University, 1945), p. 17.

50. Stampp, p. 201.

51. Fisk, *Unwritten . . .* , p. 76.

52. *Ibid.*, p. 9.

53. James Williams, *Narrative of James Williams an American Slave, Who Was for Several Years a Driver of a Cotton Plantation in Alabama* (Boston: American Anti-Slavery Society, 1838), pp. 48–49.

54. Eppes, p. 48.

55. Genovese, *Roll, Jordan, Roll . . .* , p. 374. Here Genovese is drawing from

The Southern Agriculturalist, IV (July, 1831), pp. 350–54. Louis Hughes, who had been a slave in both Virginia and Mississippi, though agreeing that some owners did not like to whip their slaves themselves, suggests a different reason for their preference. "Owners who affected culture and refinement preferred to send a servant to the yard for punishment to inflicting it themselves. It saved them trouble, they said, and possibly a slight wear and tear of feeling." Louis Hughes, p. 9.

56. Bibb, p. 112. See also, Olmsted, *Seaboard . . . ,* p. 438; Watson, p. 15; and Moses Grandy, *Narrative of the Life of Moses Grandy, Late a Slave in the United States of America* (Boston: Oliver Johnson, 1844), p. 17.

57. In discussing this buffer role played by the overseer Bassett comments: "From his decision an appeal was to the owner who as a dispenser of mercy and forgiveness had some degree of affection from the slaves. . . . It was the fate of this man, standing in the place of the owner, to absorb the shock of bitterness felt by the slaves for their enslavers and in doing so keep it away from whose who were in reality the responsible parties." Bassett, pp. 3–4.

58. Harriet Martineau, in observing that masters liked to be seen in the role of the merciful provider, adds that though they loved to deal out mercy they were in no position to administer justice. Harriet Martineau, *Society in America,* Vol. 2 (London: Saunders and Otley, 1837), p. 314.

59. See, for example, Israel Campbell, *Bond and Free: or, Yearnings for Freedom, from My Green Briar House. Being the Story of My Life in Bondage and My Life in Freedom* (Philadelphia: by the author, 1861), pp. 68–69.

60. Olmsted, *Seaboard . . . ,* p. 660.

61. See Henry Banks quoted in Drew, *A North-Side View . . . ,* p. 74.

62. Douglass, *Life and Times . . . ,* p. 147.

63. Many masters, of course, saw clearly that "if emancipation were a suitable reward for meritorious service, then the idea that slavery benefited the blacks had to be wrong." Genovese, *Roll, Jordan, Roll . . . ,* p. 52.

64. H. N. McTyeire, *Duties of Christian Masters* (Nashville: Southern Methodist Publishing House, 1859), p. 88.

65. See, for example, Moses Grandy, p. 39.

66. McTyeire, p. 87.

67. For some examples and vivid descriptions of the tortures sometimes given to slaves see: Phillips, p. 511; Ball, pp. 225, 256–57, 499–500; and Sam and Louisa Everett in Rawick, ed., *Florida,* XVII, p. 127.

68. Yetman, pp. 107–8.

69. Conway, p. 10.

70. Genovese, *Roll, Jordan, Roll . . . ,* pp. 64–65. Harriet Tubman is reported to have told Sarah Bradford that some masters made a habit of beating their newly acquired slaves immediately upon purchase informing them that: "I have no complaint to make of you. You're a good nigger, an' you've always worked well. But you belong to *me* now; you're *my* nigger, and the first lesson my niggers have to learn is that I am master and they belong to me, and are never to resist any-

thing I order them to do. So I always begin by giving them a good licking. Now strip and take it." Sarah Bradford, *Harriet Tubman: The Moses of Her People* (New York: By the author, 1886), pp. 40–41.

71. Stampp, p. 145. Stampp is here quoting from *Farmers' Register,* I (1834), 564–65.

72. H., *The Farmer's Register,* V (Sept., 1837) p. 302.

Chapter 3

1. Thomas Affleck, "The American Cotton Planter," II (December, 1854), 353–56.

2. Phillips, *American Negro Slavery . . . ,* p. 32.

3. C. C. Jones, p. 209.

4. Joseph D. Brokhage, *Francis Patrick Kenrich's Opinion on Slavery* (Washington, D.C.: Catholic University of America Press, 1955), p. 173. Brokhage is here stating Kenrich's view. Francis Kenrich was a noted Roman Catholic scholar and the Archbishop of Baltimore from 1851–1863.

5. McDougle, pp. 80–81. McDougle is here quoting from the *Presbyterian Herald* of April 16, 1846.

6. Luther P. Jackson, "Religious Instruction of Negroes, 1830–1860, with Special Reference to South Carolina," *Journal of Negro History,* XV (1930), p. 79. Jackson is here quoting from the *Southern Presbyterian Review.*

7. James Russell Johnson, "The Usefulness of Religious Training on the Southern Plantation as a Means of Inculcating Servility and a Deep Sense of Inferiority in Black Folks During the Thirty Years Preceding the American Civil War," (Unpublished paper, Teachers College, Columbia University, 1970), p. 56. Johnson is quoting from William S. Plumer, "Thoughts on the Religious Instruction of Negroes," *Savannah* (1848), 4.

8. *Ibid.,* p. 57.

9. C. C. Jones, pp. 196–97.

10. Charles S. Davis, *The Cotton Kingdom in Alabama* (Montgomery: Alabama State Department of Archives and History, 1939), p. 89.

11. See William Sumner Jenkins, *Pro-Slavery Thought in the Old South* (Chapel Hill: University of North Carolina Press, 1935), pp. 18–19.

12. Botkin, p. 91.

13. Henry Box Brown, *Narrative of Henry Box Brown* (Boston: Brown and Stearns, 1849), p. 46.

14. Olmsted, *Seaboard . . . ,* p. 93.

15. Joseph B. Earnest, Jr., *The Religious Development of the Negro in Virginia* (Charlottesville: The Michie Company, 1914), p. 91.

16. See C. C. Jones, p. 192.

17. Yetman, pp. 231–32.

18. See Stampp, p. 156; Phillips, p. 321; Susan Markey Fickling, "Slave-Con-

version in South Carolina 1830–1860 (Columbia, South Carolina: Bulletin of the University of South Carolina, 1924), pp. 17–18; Jackson, pp. 83–84; James Johnson, p. 57; Genovese, *Roll, Jordan, Roll* . . . , pp. 186–89, 190; and E. Franklin Frazier, *The Negro in the United States* (New York: Macmillan, 1949), pp. 52–53.

19. Flanders, p. 173.

20. Fickling, pp. 17–18.

21. Jenkins, p. 212. Jenkins is here referring to C. C. Pinckney.

22. Bethany Veney, *The Narrative of Bethany Veney, a Slave Woman* (Worcester, Mass.: Press of George H. Ellis, 1889), pp. 7–8.

23. Henry Box Brown, p. 45.

24. James Johnson, pp. 51–52. Johnson is here drawing from one of the sermons of the Reverend A. F. Dickson entitled "The Hard Way."

25. Lunsford Lane, p. 20.

26. J. D. Green, *Narrative of the Life of J. D. Green, a Runaway Slave, from Kentucky, Containing an Account of His Three Escapes, in 1839, 1846, and 1848* (Huddersfield: Printed by Henry Fielding, 1864), p. 6.

27. James Roberts, *The Narrative of James Roberts, Soldier in the Revolutionary War and at the Battle of New Orleans* (Chicago: Printed for the author, 1858), p. 12.

28. Lunsford Lane, p. 21.

29. Henry Watson, pp. 28–31.

30. *Ibid.*

31. Peter Randolph, *Sketches of Slave Life; or, Illustrations of the "Peculiar Institution". By Peter Randolph, an Emancipated Slave, 2nd ed.* (Boston: For the author, 1855), p. 62.

32. Yetman, pp. 12–13. See also, pp. 53, 181.

33. Ball, p. 70.

34. Emma Tidwell in Rawick, ed., Arkansas, X (6), p. 332.

35. John W. Blassingame, *The Slave Community: Plantation Life in the Antebellum South* (New York: Oxford University Press, 1972), p. 63.

36. Stampp, p. 162.

37. Campbell, p. 12.

38. T. D. Ozanne, *The South as It Is, or Twenty One Years' Experience in the Southern States of America* (London: Saunders, Otley and Company, 1863), pp. 133–34.

39. Fickling, p. 17.

40. C. C. Jones, p. 235.

41. *Ibid.*, p. 254.

42. Genovese, *Roll, Jordan, Roll* . . . , p. 206.

43. Jackson, p. 85.

44. C. C. Jones, p. 266.

45. Blassingame, p. 61.

46. Johnson, pp. 53–54.

47. James Pennington, who spent the first 21 years of his life as a slave in Maryland, recalls having heard but two sermons during this time "but heard no mention in them of Christ, or the way of life by him." James W. C. Pennington, pp. 43–44.

48. Kemble, pp. 106–7.

49. C. C. Jones, p. 261.

50. *Ibid.*, p. 265. After listing a number of songs which he felt proper for the edification of blacks, Jones continues: "The tunes should be plain and awakening. One great advantage in teaching them good psalms and hymns, is that they are thereby induced to lay aside the extravagent and nonsensical chants, and catches and hallelujah songs of their own composing; and when they sing, which is often while about their business or of an evening in their houses, they will have something profitable to sing."

51. Johnson, pp. 49–50.

52. C. C. Jones, p. 255.

53. *Ibid.*, p. 262.

54. James Johnson, p. 69.

55. C. C. Jones, p. 245.

56. Of the many elaborate theological discussions of the biblical position with regards to slavery, among the best is George D. Armstrong, *The Christian Doctrine of Slavery* (New York: Charles Scribner, 1857).

57. Mrs. Henry Rowe Schoolcraft, *Plantation Life: The Narratives of Mrs. Henry Rowe Schoolcraft* (New York: Negro Universities Press, 1960), p. 47. (Originally published, 1852.)

58. Martineau, Vol. 2, p. 314.

59. Clayton, pp. 51–52.

60. Jonathan Boucher, *Reminiscences of an American Loyalist 1738–1789. Being the Autobiography of the Rev. Jonathan Boucher Rector of Annapolis in Maryland and Afterwards of Eprom, Surrey, England* (New York: Houghton Mifflin, 1925), p. 98.

61. R. Q. Mallard, *Plantation Life Before Emancipation* (Richmond, Va.: Whittet and Shepperson, 1892), pp. 35–36.

62. Jenkins, p. 112. Here he is quoting from a letter of Governor Hammond to L. Tappan, August 1, 1845. In the Library of Congress.

63. Quoted in C. P. Patterson, *The Negro in Tennessee, 1790–1865* (New York: Negro Universities Press, 1968), p. 79.

64. Genovese, *Roll, Jordan, Roll . . .* , p. 76. Genovese is here quoting from E. N. Elliott, president of Planters' College in Mississippi.

65. B. M. Palmer, *The South: Her Peril and Her Duty. A Discourse, Delivered in the First Presbyterian Church, New Orleans, on Thursday, November 29, 1860* (New Orleans: The Office of the Time Witness and Sentinel, 1860), pp. 8–9.

66. Jenkins, p. 218.

Chapter 4

1. Lewis and Milton Clarke, *Narratives of the Sufferings of Lewis and Milton Clarke, Sons of a Soldier of the Revolution During a Captivity of More Than Twenty Years Among the Slaveholders of Kentucky, One of the So-Called Christian States of North America.* (Boston: Bela Marsh, 1846), p. 119.

Notes to pages 64–67

2. John Brown, *Slave Life in Georgia*, p. 83.

3. Campbell, p. 38. James Williams, *Narrative* . . . p. 66.

4. Orland Kay Armstrong, *Old Massa's People: The Old Slaves Tell Their Story* (Indianapolis: Bobbs-Merrill, 1931) pp. 160–63. C. C. Jones, though pointing to it as an illustration of the slaves' general immorality, writes that "the Negroes are scrupulous on one point; they make a common cause, as servants, in concealing their faults from their owners. Inquiry elicits no information, no one feels at liberty to disclose the transgressor of a 'professional secret': for they remember that they may hereafter require the same concealment of their own transgressions from their fellow servants and if they tell upon them *now,* they may have the like favor returned *them;* besides, in the meanwhile, having their names cast out as evil from among their brethren, and being subjected to scorn, and perhaps personal violence or pecuniary injury." C. C. Jones, *Religious Instruction*, p. 130. Genovese implies that most of the leading slaveholders agreed with Jones and argues that whatever reputation for violence against each other slaves acquired was due to the behavior of town slaves, who had an easy access to liquor, and to acts of violence against black informers. Genovese also argues that whatever the level of violence among slaves it "fell far short of the appalling southern norm, whereas their kindness and courtesy equaled or exceeded it." Genovese, *Roll, Jordan, Roll* . . . , pp. 622–37.

5. Jake McLeod in Rawick, ed., *South Carolina*, III (3), p. 157.

6. Campbell, p. 148.

7. Drew, *A North-Side View* . . . , pp. 53, 263.

8. Susan Davis Rhodes in Rawick, ed., *Missouri*, XI, p. 284.

9. Drew, *A North-Side View* . . . , p. 211.

10. Steward, p 32.

11. See Chapter 17.

12. See Robert Anderson, p. 31, James Campbell, p. 22, James Bolton in Rawick ed., *Georgia*, XII (1), p. 99, Fisk, *Unwritten* . . . , p. 37.

13. Orland Armstrong, p. 219, Fisk, *Unwritten* . . . , p. 201.

14. Northup, *Twelve Years a Slave*, p. 219. Several of the white commentators observed the tendency of blacks to prefer working in groups. Susan Dabney Smedes wrote: "With Negro slaves it seemed impossible for one of them to do a thing, it mattered not how insignificant, without the assistance of one or two others. It was often said with a laugh by their owners that it took two to help one do anything." (Smedes, *A Southern Planter*, p. 44). Edmund Ruffin, the noted Virginia agriculturalist and ardent secessionist, wrote in his diary of April 5, 1857, "A negro cannot abide being alone—and will prefer work of much exposure and severe toil, in company, to any lighter work, without any company." (William Kauffman Scarborough ed., *The Diary of Edmund Ruffin*, Vol. I [Baton Rouge: Louisiana State University Press, 1972], p. 52.)

15. See Part III.

16. Grandy, p. 32.

17. Douglass, *Life and Times* . . . , p. 42. The sense of kinship which permeated all the affairs of quarter slaves who had grown up together probably

helps explain why many slaves preferred to marry slaves from plantations other than their own. Although some of the informants explain the preference for "broad wives" by the fact that few men wanted to see their wives whipped or overworked, other informants suggest that to marry one of the slaves with whom one had grown up would be like marrying one's sister. See Orland Armstrong, p. 155. One white traveller was also struck by the fact that ". . . negroes have a peculiarly strong affection for the old people of their color. Veneration for the aged is one of their strongest characteristics." Joseph Holt Ingraham, *The South-West: by a Yankee* (Harper & Brothers, 1835), p. 241.

18. Fisk, *Unwritten . . .* , pp. 11–12.

19. Fanny Johnson in Rawick, ed., Arkansas, IX (4), p. 87.

20. Marion Starling who did one of the earlier and most exhaustive studies of the slave narratives wrote: "The record of slaves who refused succor to fugitive slaves is very meager. Even when discovery meant certain flagellation, and his own food allotment barely provided him with the strength needed to keep up with his 'task work,' a slave asked for help by a pitifully hungry, haunted-looking fugitive would give all he had. The few slaves who betrayed their fellow slaves, through jealousy of their scheme or through hope of ingratiating themselves with their masters seem abnormally few, considering the proportionate distribution of such natures in ordinary society." Starling, p. 41. See also, Fisk, *Unwritten . . .* , p. 9.

21. Aunt Sally, pp. 64–65.

22. Adeline in Rawick, ed., Arkansas, VII (1), p. 12. Avirett talks not only of the family and plantation pride he noticed among his slave population but also of their racial pride. Avirett, p. 111.

23. Drew, *A North-Side View . . .* , p. 53.

24. Douglass, *Life and Times . . .* , p. 193.

25. Bibb, p. 47.

26. William Parker, "The Freedman's Story," *Atlantic Monthly,* 17 (February, 1866), p. 154.

27. Drew, *A North-Sice View . . .* , pp. 113, 30.

28. George Buckner in Rawick, ed., Kentucky, XVI, p. 29.

29. Langston Hughes and Anna Bontemps, eds., *The Book of Negro Folklore.* (New York: Dodd, Mead and Company, 1958), pp. 295–96.

30. Douglass, *Life and Times . . .* , p. 97.

31. Isaac Williams, *Sunshine and Shadow of Slave Life. Reminiscences as Told by Isaac D. Williams,* (East Saginaw, Mich.: Evening News Printing and Binding Company, 1885), p. 6.

Chapter 5

1. Unknown whites could, for example, be slave traders or slave stealers. It was this fear that caused Milly Robinson to relate: "I never see a white man come

onto the place that I didn't think, 'There, now, he's coming to look at my children'; and when I saw any man going by I've called in my children and hid 'em for fear he'd see 'em and want to buy 'em." Quoted in Frederic Bancroft, *Slave Trading in the Old South* (New York: Frederick Unger, 1931), p. 370.

2. Douglass, *Life and Times . . .* , p. 64.

3. *Ibid.*

4. Lewis and Milton Clarke, p. 114.

5. Anderson, p. 29.

6. Peter Bruner, *A Slave's Adventures toward Freedom: Not Fiction, but the True Story of a Struggle* (Oxford, Ohio: n.p., n.d.), p. 29. Bruner even trusted these mountain whites enough to hide in their cabin when he decided to "absent" himself from the plantation.

7. William Henry Singleton, *Recollections of Slavery Days by William Henry Singleton* (New York: Highland Democratic Company, 1922), p. 6.

8. For a good general description of the overseer/quarter relationship based on white sources see Kenneth Stampp, pp. 106–108.

9. Lewis Paine, the author of *Six Years in a Georgia Prison*, was put in jail for attempting to assist a black man to escape from slavery.

10. Josiah Henson, *Truth Stranger Than Fiction. Father Henson's Story of His Own Life* (Boston: John P. Jewett, 1858), p. 8.

11. Ball, among others, writes that a resident of the quarters could often live his whole life upon the same plantation without once stepping inside the great house. Ball, p. 280. See also Douglass, *Life and Times . . .* , p. 63.

12. Warren McKinney in Rawick, ed., Arkansas, X (5), p. 27.

13. Drew, A *North-Side View . . .* , p. 285.

14. Work Projects Administration, *The Negro in Virginia* (New York: Hastings House, 1940), p. 34.

15. Sterling A. Brown, Arthur P. Davis, and Ulysses Lee, eds., *The Negro Caravan* (New York: Citadel, 1941), pp. 447–48.

16. Steward, p. 86.

17. Josephine Howard in Rawick, ed., Texas IV (2), p. 163. See also, Douglass, *Life and Times . . .* , p. 50; and W. W. Brown, pp. 50–52.

18. John Brown, p. 201.

19. Drew, *The North-Side View . . .* , p. 281.

20. Douglass, *Life and Times . . .* , p. 146.

21. William Wells Brown, *Clotel; or, The President's Daughter: A Narrative of Slave Life in the United States with a Sketch of the Author's Life* (London: Partridge and Oakey, 1856), p. 138.

22. Alan Lomax, *The Folk Songs of North America* (Garden City, N.Y.: Doubleday, 1960), p. 527.

23. See Bruner, p. 22.

24. Drew, *A North-Side View . . .* , p. 343.

25. *Ibid.*, p. 345.

26. This ability to both love a master and see him as the political oppressor is best exemplified by the slave who, admitting to planning a bloody insurrection,

insisted that he dearly loved his master and mistress though he would have slain them first. Genovese, *Roll, Jordan, Roll . . .* , p. 378.

27. Northup, p. 249.

28. Drew, *A North-Side View . . .* , p. 200.

29. Henry L. Swint, *Dear Ones at Home; Letters from Contraband Camps* (Nashville: Vanderbilt University Press, 1966), p. 124.

Chapter 6

1. By the late years of slavery nearly all slaves seemed to have been influenced by Christianity and most expressed their religious views in Christian terms. One does read occasionally, however, of a slave or group of slaves who chose to reject Christianity. This happened most often when slaveholders were successful in their attempts to censor the nature of the religious precepts which reached black ears. Thus Bibb relates that on those plantations where blacks were not able to learn more of the Bible or of Christianity than that taught by plantation authorities many slaves rejected Christianity completely. "This is where they have no Sabboth Schools; no one to read the Bible to them; no one to preach the gospel who is competent to expound the Scriptures, except slaveholders. And the slaves, with but few exceptions, have no confidence at all in their preaching, because they preach a pro-slavery doctrine. They say, 'Servants be obedient to your masters;—and he that knoweth his master's will and doeth it not, shall be beaten with many stripes;'—means that God will send them to hell, if they disobey their masters. This kind of preaching has driven thousands into infidelity. . . . They cannot believe or trust in such a religion. . . ." Bibb, pp. 23–24. Charles Ball's grandfather steadfastly maintained his African religion. "He never went to church or meeting, and held that the religion of this country was altogether false, and indeed, no religion at all; being the mere invention of priests and crafty men, who hoped thereby to profit through the ignorance and credulity of the multitude." Ball, p. 22.

2. Douglass, *Life and Times . . .* , p. 157.

3. Watson, p. 28.

4. Louis Hughes, p. 90.

5. Drew, *A North-Side View . . .* , p. 97.

6. John Brown, pp. 202–3.

7. William Craft, p. 10.

8. Lewis Clarke, p. 70.

9. WPA, *Negro in Virginia*, p. 80.

10. Bibb, p. 39.

11. Drew, *A North-Side View . . .* , p. 178.

12. Charles Emery Stevens, *Anthony Burns; A History,* (Boston: John P. Jewett and Company, 1856), pp. 174–75.

13. Henson, *The Life of . . .* , pp. 11–12.

14. *Ibid.*, pp. 12–13.

15. Thompson, pp. 18–19.

16. Drew, *A North-Side View . . .* , p. 271.

17. Douglass, *Life and Times . . .* , p. 73.

18. Drew, *A North-Side View . . .* , p. 81.

19. *Ibid.*, p. 82.

20. Lane, p. 20.

21. Aaron, *The Light and Truth of Slavery. Aaron's History* (Worcester, Mass.: printed for Aaron, 1843?), p. 6.

22. Douglass, *Life and Times . . .* , p. 109.

23. Mary Gladding in Rawick, ed., Georgia, XII (2), pp. 22–23. Some of the white sources also note that the concern of the slaves for the conversion of their masters was "strong and lively." See Mallard, p. 137.

24. Stroyer, p. 99. When I first came upon this line early in my study of the narratives I completely misunderstood its significance. (I had not yet learned to recognize the distinction drawn by the quarter community between "true Christianity" and "slaveholding priestcraft.") Thus, at first, I assumed that Reverend Stroyer was so inculcated with the tenets of white religious training that he failed to realize that a Christian South had held slaves for over two hundred years and that their actions, at least after 1831, were strongly supported by Southern Churches. Only later, after reading similar statements by other informants, did it become clear to me that blacks were not willing to call those who supported slavery and held slaves "Christian."

25. Douglass, *Life and Times . . .* , p. 41.

26. Fisk, *God . . .* , p. 215.

27. James Roberts, p. 12.

28. Fisk, *Unwritten . . .* , p. 136.

29. Drew, *A North-Side View . . .* , p. 87.

30. Henry Brown, pp. 18–19.

31. Orland Armstrong, p. 231.

32. John Thompson, p. 57.

33. Douglass, *Life and Times . . .* , p. 89.

34. Thomas H. Jones, *The Experience of Thomas H. Jones, Who Was a Slave for Forty-Three Years* (Boston: Bazin & Chandler, 1862), p. 6.

35. Ball, pp. 220–21. DuBois suggests that this is a theme which pervades the slave spirituals. "Through all the sorrow of the Sorrow Songs there breathes a hope—a faith in the ultimate justice of things. The minor cadences of despair often change to triumph and calm confidence. Sometimes it is faith in life, sometimes a faith in death, sometimes assurances of boundless justice in some fair world beyond. But whatever it is, the meaning is always clear: that sometime, somewhere, men will judge men by their souls and not by their skins." W. E. Burghardt DuBois, *The Souls of Black Folk* (New York: Fawcett Publications, 1961), p. 183. (Originally published in 1903.)

36. One of the best expressions of this theme is that neither the mother of an illegitimate child (that is, illegitimate in the eyes of whites) nor the child himself

was socially ostracized by the quarter community. See, for example, Fisk, *Unwritten* . . . , p. 42. Incest, however, a matter not coerced by the slave system, was soundly condemned, and those blacks who committed it were severely ostracized if not physically punished. See Julia Brown in Rawick, ed., Georgia, XII (1), p. 142.

37. Ball, p. 299.

38. Bibb, p. 122.

39. Douglass, *Life and Times* . . . , p. 105.

40. Henson, *Truth* . . . , pp. 21–22. White observers also noted this attitude on the part of slaves. Olmsted, for example, writes: "It is told me as a singular fact, that everywhere on the plantations, the agrarian notion has become a fixed point of the negro system of ethics: that the result of labor belongs of right to the laborer, and on this ground, even the religious feel justified in using 'Massa's' property for their own temporal benefit. This they term 'taking' and it is never admitted to be a reproach to a man among them that he is charged with it, though 'stealing,' or taking from another than their master, and particularly from one another, is so." Olmsted, *Seaboard* . . . , p. 117.

41. See, for example, Drew, *A North-Side View* . . . , p. 198.

42. Douglass, *Life and Times* . . . , pp. 105–6.

43. See James Williams, *Narrative* . . . , p. 51; Thomas Jones, p. 9; Ball, p. 265, and WPA, *Negro in Virginia*, p. 172.

44. William F. Allen, *Slave Songs of the United States* (New York: A. Simpson and Company, 1867), p. 46.

45. Stroyer, p. 41.

46. Steward, p. 95.

47. Grandy, p. 41.

Chapter 7

1. Josephine Bacchus in Rawick, ed., South Carolina, II (1), p. 22.

2. Felix Heywood in Rawick, ed., Texas, IV (2), p. 134.

3. Quoted in Marion Starling, p. 337.

4. Emma Foster in Rawick, ed., Arkansas, VIII (2), p. 331.

5. See "Family" chapters in Parts II and III.

6. Henson, *The Life of* . . . , p. 14.

7. James Redpath, *The Roving Editor: or Talks with Slaves in Southern States* (New York: A. B. Burdick, 1859), p. 45.

8. Fisk, *Unwritten* . . . , p. 75.

9. See, for example, *Ibid.,* p. 84.

10. *Ibid.,* p. 7.

11. Emmaline Kilpatrick in Rawick, ed., Georgia, XIII (3), p. 9.

12. Steward, pp. 108, 86.

13. Henry Brown, p. 26. Northerners who became slaveholders had an espe-

cially bad reputation among slaves. "It is true," writes Bethany Veney, "that many Northern men came South very bitter in their opposition to slavery, and after a little while came to be the hardest and most cruel slaveholders." Veney, p. 13.

14. Pennington, pp. 72, 69.

15. Anthony Dawson in Rawick, ed., Oklahoma, VII, p. 69.

16. Lizzie Hughes in Rawick, ed., Texas, IV (2), p. 47; See also Charlie Meadow in Rawick, ed., South Carolina, III (3), pp. 180–81; Pat Franks in Rawick, ed., Mississippi, VII (2), p. 58, and Walter Calloway in Rawick, ed., Alabama, VI (1), p. 52.

17. Dorothy Scarborough, *On the Trail of Negro Folk Songs* (Cambridge: Harvard University Press, 1925), p. 168.

18. Bruce, p. 96.

19. Henry Green in Rawick, ed., Arkansas, IX (3), p. 96.

20. WPA, *The Negro in Virginia*, p. 146. See also, Fisk, *Unwritten . . .* , p. 78.

21. Anderson, p. 22. Such behavior was often noted by white observers. Olmsted noticed several times that despite the constant "directing and encouraging" of an overseer carrying a rawhide whip, "as often as he visited one end of the line of operations, the hands at the other end would discontinue their labor, until he turned to ride towards them again." (Olmsted, *Seaboard . . .* , p. 388.) One Virginia planter with whom Olmsted talked did not think that slaves "ever did half a fair day's work. They could not be made to work hard: they never would lay out their strength freely, and it was impossible to make them do it." Olmsted, himself, concludes that: "This is just what I have thought when I have seen slaves at work—they seem to go through the motions of labor without putting strength into them. They keep their powers in reserve for their own use at night, perhaps." Olmsted, *Ibid.*, p. 91. See also, Schoolcraft, p. 49.

22. John Brown, pp. 196–97

23. Yetman, p. 53.

24. Ira Foster in Rawick, ed., Arkansas, VIII (2), p. 335.

25. Fisk, *Unwritten . . .* , p. 256.

26. Lewis and Milton Clarke, p. 26.

27. Fisk, *God . . .* , p. 178.

28. Randolph, p. 199.

29. WPA, *The Negro in Virginia*, pp. 127–28. See also John Brown, p. 147. Fisk, *Unwritten . . .* , p. 245. Bibb says he spent half of his time while a slave in the woods. One of his favorite ploys was to take a bridle with him and if discovered say he was hunting the old mare. (Bibb, p. 66) It was this penchant for running off that prompted the infamous D. Cartwright to propound his now famous theory that slaves were highly susceptible to a disease which he termed "Drapetomania," and which caused them to run off. (See Stampp, p. 109)

30. Fisk, *Unwritten . . .* , p. 194. Isaac Williams, p. 10.

31. Hilliard Johnson in Rawick, ed., Alabama, VI, p. 229.

32. Ellis Jefson in Rawick, ed., Arkansas, IX (4), p. 4.

33. Fisk, *Unwritten . . .* , p. 285.

34. Quoted in Botkin, *Lay My Burden Down*, pp. 4–5.
35. Genovese, *Roll, Jordan, Roll . . .* , pp. 265–66. On the topic of slaves using language to deceive masters Genovese writes: "The slaves, in effect learned to communicate with each other in the presence of whites with some measure of safety, and the studied ambiguity of their speech, reinforced by reliance upon tone and gesture, helped immeasurably to prevent informers from having too much to convey to the masters beyond impressions and suspicions. If a slave informer heard a black preacher praise a runaway by calling him a '*ba-ad* nigger,' what could he tell his master beyond saying that he thought the preacher meant the opposite of what he had said? Even slaveholders usually required better evidence." Genovese, *Roll, Jordan, Roll . . .* , p. 437.
36. Allen, *Slave Songs*, p. 53.
37. Thomas Higginson, *Army Life in a Black Regiment* (Chapel Hill: University Press, 1937), p. 12.
38. Drew, *A North-Side View . . .* , p. 41. See also, Yetman, p. 37.
39. Ball, p. 130.
40. Duncan Clinch Heyward, *Seed from Madagascar* (Chapel Hill: University of North Carolina Press, 1937), p. 165.

Chapter 8

1. Douglass, *Narrative . . .* , p. 87.
2. John Brown, pp. 192–93.
3. Grandy, p. 37.
4. Grimes, p. 36.
5. Lewis Clarke, pp. 14–16.
6. Watson, p. 23.
7. Drew, *A North-Side View . . .* , p. 42.
8. Loguen, p. 162.
9. Henry Box Brown, p. 15.
10. Drew, *A North-Side View . . .* , p. 30.
11. Bibb, p. 44.
12. Thomas Jones, pp. 5–6.
13. Fisk, *Unwritten . . .* , pp. 43–44.
14. Steward, p. 97.
15. Bibb, p. 42.
16. Grandy, p. 25.
17. John Brown, p. 201.
18. Bruce, p. iv.
19. Drew, *A North-Side View . . .* , p. 73.
20. Ball, p. 379.
21. Drew, *A North-Side View . . .* , pp. 40–41.
22. John Brown, p. 158.

23. See Chapter 13.

24. William Wells Brown, pp. 17–18. See also Bruner, p. 16; Thompson, pp. 26, 35; and Campbell, p. 39.

25. Douglass, *Life and Times* . . . , p. 52.

26. Northup, pp. 224–25. Also Steward, p. 58.

27. Stroyer, pp. 62–63.

28. Steward, pp. 33–37.

29. Northup, pp. 248–49.

30. Fisk, *God* . . . , 198.

31. Quoted in Julius Lester, *To Be a Slave* (New York: Dell, 1968), p. 29. Many slaves probably thought of such open resistance as selfish as well as foolhardy. Not only were men needed to help care for and protect their families but such action placed the whole quarters under added scrutiny and possible retaliation. See Bibb, p. 79; Steward, pp. 33–38; Pennington, pp. 12–13; Henry Box Brown, pp. 38–40.

32. Douglass, *Life and Times* . . . , p. 81.

33. Bibb, p. 17. See also *Farmer's Register* (May, 1837), p. 32.

34. Ball, p. 298.

35. John Brown, p. 106.

Chapter 9

1. Most of the black informants use the word "family" to indicate the nuclear, blood-tied grouping of husband, wife, children, and sometimes grandparents and grandchildren. Although this was the ideal norm, as seen in the present chapter, the exigencies of slavery caused the creation of different forms. See Chapter 13.

2. Fisk, *Unwritten* . . . , p. 284.

3. Adeline Willis in Rawick, ed., Georgia, XIII (4), p. 162.

4. Lina Hunter in Rawick, ed., Georgia, XII (2), p. 266.

5. Allen, *Slave Songs*, p. 6.

6. Archer Alexander, *The Story of Archer Alexander From Slavery to Freedom, March 30, 1863* (Boston: Cupples, Upham & Company, 1885), p. 32. Alexander was born in Virginia but spent most of his slave life in Missouri.

7. Thompson, p. 48.

8. Steward, p. 126.

9. James Mars, p. 3.

10. Elijah Marrs, p. 11.

11. Fisk, *God* . . . , p. 161.

12. Ball, quoted in Blassingame, p. 102.

13. Ball, pp. 18–19.

14. Clarke, p. 22.

15. Northup, pp. 85–88. Similar references would take several pages. For but

a small sample see James Watkins, *Narrative of the Life of James Watkins, Formerly a Chattel in Maryland, United States* (Bolton, England: Kenyon and Abbott, 1852), pp. 6–8; Thompson, p. 16; Henry Brown, pp. 46–47; and Henson, *Truth . . .*, p. 11; WPA, *The Negro in Virginia,* p. 173; Grandy, p. 11; Drew, *A North-Side View . . .*, p. 198; Cade, p. 306.

16. Eileen Southern, *The Music of Black Americans: A History* (New York: W. W. Norton, 1971), p. 176.

17. W. W. Brown, p. 51.

18. Cade, p. 324.

19. John Brown, pp. 5–6.

20. WPA, *The Negro in Virginia*, p. 11.

21. Drew, *A North-Side View . . .*, p. 133.

22. Bibb, p. 56. In all Bibb returned to the slave South five times, being recaptured four times, in a fruitless attempt to bring his family away with him. He ceased his attempts only after learning that his wife had been living in forced concubinage with her master for three years.

23. Drew, *A North-Side View . . .*, pp. 52–53.

24. *Ibid.*, p. 81.

25. Ball, p. 466.

26. Pennington, pp. 12–13.

27. Bibb, p. 192.

28. Drew, *A North-Side View . . .*, p. 187.

29. Yetman, p. 291.

30. H. B. Holloway in Rawick, ed., Arkansas, IX (3), p. 288.

31. Jones, p. 30.

Chapter 10

1. Some slaves made a distinction between ghosts and witches. "Yuh know ghos an witches is diffunt. Witches is libin people and ghos is spirits uh duh dead." (WPA, Drums and Shadows, p. 6.) Most informants use the word "haunt," or "hant," interchangeably with spirit.

2. Stroyer, p. 54.

3. William Wells Brown, *My Shouthern Home; or, The South and Its People* 1880; rpt. (Upper Saddle River, New Jersey: Gregg Press, 1969), p. 68.

4. Ball, p. 260.

5. Douglass, *Life and Times . . .*, pp. 137–38.

6. Bibb, pp. 26–28.

7. Grimes, p. 15.

8. Abram Harris in Rawick, ed., Arkansas, IX (3), p. 174.

9. Yetman, p. 63.

10. Botkin, p. 39.

11. Kemble, p. 119.

12. Orland Armstrong, p. 250.

13. Botkin, p. 30.

14. Bruce, p. 52.

15. Stroyer, pp. 57–59. Stroyer adds that these things were always done at night "as it was the only time they could attend to such matters as concerned themselves" and that "these customs were among the negroes for their own benefit, for they did not consider it stealing when they took anything from their master."

16. Will Sheets in Rawick, ed., Georgia, XIII (3), p. 242. Also Cheney Cross in Rawick, ed., Alabama, VI, p. 98. Angie Garrett in Rawick, ed., Alabama, VI, p. 134.

17. Amanda McCray in Rawick, ed., Florida, XVII, p. 213.

18. Hughes, p. 108.

19. Josephine Anderson in Rawick, ed., Florida, XVII, pp. 8–9.

20. Mildred Heard in Rawick, ed., Georgia, XII (2), p. 168.

21. Doc Quinn in Rawick, ed., Arkansas, X (6), p. 7.

22. Ball, p. 265. The white Mrs. Telfair Hodgson says that on her father's Georgia plantation in the 1850's: "Negro graves were always decorated with the last article used by the departed, and broken pitchers, and broken bits of colored glass were considered even more appropriate than the white shells from the beach nearby. Sometimes they carved rude wooden figures like images of idols, and sometimes a patchwork quilt was laid upon the grave." Sarah H. Torian, ed., "Ante-Bellum and War Memories of Mrs. Telfair Hodgson," *Georgia Historical Quarterly*, XXVII (December, 1943), 352.

23. Botkin, p. 34.

24. Julia Bunch in Rawick, ed., Georgia XII (1), p. 158; Fisk, *Unwritten* . . . , pp. 39, 224; Jack Atkinson in Rawick, ed., Georgia, XII (1), p. 18; Alice Bradly, Georgia, XII (1), p. 119.

25. Ellis Kannon in Rawick, ed., Tennessee, XVI, p. 38.

26. Patsy Hyde in Rawick, ed., Tennessee, XVI, p. 34. See also Orland Armstrong, p. 251.

27. Fisk, *God* . . . , p. 159.

28. Drew, *A North-Side View* . . . , p. 60.

29. Fisk, *Unwritten* . . . , pp. 164–65.

30. Fisk, *God* . . . , pp. 3, 16, 20, 99.

31. Paul Radin, who as Research Professor of Anthropology at Fisk University guided A. P. Watson in his recording of the conversion experiences, writes: ". . . it was not so much the Negro who sought God as God who sought the Negro. The difficulty the latter experienced was how to recognize who was talking to him. In many instances the conversion experiences indicate quite clearly that God had literally to struggle with him, not to persuade him to give up his sins but to force him to be willing to express himself, to fulfill his mission, in other words to attain individuation. The sins would take care of themselves." Fisk, *God* . . . , p. viii.

32. *Ibid.*, p. 99.

33. *Ibid.*, p. 7.

34. *Ibid.*, p. 18.

35. Henry Brown, p. 18. Here once again we note the frequency with which the slaves combined their folk beliefs with the practice of Christianity.

36. Quoted in Genovese, *Roll, Jordan, Roll* . . . , p. 238.

37. Allen, *Slave Songs* . . . , p. 13.

38. *Ibid.*, p. 5.

39. *Ibid.*, p. 17.

40. Henry H. Mitchell writes: "Black tradition holds that the Holy Spirit does not follow white clocks. The Spirit must have its way, and whatever God does is right on. It is believed that the true Presence is intellectually as well as emotionally enlightening, and that it takes *time* for the Spirit to involve a congregation which must first be emptied of private concerns for mundane interests." Henry H. Mitchell, *Black Preaching* (New York: J. P. Lippincott, 1970), p. 107.

41. Mary Gladdy in Rawick, ed., Georgia, XII (2), pp. 26–27.

42. Botkin, p. 214.

43. Emoline Glasgow in Rawick, ed., South Carolina, II (2), p. 135.

44. Fannie Moore in Rawick, ed., North Carolina, XIV (2), p. 130.

45. Yetman, p. 13.

46. Cade, p. 331.

47. Allen, *Slave Songs* . . . , p. 71.

48. Minerva Lofton in Rawick, ed., Arkansas, IX (4), p. 265.

49. Wes Woods in Rawick, ed., Kentucky, XVI, p. 26.

50. Fisk, *God* . . . , p. 101.

51. *Ibid.*, p. 12.

52. WPA, *The Negro in Virginia*, p. 109.

53. *Ibid.*, p. 108.

54. Cordelia Jackson in Rawick, ed., South Carolina, III (3), p. 5. Jackson is commenting here on her perception of whites as outside of the religious fold.

55. Southern, p. 186.

56. Emma Fraser in Rawick, ed., South Carolina, II (2), p. 87.

57. W. W. Brown, *My Southern Home*, p. 68.

58. Linda Brent, *Incidents in the Life of a Slave Girl* (Boston: For the author), p. 109.

59. *Ibid.*, p. 108. See also G. W. Offley, *Narrative of the Life and Labors of the Reverend G. W. Offley, a Colored Man and Preacher, Written by Himself* (Hartford: By the author, 1860), p. 50; and Allen, *Slave Songs* . . . , p. 51.

60. Fisk, *God* . . . , p. 11.

61. *Ibid.*, p. 10. In an interesting passage Mary Banks, the white daughter of a Southern cotton planter, remarks that she never knew "one negro in whom this religious element was not strongly marked." Blacks, she continues, have a greater "intimacy with the 'Great Unseen.' I have often wished that with the white race He might be more of a living presence, and less an object to be adored at a distance, and in places set apart for worship." Banks, p. 2.

62. Botkin, p. 34.

63. William ´Webb, *History of William Webb, Composed by Himself* (Detroit: E. Hokstra, 1873), p. 5.

64. Sam Aleckson, p. 131.

65. Fisk, *God . . .* , p. 83.

66. Botkin, p. 38.

67. Allen, *Slave Songs . . .* , p. 55.

68. Fisk, *God . . .* , p. 22.

69. Allen, *Slave Songs . . .* , p. 15.

70. *Ibid.*, p. 73.

71. Brown, *Folklore . . .* , p. 46.

72. Fisk, *Unwritten . . .* , p. 166.

73. Allen, *Slave Songs . . .* , pp. 10–11.

Chapter 11

1. Genovese says that W. E. B. DuBois' estimate of five percent "is entirely plausible and may even be too low." Genovese, *Roll, Jordan, Roll . . .* , p. 563.

2. Yetman, p. 145.

3. Washington, p. 18.

4. Grandy, p. 36.

5. James Graham in Rawick, ed., Arkansas, IX (3), p. 70.

6. Drew, *A North-Side View . . .* , p. 97.

7. Thompson, p. 103–4. Thompson finishes the story by relating how his father gave Henry money to buy him a book, and how he finished this book, *Webster's Spelling Book,* and proceeded to the *Introduction to the English Reader.*

8. J. H. Curry in Rawick, ed., Arkansas, VIII (2), p. 84.

9. Marrs, p. 15.

10. Noah Davis, *A Narrative of the Life of Rev. Noah Davis, a Colored Man, Written by Himself, at the Age of Fifty-four* (Baltimore: John F. Wiishampel, Jr., 1859), p. 17; Fisk, *God . . .* , and Nat Turner, *The Confessions of Nat Turner, the Leader of the Late Insurrection in Southhampton, Va. As Fully Made to Thomas R. Gray, in the Prison where He Was Confined, and Acknowledged by Him to Be Such when Read before the Court of Southhampton: With the Certificate under the Seal of the Court Convened at Jerusalem, Nov. 5, for His Trial* (Baltimore: Thomas R. Gray, Lucas and Deaver, 1831), p. 147.

11. "Gate-eye" Fisher in Rawick, ed., Arkansas, VIII (2), p. 301.

12. Hughes, pp. 100–1.

13. Guion Griffie Johnson, *A Social History of the Sea Islands with Special Reference to St. Helena Island,* (Chapel Hill: University of North Carolina Press, 1930), p. 153.

14. Douglass, *Life and Times . . .* , p. 151.

15. W. E. Northcross in Rawick, ed., Alabama, VI, p. 300.

16. Steward, p. 82.

17. Davis, p. 17.

18. Douglass, *Life and Times* . . . , pp. 92–93.

19. Bibb, pp. 134–35.

20. Titus Byrnes in Rawick, ed., Florida, XVII, pp. 52–53.

21. Lewis and Milton Clarke, p. 104.

22. Leonard Black, *The Life and Sufferings of Leonard Black, a Fugitive from Slavery, Written by Himself* (New Bedford: Press of Benjamin Lindsey, 1847), p. 18.

23. Thompson, pp. 49–50.

24. Douglas Dorsey in Rawick, ed., Florida, XVII, pp. 95–96.

25. Yetman, p. 257.

26. Thomas Jones, p. 15.

27. *Ibid.,* pp. 20–21.

28. Steward, p. 83.

29. Douglass, *Life and Times* . . . , pp. 79–80.

30. Bruce, p. 86.

31. Douglass, p. 136.

32. Drew, *A North-Side View* . . . , p. 177.

33. *Ibid.,* p. 355.

34. *Ibid.,* p. 298.

35. Fisk, *Unwritten* . . . , p. 240.

36. Pennington, p. 56.

37. Willie Lee Rose, *Rehearsal for Reconstruction: The Port Royal Experiment* (New York: Vintage Books, 1964), p. 22.

38. *Ibid.,* p. 230.

39. *Ibid.,* p. 88.

40. W. E. B. DuBois, *Black Reconstruction* (New York: Harcourt, Brace, 1935), pp. 641–42.

Chapter 12

1. Some of the WPA informants do speak with a certain wistfulness of the times they had back on the old plantation, and some even of a desire to be back under slavery. Even most of these, however, do not deny that as slaves they longed for freedom.

2. Lane, p. 8.

3. Hughes, p. 100.

4. Clayborn Gantling in Rawick, ed., Florida, XVII, p. 142.

5. Laura Abromson in Rawick, ed., Arkansas, VIII (1), p. 9.

6. Thompson, pp. 37–38.

7. Willis Dukes in Rawick, ed., Florida, XVII, pp. 121–22.

8. Botkin, p. 121.

9. Drew, *A North-Side View* . . . , p. 35.

10. Steward, p. 107.

11. Drew, *A North-Side View* . . . , p. 270.

12. James Williams, *Life and Adventures* . . . , p. 11.

13. Allen, *Slave Songs* . . . , pp. 45–46.

14. Quoted in Blassingame, p. 72.

15. Tom Robinson in Rawick, ed., Arkansas, X (6), p. 64.

16. Douglass, *Life and Times* . . . , p. 156.

17. Hughes, p. 79.

18. Douglass, *Life and Times* . . . , p. 150. The notion that even those slaves who were treated well desired to be free is amply evidenced in the narratives. See Tom Wilcox in Rawick, ed., North Carolina, XV (2), p. 377.

19. Steward, p. 107.

20. Northup, p. 260.

21. Webb, p. 26.

22. J. Vance Lewis, pp. 8–9.

23. Henry Brown, pp. 31–32.

24. Aaron, p. 8.

25. See Douglass, *Life and Times* . . . , p. 208; Grandy p. 37; Olaudah Equiano, *The Interesting Narrative of the Life of Olaudah Equiano, or Gustavus Vasa, The African. Written by Himself* (London: Stationers Hall, 1789), p. 140. The end of slavery and the official conferring upon them of the title "freemen" did not, of course, end the black struggle for Freedom. In this vein, it has occurred to me that the black definition of Freedom may help explain why many of the WPA informants express the thought that many blacks were better off during slavery times. To the elderly black man or woman living in the South during the Depression, with little food or clothing, little security in terms of the future, and, most important, with most of their family dead or moved north, it must have seemed that emancipation ended more freedoms than it brought. Such a view is, of course, more illustrative of black life in the rural South of the 1930's than it is of life under slavery.

26. Alexander, pp. 47–48.

27. Henry Brown, p. 59

28. Thompson, pp. 75–76.

29. Webb, p. 7.

30. Isaac Mason, *Life of Isaac Mason as a Slave* (Worcester, Massachusetts: by the author, 1893), p. 31.

31. Leonard Black, p. 6.

32. Solomon Bayley, pp. 2–3.

33. Mason, p. 43.

34. Yetman, p. 17.

35. Hughes, p. 146.

36. Stroyer, p. 99.

37. Botkin, pp. 7–8. Many slaves, of course, also supported the Northern war effort with their deeds. See, for example, James M. McPherson, *The Negro's Civil War: How Negroes Felt and Acted During the War for the Union* (New York: Pantheon Books, 1965).

38. W. B. Allen in Rawick, ed., Georgia, XII (1), p. 13.
39. Botkin, p. 240.
40. Bruce, p. 103.
41. Laura Abromson in Rawick, ed., Arkansas, VIII (1), p. 9.
42. WPA, *The Negro in Virginia,* p. 210.
43. Harriet Gresham in Rawick, ed., Florida, XVII, pp. 160–61.
44. WPA, *The Negro in Virginia,* p. 212.
45. *Ibid.,* p. 211.

Conclusion to Part II

1. Rias Body in Rawick, ed., Georgia, XII(1), p. 89.
2. The significance of the absence of certain themes would be more apparent in a study which, unlike the present one, attempted to make comparisons of quarter culture with other cultures or with black culture in America at an earlier or later time. For instance, it would be highly illuminating to attempt to determine if the culture which slaves brought with them contained a similar absence of either male superiority or female dominance. It would also be of interest to attempt to analyze what happened to this aspect of slave culture, and to the themes themselves, in the century since emancipation.
3. W. W. Brown, pp. 85–89.
4. Bibb, pp. 36–38. See also, Craft, p. 27. Loguen, p. 41. The ambivalence of the quarter community towards those slaves who physically confronted white power can be understood, in part, by the tension between the themes of Freedom and antipathy to whites on the one hand and family and community on the other.
5. According to Opler a formalized expression of a theme "refers to activities, prohibitions of activities or references which have become fixed in time or place and to which everyone to whom they apply must respond without significant variation." Opler, *Themes as Dynamics . . . ,* p. 199.
6. *Ibid.,* p. 199.

Chapter 13

1. After being assigned to a quarter household by the plantation authorities, Ball proposed to the two heads of the house, Nero and his wife, "that whilst I should remain a member of the family, I would contribute as much towards its support as Nero himself; or, at least that I would bring all my earnings into the family stock, provided I might be treated as one of its members, and be allowed a portion of the proceeds of their patch or garden. This offer was very readily ac-

cepted, and from this time we constituted one community, as long as I remained among the field hands on this plantation." Ball, pp. 192–93.

The confusion and potential distortion which occurs when historians assume that a white definition is a sociological reality in another society is clearly demonstrated in the case of the slave family. Some historians like Ulrich Phillips and Robert Fogel and Stanley Engerman found the plantation organized in nuclear family units and expostulated on the one hand that the plantation trained amoral Africans well (Phillips, p. 343) and on the other that slaves as well as masters must have actively worked for this nuclear organization (Fogel and Engerman, pp. 126–44). Others, like E. Franklin Frazier, found stronger nuclear ties among house servants, skilled slaves, and town slaves, than among fieldhands. (E. Franklin Frazier, *The Negro Family in the United States,* Chicago: University of Chicago Press, 1939.) Still others like Stanley Elkins and Kenneth Stampp found strong nuclear ties missing altogether and concluded that this was what the plantation had done to the family organization of slaves. (Elkins, pp. 128–31; Stampp, pp. 340–49.) All, by applying a white norm to slave society, missed both the value which most slaves placed upon nuclear family ties and the different family patterns which slaves created in order to deal with the instability of the nuclear family in a white slave system which did not legally recognize it.

2. DeBow cites the example of a plantation of "fifty or sixty persons . . . from the descendants of a single female in the course of the lifetime of the original purchasers." See Bancroft, p. 87. On Georgia Baker's plantation "dere was a heep of Niggers . . . all of us was kin to one another. Grandma Becky and Grandpa Stafford was de fust slaves Marse Alec ever had, and dey sho had a passel of chillun." Rawick, ed., Georgia, XII (1), p. 44. Herbert Gutman cites several similar examples. Gutman, *The Black Family,* Part I.

3. Yetman, p. 112.

4. *Ibid.*, p. 125.

5. This is one verse of a song entitled "A Slave Mammy's Lullaby," recorded by Katie Sutton in Rawick, ed., Indiana, VI, p. 195.

6. Orland Armstrong, p. 58.

7. Allen, *Slave Songs . . .* , p. 60.

8. Fisk, *Unwritten . . .* , p. 115. See also Fisk, *God . . .* , p. 214.

9. Botkin, p. 113.

10. Shack Thomas in Rawick, ed., Florida, XVII, p. 338; Emily Mays in Rawick, ed., Georgia, XIII (3), p. 119; and Fisk, *Unwritten . . .* , p. 112.

11. Matilda Brooks in Rawick, ed., Florida, XVII, p. 48. Ball says that in place of soap slaves sometimes washed their clothes with "a very fine and unctious kind of clay, resembling fullers' earth, but of a yellow color, which was found on the margin of a small swamp near the house." Ball, p. 97.

12. Fisk, *Unwritten . . .* , p. 112.

13. Henry Green in Rawick, ed., Arkansas, IX (3), p. 97; Simeon Andrews in Rawick, ed., Florida, XVII, p. 12; and Fisk, *Unwritten . . .* , p. 46.

14. Doc Quinn in Rawick, ed., Arkansa, X (6), p. 8.

15. Robert Grinstead in Rawick, ed., Oklahoma, VII, pp. 125–26.
16. Harriet Cheatam in Rawick, ed., Indiana, VI, p. 54.
17. Austin Parnell in Rawick, ed., Arkansas, X (5), pp. 264–65.
18. Drew, *A North-Side View* . . . , p. 28.
19. Henson, *Truth* . . . , p. 10.
20. Fisk, *God* . . . , p. 146.
21. *Ibid.,* p. 98.
22. Campbell, p. 23.
23. Fannie Moore in Rawick, ed., North Carolina, XIV (2), p. 130.
24. Duncan Gaines in Rawick, ed., Florida, XVII, p. 135.
25. Washington, pp. 18–19. See also chapter on "Freedom."
26. Douglass, *Life and Times* . . . , p. 36.
27. Bruce, p. 67.
28. Yetman, p. 45.
29. Richard Crump in Rawick, ed., Arkansas, VIII (2), p. 63.
30. Yetman, p. 323.
31. Botkin, p. 175.
32. Fisk, *Unwritten* . . . , p. 284.
33. Fisk, *God* . . . , p. 216.
34. Cora Armstrong in Rawick, ed., Arkansas, VIII (1), p. 75.
35. Marriah Hines in Rawick, ed., Virginia, XVI, p. 29.
36. Jane Lassiter in Rawick, ed., North Carolina, XIV (2), p. 40 and Talley, *Negro Folk* . . . , p. 174. See also William Towns in Rawick, ed., Alabama, VI, p. 387 and Rachel Adams in Rawick, ed., Georgia, XII (1) p. 6.
37. Marrs, p. 11.
38. Fisk, *Unwritten* . . . , p. 51.
39. For a discussion of the difference between authoritative and authoritarian parental relationships see Kurt Danziger, *Socialization* (Baltimore: Penguin, 1971), pp. 83–84.
40. Bruner, p. 11.
41. Yetman, p. 302.
42. Loguen, pp. 128–29.
43. Grandy, p. 5.
44. Aunt Sally, p. 47.
45. Fisk, *Unwritten* . . . , p. 108.
46. Harrison Beckett in Rawick, ed., Texas, IV (1), p. 54.
47. Ball, p. 18.
48. Booker T. Washington, p. 17.
49. David Goodman Gullins in Rawick, ed., Georgia, XII (2), pp. 81–82.
50. Wash Ford in Rawick, ed., Arkansas, VIII (2), p. 324.
51. Thomas Jones, p. 31.
52. Duncan Gaines in Rawick, ed., Florida, XVII, p. 136.
53. Mary Biddle in Rawick, ed., Florida, XVII, p. 33.
54. Molly Ammond in Rawick, ed., Alabama, VI, p. 10.
55. Quoted in Genovese, p. 644.

56. Ball, p. 108.

57. *Ibid.*, p. 18.

58. Aunt Sally, p. 47.

59. Ida May Fluker in Rawick, ed., Arkansas, VIII (2), p. 322.

60. Newbell Niles Puckett, *Folk Beliefs of the Southern Negro* (Chapel Hill: University of North Carolina Press, 1926), p. 75.

61. Zenie Cauley in Rawick, ed., Arkansas, VIII (2), p. 4 and Ball, p. 190.

62. Lulu Jackson in Rawick, ed., Arkansas, IX (4), p. 19 and Frank Cannon in Rawick, ed., Arkansas, VIII (2), p. 1. Jackson says that to fix a gourd for drinking slaves would take the seeds out, boil the gourd, and then scrape it out and sun it.

63. Pennington, pp. 8–9.

64. Mittie Freeman in Rawick, ed., Arkansas, VIII (2), p. 348.

65. Louisa Adams in Rawick, ed., North Carolina, XIV (1), p. 3.

66. Yetman, p. 268.

67. Fisk, *Unwritten . . .* , p. 285.

68. Fisk, *God . . .* , p. 147. Rebecca Hooks in Rawick, ed., Florida, XVII, p. 175; Noah Davis, p. 17; and Isaac Williams, p. 62.

69. Yetman, p. 89.

70. Shack Thomas in Rawick, ed., Florida, XVII, p. 336.

71. Aleckson, pp. 61–62.

72. Ball, p. 18.

73. Randel Lee in Rawick, ed., Florida, XVII, p. 199.

74. Yetman, p. 13.

75. Adeline Hodges in Rawick, ed., Alabama, VI, p. 184.

76. Thompson, p. 48.

77. Davis, p. 10.

78. Stroyer, p. 21.

79. Garret Buster, *Brighter Sun. An Historical Account of the Struggle of a Man to Free Himself and His Family from Bondage. By his grandson, Green B. Buster* (New York: Pageant Press, 1945), p. 6.

80. Archer Alexander, pp. 19–24. Archer's father was sold when it was learned that at a prayer meeting "He had gone so far as to say that 'by the 'Claration of 'Dependence all men was ekal,' and that 'to trade in men and women, jes like hogs and horses, wasn't 'cordin' to gospel, nohow.' " p. 19.

81. Fisk, *God . . .* , p. 162.

82. W. H. Robinson, *From Log Cabin to the Pulpit* (Eau Claire, Wisconsin: 1913), p. 25.

83. Fredrika Bremer, *The Homes of the New World: Impressions of America*, Vol. 1 (New York: Harper & Brothers, 1853), pp. 251–52.

84. W. W. Brown, pp. 95–96.

85. Ball, pp. 16–23.

86. Roxy Pitts in Rawick, ed., Alabama, VI, p. 317.

87. Fisk, *God . . .* , p. 162.

88. Betty Guwn in Rawick, ed., Indiana, VI, p. 99.

89. Irella Walker in Rawick, ed., Texas, V (4), p. 123.

90. Margaret Nickerson in Rawick, ed., Florida, XVII, p. 253.

91. Oscar James Rogers in Rawick, ed., Arkansas, X (6), p. 70.

92. Lane, pp. 11–12. Aunt Sally, p. 59. Campbell, p. 39. Grandy, pp. 17–18. Orland Armstrong, pp. 266–68. Fisk, *Unwritten* . . . , pp. 2, 64, 285. Bill Austin in Rawick, ed., Florida, XVII, pp. 22–23.

93. John Collins in Rawick, ed., South Carolina, II (2), pp. 224–25.

94. Fisk, *God* . . . , p. 161.

95. See Genovese, *Roll, Jordan, Roll* . . . , p. 493. Interestingly enough, the myth of the typical fatherless slave family seems to have originated in the black sources themselves; in the well read autobiographies of Frederick Douglass, Henry Bibb, and William Wells Brown. "It is almost impossible," writes Bibb, "for slaves to give a correct account of their male parentage." Bibb, p. 14. Douglass writes: "A person of some consequence in civilized society, sometimes designated as father, was literally unknown to slave law and to slave practice." Douglass, p. 27. Brown relates that he knew little of his father and only learned his name by being told it by his mother. W. W. Brown, p. 13. It seems more than coincidental that all three were the biological sons of white men.

96. Mingo White in Rawick, ed., Alabama, VI, pp. 413–14.

97. Georgia Baker in Rawick, ed., Georgia, XII (1), p. 40.

98. Martha Colquitt in Rawick, ed., Georgia, XII (1), p. 243.

99. Callie Elder in Rawick, ed., Georgia, XII (1), p. 307.

100. Perry Sid Jemison in Rawick, ed., Ohio, XVI, pp. 50–51.

101. Austin Grant in Rawick, ed., Texas, IV (2), p. 84.

102. Parker, pp. 20–22.

103. Aleckson, p. 19.

104. Eliza White in Rawick, ed., Alabama, VI, p. 412.

105. Fannie Moore in Rawick, ed., North Carolina, XIV (2), pp. 134–35.

106. Eli Boyd in Rawick, ed., Florida, XVII, p. 40.

107. Davenport, Yetman, p. 7.

108. Phil Towns in Rawick, ed., Georgia, XIII (4), p. 37. Also Martha King in Rawick, ed., Oklahoma, VII, p. 169; and John Brown in Rawick, ed., Oklahoma, VII, pp. 24–25.

109. Orland Armstrong, p. 93.

110. Ball, pp. 38–39, 24.

111. Douglass, p. 30.

112. Ellen Briggs Thompson in Rawick, ed., Arkansas, X (6), pp. 309–314.

113. Dosia Harris in Rawick, ed., Georgia, XIII (2), p. 105.

114. Sylvia Witherspoon, Alabama, VI, p. 429. Sometimes, of course, the care given their younger siblings by older brothers and sisters was not the most attentive. See John Brown, p. 4.

115. Everett Ingram in Rawick, ed., Alabama, VI, p. 215. Fisk, *God* . . . , pp. 108–9. Henry Waldon, Rawick in ed., Arkansas, XI (7), p. 16.

116. Orland Armstrong, p. 76.

117. Charlie King in Rawick, ed., Georgia, XIII (3), p. 18.

118. Washington, pp. 21–22.

119. Pennington, p. 15.
120. Yetman, p. 237.
121. Loguen, p. 115.
122. Mack Brantley in Rawick, ed., Arkansas, VIII (1), p. 243.
123. Robert Anderson, p. 5.
124. William Parker, p. 158. Fisk, *God* . . . , pp. 112–14, 109. Fisk, *Unwritten* . . . , p. 217. Hughes, p. 24. Black, p. 22.
125. Fisk, *Unwritten* . . . , pp. 277, 283. Frank Gill in Rawick, ed., Alabama, VI, p. 150. A. J. Mitchell in Rawick, ed., Arkansas X (6), p. 103.

Chapter 14

1. Yetman, p. 72.
2. Tom Hawkins in Rawick, ed., Georgia, XII (?), p. 132.
3. Sally Murphy in Rawick, ed., Alabama, VI, p. 296.
4. Fisk, *Unwritten* . . . , p. 15.
5. Bert Mayfield in Rawick, ed., Kentucky, XVI, p. 15.
6. Hannah Davidson in Rawick, ed., Ohio, XVI, p. 29.
7. Callie Elder in Rawick, ed., Georgia, XII (1), p. 307.
8. Anna Parkes in Rawick, ed., Georgia, XIII (3), p. 159.
9. Katherine Eppes in Rawick, ed., Alabama, VI, p. 120.
10. Yetman, p. 63.
11. William Henry Towns in Rawick, ed., Alabama, VI, pp. 387–388.
12. Josephine Hamilton in Rawick, ed., Arkansas, IX (3), p. 134.
13. Frank Gill in Rawick, ed., Alabama, VI, p. 150.
14. Yetman, p. 279.
15. Botkin, p. 238.
16. Banks, pp. 175–76.
17. Dinah Perry in Rawick, ed., Arkansas, X (5), pp. 320–21. See also Mary Colbert in Rawick, ed., Georgia, XII (1), p. 221.
18. See Genovese, *Roll, Jordan, Roll* . . . , p. 506.
19. Fisk, *Unwritten* . . . , p. 15.
20. Robert Shepherd in Rawick, ed., Georgia, XIII (3), p. 249.
21. Acie Thomas in Rawick, ed., Florida, XVII, p. 328.
22. Julia Cole in Rawick, ed., Georgia, XII (1), p. 233.
23. Yetman, p. 260.
24. Tom Hawkins in Rawick, ed., Georgia, XII (2), p. 129.
25. Bruce, pp. 17–18.
26. Allen Johnson in Rawick, ed., Arkansas, IX (4), p. 64.
27. Silas Jackson in Rawick, ed., Maryland, XVI, p. 33.
28. Perry in Rawick, ed., Arkansas, X (5), p. 249.
29. Benny Dilliard in Rawick, ed., Georgia, XII (1), p. 290.
30. Yetman, pp. 205–6.

31. Lucindy Jurdon in Rawick, ed., Alabama, VI, p. 243.

32. Randel Lee in Rawick, ed., Florida, XVII, p. 197.

33. Watson, p. 7.

34. Jaspar Battle in Rawick, ed., Georgia, XII (1), p. 64. Shepherd in Rawick, ed., Georgia, XIII (3), p. 250. Yetman, p. 72.

35. Tom Hawkins in Rawick, ed., Georgia, XII (2), p. 129.

36. David Goodman Gullins in Rawick, ed., Georgia, XII (2), p. 87.

37. Acie Thomas in Rawick, ed., Florida, XVII, p. 328.

38. Aleckson, p. 48.

39. Campbell, p. 60.

40. Isaac Mason, p. 40.

41. Yetman, p. 202.

42. Douglass, *Life and Times* . . . , p. 153.

Chapter 15

1. Harriet Gresham in Rawick, ed., Florida, XVII, p. 159.

2. There were those sanctioned preachers who gained a black following, and sometimes even a white one. See, for example, William White, *The African Preacher. An Authentic Narrative by the Rev. William S. White, Paster of the Presbyterian Church, Lexington, Virginia* (Philadelphia: Presbyterian Board of Publication, 1849); Campbell, pp. 91–92; and Noah Davis, pp. 27–28. As noted throughout this chapter, however, when slaves gathered together in secret they desired a preacher who could not only speak with passion and perform with style but whose preaching delivered the message of what slaves felt was true Christianity.

3. Yetman, p. 337.

4. Botkin, p. 26.

5. Pet Frank in Rawick, ed., Mississippi, VII, p. 58.

6. Yetman, p. 335.

7. Cade, p. 330.

8. W. E. B. DuBois, *The Negro Church: A Social Study* (Atlanta, Georgia: Atlanta University Press, 1903), p. 5.

9. Henry Mitchell, *Black Preaching* (Philadelphia and New York: J. B. Lippincott Company, 1970), p. 36.

10. W. E. B. DuBois, *The Souls of Black Folks*, Crest rpt. (Greenwich, Conn.: Fawcett Publications, 1961), p. 141.

11. Yetman, p. 299.

12. Cade, p. 330.

13. Amanda McCray in Rawick, ed., Florida, XVII, p. 215.

14. Yetman, p. 53.

15. Cade, p. 33.

16. *Ibid.*, pp. 330–31.

17. Yetman, p. 13.

18. Fisk, *Unwritten . . .*, p. 162.

19. John Hunter in Rawick, ed., Arkansas, IX (3), p. 364. Rawick says that singing into pots is a custom of definite African origin. See Rawick, pp. 39–45.

20. James Reeves in Rawick, ed., Arkansas, X (6), p. 27A.

21. Cade, p. 329.

22. Yetman, p. 225.

23. Allen, *Slave Songs . . .* , p. 9.

24. *Ibid.*, p. 21.

25. For more on the use of songs see Chapter 16.

26. Mitchell, p. 101.

27. Both the white and the black sources give examples of exhorters who were allowed by plantation authorities to travel from plantation to plantation. Such men were careful to go easy on instruction and heavy on performance. If they preached too much white doctrine they lost their black followers; if they preached the concepts of true Christianity, they were sure to lose the privilege of openly preaching, or worse. Pennington recalls one such exhorter who used to travel fifty miles to voluntarily give his exhortations. "He could not read, and I never heard him refer to any Scripture, and state discourse upon any fundamental doctrine of the gospel; but he knew a number of 'spiritual songs' by heart, of these he would give two lines at a time very exact, and set and lead them himself; he would pray with great fervour, and his exhortations were among the most impressive I have heard." Pennington, p. 67. See also William Ward in Rawick, ed., Georgia, XIII (4), p. 129 and Harriet Gresham in Rawick, ed., Florida, XVII, p. 159.

28. As we have seen in the chapter on the theme of the reality and significance of the spirit world, most blacks under slavery believed that the feelings and ecstasy of true religion were too powerful to experience quietly and that their shouted expression left not only the soul satisfied but God satisfied as well. They believed that the harder you preached, prayed and sang, the harder it would be for God to resist your petition, or for the Holy Spirit to resist making his wondrous presence felt.

29. Isaac Williams, p. 67.

30. Cade, p. 329.

31. Anderson, pp. 25–26.

32. James L. Smith, *Autobiography of James L. Smith* (Norwich: Press of the Bulletin Company, 1881), p. 27.

33. Callie Williams in Rawick, ed., Alabama, VI, p. 427.

34. Battle, p. 9.

35. H. G. Spaulding, "Under the Palmetto," *Continental Monthly*, IV (August, 1863), 196–97.

36. Yetman, p. 263.

37. Allen, p. 52. To this song Mrs. Charles J. Bowen has added the note: "This

is sung at the breaking up of a meeting, with a general shaking of hands, and the name of him or her pronounced, whose hand is shaken; of course there is seeming confusion."

38. Henry Brown, pp. 23–24.

39. Allen, *Slave Songs* . . . , p. 74.

40. Isaac Williams, p. 66.

41. Yetman, p. 229.

42. Allen, *Slave Songs* . . . , p. 15.

43. Yetman, p. 92.

44. *Ibid.*, pp. 252–53.

45. Higginson, p. 44. To this information provided by Higginson, Genovese adds: "For the slaves of the eastern seaboard, and for many of the interior as well, graves had to be dug east-west, with the deceased's head to the west, for a man should neither sleep nor be buried with his head 'crossways uv de world.' The dead should not have to turn around when Gabriel blows his trumpet in the eastern sunrise. African burial customs lingered on in the Old South and in fact into the twentieth century, although by the end of the first decade of the nineteenth century the slaves had merged them with white and Indian customs to form new ones." Genovese, *Roll, Jordan, Roll* . . . , p. 198.

46. Ball, p. 265.

47. Bill Crump in Rawick, ed., North Carolina, XIV (1), p. 210.

48. Allen, *Slave Songs* . . . , p. 47. Rogers adds here: "These midnight 'wails' are very solemn to me, and exhibit the sadness of the present mingled with the joyful hope of the future."

49. Randolph, pp. 49–50.

50. Allen, *Slave Songs* . . . , p. 101.

51. Mary Jane Drucilla Davis in Rawick, ed., Arkansas, VIII (2), p. 124.

52. Fisk, *Unwritten* . . . , p. 57.

53. Yetman, p. 13.

54. Estella Jones in Rawick, ed., Georgia, XII (2), p. 350.

55. Mary Dickson Arrowood and T. F. Hamilton, "Nine Negro Spirituals, 1850–1861, from Lower South Carolina," *Journal of American Folklore,* XLI (October–December, 1928), 582.

56. Mingo White in Rawick, ed., Alabama, VI, p. 416.

57. Yetman, p. 37.

58. Amanda McCray in Rawick, ed., Florida, XVII, p. 215.

59. Mary Gladdy in Rawick, ed., Georgia, XII (2), pp. 26–27.

60. C. C. Jones, p. 126.

61. Mitchell, p. 111.

Chapter 16

1. Sterling Stuckey, "Through the Prism of Folklore: The Black Ethos in Slavery," *The Massachusetts Review,* 9 (1968), p. 419. Alan Lomax, *Folk Songs of North America* (Garden City, New York: Doubleday, 1960). Howard Thurmond, *Deep River: Reflections on the Religious Insights of Certain of the Negro Spirituals* (New York: Harper & Brothers, 1945). Sterling Brown, "Negro Folk Expression: Spirituals, Seculars, Ballads, and Work Songs," *Phylon, The Atlanta University Review of Race and Culture* (October, 1953), pp. 45–61. Orlando Patterson, "Rethinking Black History," *Harvard Educational Review,* Vol. 41, 3 (August, 1971). The present chapter is greatly indebted to the research and insights of these works.

2. T. W. Higginson, "Negro Spirituals," *Atlantic Monthly,* Vol. 19 (June, 1867), 693.

3. Quoted in Blassingame, pp. 50–51. Blassingame is here quoting from Nicholas Cresswell, *The Journal of Nicholas Cresswell, 1774–1777* (New York, 1924), pp. 17–19, and, William Faux, *Memorable Days in America* (London, 1823), pp. 77–78.

4. Quoted in Jeanette R. Murphy, "The Survival of African Music in America," *Popular Science Monthly,* LV (September, 1899), 662.

5. James Miller McKim, "Negro Songs," in Katz, ed., *Social Implications of Early Negro Music,* p. 2.

6. Yetman, pp. 113–14.

7. Higginson, "Negro Spirituals," pp. 692–93.

8. Hughes, p. 146.

9. Higginson, "Negro Songs," p. 692. Higginson writes that the negroes had been put in jail for singing this song at the outbreak of the Civil War. " 'We'll soon be free,' was too dangerous an assertion; and though the chant was an old one, it was no doubt sung with redoubled emphasis during the new events. 'De Lord will call us home,' was evidently thought to be a symbolic verse; for, as a little drummer-boy explained to me, showing all his white teeth as he sat in the moonlight by the door of my tent, 'dey tink *de Lord* mean for say *de Yankees*.' "

10. WPA, *The Negro in Virginia*, p. 211.

11. *Ibid.,* p. 212.

12. Southern, p. 179. Southern writes: "Each plantation had its own repertory of worksongs, which grew out of the work activities of the plantation." The above example "was sung in a woods, where hundreds of slaves, paired off in twos in front of the trees, 'marked the blows by the song.' "

13. Quoted in Thomas W. Talley, *Negro Folk Rhymes: Wise and Otherwise* (New York: The Macmillan Company, 1922), pp. 23–24.

14. Allen, *Slave Songs . . . ,* p. 68.

15. Marshall Butler in Rawick, ed., Georgia, XII (1), p. 164.

16. Fisk, *Unwritten . . . ,* p. 118.

17. Brent, p. 180.

18. Talley, p. 88. Talley adds to this song the note: "The story went among Negroes that a runaway slave husband returned every night, and knocked on the

window of his wife's cabin to get food. Other slaves having betrayed the secret that he was still in the vicinity, he was sold in the woods to a slave trader at reduced price. This trader was to come next day with bloodhounds to hunt him down. On the night after the sale, when the runaway slave husband knocked, the slave wife pinched their baby to make it cry. Then she sang the above song (as if singing to the baby), so that he might, if possible, effect his escape."

19. Douglass, *Life and Times* . . . , p. 159. Douglass writes that to himself and his friends who were planning an escape the North was their Canaan. "On the lips of some it meant the expectation of a speedy summons to a world of the spirit, but on the lips of our company it simply meant a speedy pilgrimage to a free state, and deliverance from all the evils and dangers of slavery." *Ibid.,* pp. 159–60.

20. Bradford, p. 28. Harriet Tubman is said to have sung this song to announce to the other slaves of her quarters her impending escape.

21. Yetman, p. 335.

22. Fisk, *God Struck Me Dead* . . . , p. 171.

23. Botkin, p. 146.

24. Ball, pp. 200–01.

25. Alan Lomax, "Folk Song Style," *The American Anthropologist*, Vol. 61, No. 6 (December, 1959), 930–31. To the performance ingredients of black singers listed by Lomax, Harold Courlander adds that many black song performances contain humming or "moaning and groaning passages," the softening of various ultimate consonants to produce a humming effect, and various muted sounds which produce a "buzzing effect." Harold Courlander, *Negro Folk Music, U.S.A.* (New York: Columbia University Press, 1960), pp. 24–29. Though both Courlander and Lomax are referring to twentieth-century black music, Lomax himself argues that folksinging, "an art so deeply rooted in the security patterns of the community should not, in theory, be subject to rapid change, and in fact this seems to be the case. Musical style appears to be one of the most conservative of culture traits." Lomax, p. 930.

26. Hannah Davidson in Rawick, ed., Ohio, XVI, p. 28. Davidson was born in 1852 as a slave on a large Kentucky plantation of between 30 and 35 slave families.

27. Courlander, p. 27.

28. Emma M. Backus, "Folk Tales from Georgia," *Journal of American Folklore*, XLVIII (January-March, 1900), 32.

29. Sarah Byrd in Rawick, ed., Georgia, XII (1), p. 170. Fisk, *Unwritten* . . . , p. 131. Scarborough, p. 102. Lucindy Jurdon in Rawick, ed., Alabama, VI, p. 243. Betty Curlette says that some slaves made their own banjos. "Take a bucket or pan and a long strip of wood. Three horsehairs twisted made the base string. Two horsehairs twisted made the second string. One horsehair twisted made the fourth and the fifth string was the fine one, it was not twisted at all but drawn tight. They were all bees waxed." Betty Curlette in Rawick, ed., Arkansas, VIII (2), p. 81. Isaac Williams writes: "We generally made our own banjos and fiddles, and I had a fiddle that was manufactured out of a gourd, with horsehairs and a

bow made out of the same material. If you put plenty of rosin on the strings, it would compare favorably with an ordinary violin and make excellent music. When we made a banjo we would first of all catch what we called a ground hog, known in the north as a woodchuck. After tanning his hide it would be stretched over a piece of timber fashioned like a cheese box, and you couldn't tell the difference in sound between that homely affair and a handsome store bought one." Isaac Williams, p. 62. Hammett Dell describes how he made quills: "I took cane cut four or six made whistles then I tuned 'em together and knit them together in a row . . . like a mouth harp you see. Another way get a big long cane cut holes long down to the joint, hold your fingers over the different holes and blow." Hammett Dell in Rawick, ed., Arkansas, VIII (2), p. 141.

30. James Southall in Rawick, ed., Oklahoma, VII, p. 308.

31. Sterling A. Brown, Arthur P. Davis, and Ulysses Lee, eds., *The Negro Caravan* (New York: The Citadel Press, 1941), p. 439.

32. Yetman, p. 192.

33. Robert Solomon in Rawick, ed., Arkansas, X (6), p. 208.

34. Adelaide Vaughn in Rawick, ed., Arkansas, XI (7), p. 9.

35. Brown, Davis, and Lee, *The Negro Caravan*, p. 439.

36. Lomax, *The Folk Songs of North America*, p. 475.

37. For numerous examples of the attitudes and values expressed in the songs of the quarter community see each of the chapters in Part II of the present study.

38. Langston Hughes and Arna Bontemps, eds., *The Book of Negro Folklore* (New York: Dodd, Mead & Company, 1958), p. ix.

39. Interestingly enough, they seemed to suggest nothing of the sort to white listeners. "While masters of slaves went to some length to get rid of tribal languages and some tribal customs, like certain practices of sorcery, they accepted the animal stories as a harmless way to ease the time or entertain the master's children. That the folk tales of these Negro slaves were actually projections of personal experiences and hopes and defeats in terms of symbols appears to have gone unnoticed." Hughes and Bontemps, p. viii.

40. Zora Neale Hurston says that "Jack or John (not John Henry) is the great culture hero in Negro folk-lore. He is like Daniel in Jewish folk-lore, the wish-fulfillment hero of the race. The one who, nevertheless, or in spite of laughter, usually defeats Ole Massa, God and the Devil. Even when Massa seems to have him in a hopeless dilemma he wins out by a trick." Zora Neale Huston, *Mules and Men* (New York: Harper & Row, 1935), p. 305. Elsewhere Ms. Huston writes that John stories, unlike the animal stories, were never told to whites. She adds that "there is no established picture of what sort of looking-man this John de Conquer was. To some he was a big, physical-looking man like John Henry. To others, he was a little, hammered down low built man like the Devil's doll-baby." Zora Neal Huston, "High John de Conquer," in Hughes and Bontemps, pp. 94–96.

41. Quoted in Blassingame, p. 59.

42. For examples of such stories see pages 94–100, 230–233.

43. Fisk, *Unwritten . . .* , p. 16.

44. Howard W. Odum, "Religious Folk-Songs of the Southern Negroes," *The American Journal of Religious Psychology and Education,* Vol. 3 (July, 1909), 5.

45. Whatever the merit or demerits of the thesis that white folk music and black folk music are similar in origin and textual content, the importance of the total song experience is often overlooked. The meaning of even identical texts would be different for poor whites, rich planters, and black members of the quarter community. Furthermore, neither the white or the black sources give credence to the idea that whites and blacks performed their songs and stories similarly. Lomax lists the following differences in the styles of white folk singing compared to the list of black folksinging ingredients given on pages 215–216. Lomax writes that white folksinging is:

Solo voiced.

The group sits and listens in silence, sometimes sings in poor unison on refrains, has to be taught harmony by a teacher.

The body is held tensely, as the singer sits or stands stiffly erect. The head is often thrown far back.

The singing expression is mask-like and withdrawn, normally, and agonized on high notes.

The voice is rigidly pitched, somewhat higher than the normal speaking tone, confined to a limited range of vocal color; it is often harsh, hard, nasal—the ideal being a pure violin-like tone with which the singer can make ornaments on the melody.

Tunes are extended, ornamented, considered as units; fragmentation and excessive variation are disapproved of. Simple rhythms, which sometimes wander in conformity to the demands of the text.

Texts normally dominate the song. Strict stanzaic structures. Memory slips source of embarrassment. Precise repetition the desired trait.

Lomax, "Folk Song Style . . . ," pp. 930–31.

46. Lomax, "Folk Song Style . . . ," p. 929. Lomax adds: "Thus from the point of view of its social function, the primary effect of music is to give the listener a feeling of security, for it symbolizes the place where he was born, his earliest childhood satisfactions, his religious experience, his pleasure in community doings, his courtship and his work—any or all of these personality-shaping experiences."

Chapter 17

1. See Stroyer, pp. 57–59; Campbell, pp. 125–27; and Orland Armstrong, pp. 160–63.

2. Yetman, p. 260.

3. WPA, *The Negro in Virginia*, p. 75.

4. Josephine Bacchus in Rawick, ed., South Carolina, II (1), p. 24. Although white doctors were called in by plantation authorities in cases of serious sickness, most quarter slaves displayed a strong skepticism towards white doctors and their common practices of bleeding and freezing. The success of many of these slave cures was learned by whites who sometimes incorporated them into their own medical practices or went, themselves, to visit slave doctors. See Genovese, *Roll, Jordan, Roll . . .* , pp. 224–28.

5. Dellie Lewis in Rawick, ed., Alabama, VI, p. 256.

6. Yetman, p. 47.

7. *Ibid.*, pp. 286–87.

8. For several examples of conjurors and their power among quarter slaves see pages 119–20.

9. Sarah Burke in Rawick, ed., Ohio, XVI, p. 16.

10. Bruce, p. 99.

11. Drew, *A North-Side View . . .* , pp. 141–42.

12. Douglass Dorsey in Rawick, ed., Florida, XVII, pp. 97–98.

13. WPA, *The Negro in Virginia*, p. 149.

14. *Ibid.*, p. 44.

15. Rebecca Hooks in Rawick, ed., Florida, XVII, p. 176.

16. Marrs, p. 17.

17. Victoria McMullen in Rawick, ed., Arkansas, X (5), p. 5.

18. Benjamin Russell in Rawick, ed., South Carolina, III (4), pp. 52–53.

19. WPA, *The Negro in Virginia*, p. 156.

20. Northup, p. 226.

21. James Williams, *Narrative . . .* , p. 66. Eugene Genovese argues that the drivers were forced to mediate between the master and the quarters without being able to participate in their own separate group as did many drivers in the Caribbean. Thus from the point of view of the historian and perhaps from their viewpoint "They were men between." Genovese, *Roll, Jordan, Roll . . .* , pp. 378–79. From the point of view of the quarter community, however, no such ambiguity could be tolerated. Most quarters demanded evidence that the driver felt himself primarily a member of, and responsible to, the quarter community, or he was severely ostracized. See Thomas Goodwater in Rawick, ed., South Carolina, II (2), p. 166; Josiah Henson, p. 48, and Orland Armstrong, pp. 218–19.

22. Botkin, p. 11.

23. WPA, *The Negro in Virginia*, pp. 65–66.

24. Hannah Crasson in Rawick, ed., North Carolina, XIV (1), p. 191.

25. Botkin, pp. 56–57.

26. For some examples of slaves who played the role of the trickster see pages 94–101.

27. Willis Dukes in Rawick, ed., Florida, XVII, pp. 121–22.

28. Douglass, *Life and Times* . . . , pp. 50–51.

29. Loguen, pp. 201–3.

30. Lila Nicholas in Rawick, ed., North Carolina, XIV (2), p. 149.

31. Charity Morris in Rawick, ed., Arkansas, X (5) pp. 149–50.

32. Bruner, p. 16.

33. Thompson, p. 35.

34. *Ibid.*, pp. 35–37.

35. Roberts, p. 34. Often, of course, other slaves displayed a marked ambivalence towards these rebels, especially if their actions endangered the welfare of their families or of other quarter members. The point here, however, is that whatever their status in the community they presented one more alternative role model which quarter children could follow or reject according to their own instincts and personalities.

This understanding of how the quarter community chose its leaders and other role models belies the currently in vogue "significant individuals" approach to black history. Such an approach has been championed most recently by Fogel and Engerman and has won wide acceptance in the public school system. Its focus upon famous black individuals, be they war heroes, mathematicians, poets, surgeons, athletes, businessmen, or entertainers may be inspiring in the arena of what individual men and women are capable of achieving under even the most oppressive of conditions but it does not necessarily add to, and may even distort, our understanding of the cultural experiences, and motivating factors of other black people. Indeed, the isolation of Crispus Atticus, Benjamin Banneker, Phyllis Wheatley, and even Nat Turner, reinforces the values of the larger American society which has always adulated the independent achievements of the enterprising and heroic individual more than it illuminates the values and attitudes of many slaves. When Fogel and Engerman hold up as the true heroes of the slave population Leven, the faithful, true, honest, and faultless overseer of a Louisiana plantation who oversaw his master's plantation and "done much better than any white man ever done here" or Aham, the enterprising Alabama fieldhand whose sale of peaches, apples, and cotton enabled him to accumulate "enough capital over the years so that in 1860 he held notes on loans totaling over $2,400," and offer them as the leaders "in shaping the patterns of black culture," they are using men who embody the values of the larger society to speak for a people whose own values were not nearly so individualistic or self-seeking. (Fogel and Engerman, pp. 40, 77, 152, 260.) The quarter community had other criteria in choosing those who they felt deserving of becoming role models for their children. At the very least, they would have asked of Banneker, Wheatley, Aham and Leven whether or not they provided for their families, identified with and supported their quarter communities, shared their knowledge, poems, skills, position, and money with other slaves.

36. Fisk, *Unwritten* . . . , p. 256.

37. Fisk, *God . . .* , p. 177.

38. Yetman, p. 9.

39. Easter Brown in Rawick, ed., Georgia, XII (1), p. 136.

40. Fisk, *Unwritten . . .* , p. 187.

41. Botkin, p. 121.

42. James Bolton in Rawick, ed., Georgia, XII (1), p. 99.

43. Sarah Byrd in Rawick, ed., Georgia, XII (1), p. 170.

44. Anderson, pp. 30–31.

45. Northup, p. 219.

46. Campbell, p. 22.

47. Fisk, *Unwritten . . .* , p. 8.

48. WPA, *The Negro in Virginia,* p. 95.

49. Fisk, *Unwritten . . .* , p. 137.

50. Steward, pp. 29–30.

51. Botkin, p. 46.

52. Ball, p. 202.

53. Mary Colbert in Rawick, ed., Georgia, XII (1), p. 221.

54. See pages 95–96, 109.

55. Grandy, p. 24.

56. Yetman, p. 289.

57. Grandy, p. 32.

58. Fisk, *Unwritten . . .* , p. 245.

59. *Ibid.,* p. 97.

60. Yetman, p. 49.

61. Leah Garret in Rawick, ed., Georgia, XII (2), pp. 14–15.

62. Drew, *A North-Side View . . .* , p. 53.

63. Andrew Jackson, *Narrative and Writings of Andrew Jackson of Kentucky Containing an Account of His Birth and Twenty-Six Years of His Life While a Slave. Narrated by Himself, Written by a Friend* (Syracuse: Daily and Weekly Star Office, 1847) p. 9

64. Phillips, *American Negro Slavery . . .* , p. 296.

65. See pages 120–21.

66. Orland Armstrong, p. 162.

67. See for example Willis Cofer in Rawick, ed., Georgia, XII (1), p. 20; Henry Clay in Rawick, ed., Indiana, VI, p. 139; Phil Towns in Rawick, ed. in Georgia, XIII (4), p. 39. Fisk, *Unwritten . . .* , p. 12.

68. WPA, *The Negro in Virginia,* pp. 81–83.

69. *Ibid.,* p. 76.

70. William Green, *Narrative Events in the Life of William Green, Formerly a Slave* (Springfield, Massachusetts: Guernsey, 1853), p. 9.

71. Ball, p. 306.

72. Mandy Lewis in Rawick, ed., Alabama, VI, p. 251.

73. Yetman, p. 71.

74. Anderson, p. 31.

75. Paine, pp. 142–43.

76. See pages 67–68.

77. Yetman, p. 136.

78. Katherine M. Jones, *The Plantation South* (New York: Bobbs-Merrill, 1957), p. 73.

79. Daniel Dowdy in Rawick, ed., Oklahoma, VII, p. 78.

80. Hal Hutson in Rawick, ed., Oklahoma, VII, p. 146.

81. Clarke, p. 82.

82. Bruce, p. 86.

83. Yetman, p. 17.

84. Conway, p. 112.

85. Washington, pp. 19–20.

Conclusion to Part III

1. Campbell, p. 18.

2. Douglass, *Life and Times* . . . , p. 208.

3. H. C. Bruce, p. 76. Writing of conditions in the eighteenth century, Equiano drew the following conclusion after witnessing the torture, robbery, and kidnapping of free persons of color: "Hitherto I had thought slavery only dreadful, but the state of a free negro appeared to me now equally so at least, and in some respects even worse, for they are universally insulted and plundered, without the possibility of redress. . . . In their situation is it surprising that slaves, when mildly treated should prefer even the misery of slavery to such a mockery of freedom?" Equiano, p. 140.

4. Hall, Vol. 3, p. 191.

5. Robert Anderson, p. 31.

6. Marrs, p. 11.

7. The assumption by Southern whites that what they taught was necessarily internalized by their slaves can be compared with the assumption on the part of far too many historians that what whites did to slaves is the sole explanation needed for what slaves became. One cannot assume that because "the etiquette of plantation life removed even the honorific attributes of fatherhood from the negro male," for American slaves the roles of husband and father "had virtually no meaning," "a meaningful relationship between fathers and sons was not possible," "the only real father-figure on the plantation was the master," and "the psychological implication for the young boy growing up in such a system should be obvious." (Elkins, pp. 136, 142.)

A vivid example of the ability of slaves to make their own use of white teaching is the case of Frederick Douglass when his master tried to impress upon him the conviction that learning to read and write would make him an unfit slave. See Chapter 12.

Chapter 18

1. The crux of total institution theory is that total institutions are able to create significant attitudinal readjustment in people by separating them from the world—the people and institutions—which gave rise to, and molded, at least in part, their pre-entrance attitudes and values. Thus Erving Goffman, perhaps the leading analyst of total institutions, writes: "A total institution may be defined as a place where a large number of like-situated individuals, cut off from the wider society for an appreciable period of time, together lead an enclosed, formally administered round of life." (Erving Goffman, *Asylums: Essays on the Social Situation of Mental Patients and Other Inmates* [Garden City, N.Y.: Anchor Books, 1961], p. xiii.) Incompatible with total institutions is continued membership in noninstitutional primary groups, like the family, where initial attitudes were formed; continued contact with the world outside the institution; participation in ceremonies, particularly those of a religious nature not controlled by institutional authorities. (For a discussion of this point as related to concentration camps see Eugen Kogon, *The Theory and Practice of Hell* [New York: Farrar, Straus, 1946], p. 14.) Equally important to total institution theory is the institution's willingness and ability to become the sole source of the inmate's material and psychological rewards and punishments and its skill in crushing those inmates whose behavior varies from that prescribed by institutional rules and covert behavior norms.

Stanley Elkins, who began the trend among historians of classifying the plantation as a total institution, comparing it in his now famous paradigm with the Nazi concentration camp, argues that these conditions were, in fact, a reality for most plantation slaves. By asserting that slaves were torn from their African environment and, after the brutal shock of the middle passage, forced to enter a closed institution where they were effectively cut off from contact with the outside world, while at the same time being denied participation in institutions of their own creation and control, including for all extents and purposes the family, Elkins justifies his comparison and paves the way for an explanation of what he sees as "the infantilized slave personality." (Elkins, pp. 81–139. For a discussion of the plantation as compared with other total institutions, as well as for a general critique of Elkins' theory and approach, see Ann J. Lane, ed., *The Debate Over Slavery: Stanley Elkins and His Critics* [Urbana: University of Illinois Press, 1971.])

However, despite the originality of his sociological comparison, Elkins got some of his facts wrong. Historians have been able to amply demonstrate that the plantation was never the closed institution that Elkins suggests and that slaves, especially those in the quarters, had available to them any number of black role models. Furthermore, by the 1830's all but a very few slaves had been born and raised in the American South. Though many had been sold at least once, most had experienced no shock of separation from family and community and nearly all maintained membership in a larger slave community which, wherever the slave went in the South, enabled him or her to maintain association with familiar black institutions and helped to sustain the themes of the quarter community.

321

2. When studied by Kluckhohn and Leighton, the Navaho comprised the largest Indian tribe in the United States, numbering about 55,000. Their research was part of a larger Indian Education Project undertaken jointly by the Committee on Human Development of the University of Chicago and the United States Office of Indian Affairs. The central aim of the Kluckhohn and Leighton study was to "supply the background needed by the administrator or teacher who is to deal effectively with the People [the Navaho] in human terms." (Clyde Kluckhohn and Dorthea Leighton, *The Navaho* [Cambridge: Harvard University Press, 1948], pp. xix.) In their own language Navahos refer to themselves as "diné," the People.

3. Kluckhohn and Leighton, p. 28.

4. Dorthea Leighton and Clyde Kluckhohn, *Children of the People* (Cambridge: Harvard University Press, 1947), p. 6. This book is a companion volume to *The Navaho*. "Each book is a separate study, though the two supplement each other. *The Navaho* deals primarily with the situational and cultural context. *Children of the People* deals primarily with the psychological end-product in the individual." *Ibid.*, p. viii.

5. *Ibid.*, p. 48. See also, *The Navaho*, p. 63.

6. From his observations of the Oglala Sioux of the Pine Ridge Reservation located in the southeast corner of South Dakota Erik Erikson came to similar conclusions. "In this respect two elements of Sioux education seem especially apt to prevent the dangerous accumulation of ambivalent tensions: If every maternal aunt is a 'mother,' and every paternal uncle a 'father,' and if short and long visits with them are the rule, then the tension from the ambivalent fixation on the parents most probably cannot accumulate to the dangerous point which is often reached in our narcissistic use of the one-family system of self-chosen prisons. . . . But more important, three quarters of the Sioux education was introduced at a time when the child was able to receive it from the older children rather than from the parents: example makes less ambiguous followers than commands do." Erik Homburger Erikson, "Observation on Sioux Education," *Journal of Psychology*, Vol. 7 (1939), p. 146.

7. Leighton and Kluckhohn, *Children . . .* , p. 6.

8. Kluckhohn and Leighton, *The Navaho*, p. 72.

9. *Ibid.*, p. 54.

10. Leighton and Kluckhohn, *Children . . .* , p. 39.

11. *Ibid.*, p. 41. The tests given to 211 Navahos between the ages of six and eighteen included: the Arthur Point Performance Scale, the Goodenough Draw-A-Man Test, the Stewart Emotional Response Test, the Bavelas Moral Ideology Test, Free Drawings, a modification of Murray's Thematic Apperception Test, and the Rorschach Psychodiagnostic Test.

12. Kluckhohn and Leighton, *The Navaho*, p. 84.

13. Bruner writes that Lone Hill has never been a closed, self-sufficient society since it was established by the Indian Bureau in the last decade of the nineteenth century. The people of Lone Hill live in a culture that is a mixture of the culture of their ancestors, local white, mass American, and pan-Indian cultures. "Viewed

historically, contemporary Indian culture is mixed. It consists of automobiles from Detroit, dances from the Cheyenne, medicine bundles from the Mandan, and a language from the Hidatsa. From the perspective of some individuals who share it, this mixed culture is perfectly consistent. No person in Lone Hill today knows how to stalk buffalo, scalp a Sioux, or shape a stone arrowhead. With the exception of a few old people, no one in Lone Hill had ever lived in a culture in which these activities were performed. Our task is to understand how groups of individuals in Lone Hill come to regard and participate in that historically mixed but contemporary functioning Indian culture." Edward M. Bruner, "Primary Group Experience and the Processes of Acculturation," *American Anthropologist* 58 (1956), 606–607. See also, Edward M. Bruner, "Cultural Transmission and Cultural Change," *Southwestern Journal of Anthropology,* 12 (1956), 191–99.

14. Concerning his choice of the give-away dance as his acculturation criteria, Bruner writes: "There are many superficial criteria that could be selected to divide the population of Lone Hill into groups differing in degree of acculturation, but I prefer the one that has an essential connection to the Indian value system. One well known basic value that contrasts sharply with our general American ethic is the Indian value of generosity. This difference has a readily observable behavioral manifestation—participation in the Indian ceremonial dances. The Indian 'give-away' dance is now a secular affair, featuring Indian songs and dances and the giving of war bonnets, horses, cattle, blankets, and money as gifts to prescribed relatives, distinguished visitors, societies, and the needy. It is one of the few remaining public gatherings in Lone Hill where generosity and other Indian values are expressed, reaffirmed and maintained," Bruner, "Primary Group Experience . . . ," p. 607.

15. *Ibid.,* p. 608. Bruner notes that "The presence of a white model in the nuclear family through marriage is a cultural factor, and it should not be confused with degree of blood, a biological factor. The grandfather of one woman in Lone Hill was a white man who came up the Missouri on a steamboat, stayed a few years, and then left for parts unknown. He produced an undetermined number of children by different Indian women, but all his children were raised in Indian homes. The only cultural transmission from this white man is that some of his known descendants suspect that he may have been Irish and they jokingly celebrate St. Patrick's Day in his honor. His descendants have not had a white model despite their one-fourth degree of white blood." Bruner, "Primary Group Experience . . . ," p. 609.

16. *Ibid.,* p. 611.

17. *Ibid.,* p. 612. For a similar conclusion concerning the Sioux Indians see Erikson, p. 124. Erikson writes: "This, it seems, is the most astonishing single fact to be investigated: Indian children can live for years, without open rebellion or any signs of inner conflict between two standards which are incomparably further apart than those of any two generations or two classes in our culture."

18. Bruner, "Primary Group Experience . . . ," p. 614.

19. *Ibid.,* p. 615. "Acculturated Indians," according to Bruner, "actively seek to increase their interaction with middle class whites, as they need their approval

and support. White people tend to accept the acculturated Indian because he behaves in accordance with the middle class ethic and is docile in his relations to whites. Almost without exception, when whites make their infrequent trips to Lone Hill they visit at the home of a handful of acculturated families. As a consequence, the unacculturated Indians are further isolated from white contact in the village." *Ibid.,* p. 616.

20. *Ibid.,* p. 616.

21. *Ibid.,* p. 30.

22. Peter L. Berger and Thomas Luckmann, *The Social Construction of Reality: A Treatise in the Sociology of Knowledge* (New York: Anchor Books, 1966), p. 130. See also George Herbert Mead, *Mind, Self, and Society.* (Chicago: University of Chicago Press, 1934), p. 138. Although students of culture and personality disagree sharply about the nature of the enculturation/socialization process, there is general agreement that the initial intercourse which a child has with the significant others of his family and community, in which he begins to construct his first understanding of himself and the nature of the world in which he lives, has great, and to some determining, influence upon his personality as well as his values, attitudes, and understandings. See Anthony F. C. Wallace, "Individual Differences and Cultural Uniformities," *American Sociological Review,* 17 (1952) 748–49.

Primary group is used in the sense proposed by Charles Horton Cooley. In a letter to Frederick Clow, Cooley wrote: "The primary group is simply an *intimate* group, the intimacy covering a considerable period and resulting in a habitual sympathy, the mind of each being filled with a sense of the mind of the others, so that the group as a whole is the chief sphere of the social self for each individual in it—of emulation, ambition, resentment, loyalty, etc." Frederick Clow, "Cooley's Doctrine of Primary Groups," *American Journal of Sociology,* 25 (1919), 327.

23. See Dennis H. Wrong, "The Oversocialized Conception of Man in Modern Society," *The Sociological Perspective,* ed. Scott G. McNall, Second Edition (Boston: Little, Brown and Company, 1971), pp. 120–32. Wrong writes: ". . . in psychoanalytic terms to say that a norm has been internalized, or introjected to become part of the superego, is to say no more than that a person will suffer guilt feelings if he fails to live up to it in his behavior. . . . To Freud, man is a *social* animal without being entirely a *socialized* animal. His very social nature is the source of conflicts and antagonisms that create resistance to socialization by the norms of any of the societies which have existed in human nature" (pp. 125, 130).

24. For some examples of such house servants, see the narratives of John Anderson, Robert Anderson, Israel Campbell, and William Hayden. See also: Yetman, pp. 9, 60–65, 170–72; Botkin, pp. 83–89; Eppes p. 74; and Smedes, p. 60. It should be noted that most whites, planters and travelers, like the white visitors to Lone Hill, associated almost exclusively with such house servants. One searches in vain through the diaries, letters, and plantation records of whites for references to fieldhands as anything more than a largely undistinguished mass. See Blassingame, pp. 200–1.

25. Although the sources are vague on this point, they suggest that a high proportion of such house servants either lived on plantations where they were

allowed frequent contact with the slave quarters, as with young slaves who worked in the house during the day and returned to their parents' cabin in the quarters at night, or were men and women who had been raised in the quarters becoming house servants only after their primary enculturation within the quarter community. See, for example, the narratives of Austin Steward and Frederick Douglass; also Simon Phillips in Rawick, ed., Alabama, VI, p. 312; WPA, *The Negro in Virginia,* p. 44, and Fisk, *Unwritten . . . ,* pp. 86–103.

26. The completeness of the quarter child's primary enculturation within the quarter community further explains the failure of white teaching. In order to counteract slave education within the quarters whites would have either had to prevent slave family and community relationships in the first place or to have completely isolated adult slaves from the black significant others and primary groups of their childhood enculturation. On a small but distinct minority of plantations slaves were so poorly fed, so frequently tortured and killed, and effectively disrupted in their attempts to create for themselves a secure family and community life that transmission of slave culture may have been of secondary importance to the pure physical and psychological struggle to survive. To the degree that plantations resembled concentration camps the infantilization of slaves was possible, though it should be remembered that even in concentration camps inmates were able to devise means of protecting themselves from complete dehumanization and identification with their captors.

Most plantation blacks were neither constantly physically terrorized nor removed from the sources of their primary educational experiences and relationships. Even as they became full-fledged fieldhands they continued to spend most of their time, day and night, in close association with their families and the other members of the quarter community. Indeed, many slaves, those not separated from family or community, were able to spend their entire lives as members of the primary groups that had been the most significant factors in their first conceptions of themselves and the world they lived in. For those slaves who were sold the shock of separation from family and community was softened by membership in another quarter community whose songs, stories, people and institutions espoused and perpetuated familiar themes in a familiar style.

27. In sociological terms most slaves were able to "internalize different realities *without* identifying with them. Therefore, if an alternative world appears in secondary socialization, the individual may opt for it in a manipulative manner. One could speak here of 'cool' alternation. The individual internalizes the new reality, but instead of its being his reality, it is a reality to be used by him for specific purposes. Insofar as this involves the performance of certain roles, he retains subjective detachment, vis-a-vis them—he 'puts them on' deliberately and purposefully. If this phenomenon becomes widely distributed, the institutional order as a whole begins to take on the character of a network of reciprocal manipulation." Berger and Luckmann, p. 172.

Appendix

1. See Margaret Mead and Rhoda Metraux, eds., *The Study of Culture at a Distance* (Chicago: University of Chicago Press, 1953).

2. In an article which discusses the common problems of the anthropologist and the historian, Margaret Mead writes: "The crux of the methodological differences between historians and anthropologists can be summed up in the words 'document' and 'informant.' The historian uses written materials which have been created within the ordinary ongoing social process without references to his inquiring intent, and distrusts material as probably biased, when it has been written for the purpose for which he, himself, uses it. In contrast, the anthropologist finds informants, whose place in their society he learns very carefully so that from these living human beings he can elicit materials on the culture, which traditionally he writes down, on the spot." Margaret Mead, "Anthropologist and Historian: Their Common Problems," *American Quarterly*, III, No. 1 (Spring, 1951), 10.

3. Margaret Mead, "Our Educational Emphases in Primitive Perspective," *American Journal of Sociology*, 48 (May, 1943), p. 639.

4. Bernard Bailyn, *Education in the Forming of American Society* (Chapel Hill: University of North Carolina Press, 1960), p. 14.

5. Historians of the historicist school in particular have made this point. "By capturing not some metaphysical meaning but the meaning which individuals, here and there, have perceived in, and attributed to their circumstances, the meaning which informed their actions and became embodied in their creations, the historian can tell a meaningful story." H. P. Rickman, ed., *Pattern and Meaning in History* (New York: Harper and Row, 1962), p. 62. Rickman is commenting here on the thought of Wilhelm Dilthey. Dilthey, himself, argues that autobiography and biography are immensely important to historical understanding because the individual human being is "a point where systems intersect; systems which go through individuals, exist within them, but reach beyond their life and possess an independent existence and development of their own through the content, and value, the purpose which is realized in them." Wilhelm Dilthey, *Ideal Units as the Basis of Life and Experience of It,* in Rickman, p. 78.

6. Concepts similar to themes are those of values and perspectives. For work on values see the writings of Clyde Kluckhohn, particularly "Values and Value-Orientation in the Theory of Action: An Exploration in Definition and Classification," in *Toward a General Theory of Action,* ed. Talcott Parsons and Edward Shils (Cambridge, Mass.: Harvard University Press, 1954), pp. 388–433 and "The Scientific Study of Values and Contemporary Society." Proceedings of the American Philosophical Society, 102, No. 5 (October, 1958), 469–76. For the closely associated concept of perspectives see Tamotsu Shibutani, "Reference Groups as Perspectives," *Current Perspectives in Social Psychology,* eds. E. P. Hollander and Raymond G. Glunt (New York: Oxford University Press), pp. 97–106, and Howard S. Becker, Blanche Geer, Everett C. Hughes, and Anselm L. Strauss, *Boys in White: Student Culture in Medical School* (Chicago: University of Chicago Press, 1961), pp. 34–48.

Notes to page 263

7. The presentation of Opler's theory in this chapter is drawn primarily from four of his articles. "Themes as Dynamic Forces in Culture," *The American Journal of Sociology,* 51 (1945), 198–206; "An Application of the Theory of Themes in Culture," *Journal of the Washington Academy of Sciences,* 36, (1946), 137–166; "Rejoinder," *American Journal of Sociology,* 52, (1946), 43–44; and "The Themal Approach in Cultural Anthropology and Its Application to North Indian Data," *Southwestern Journal of Anthropology,* 24, (1968), 215–27.

In recent decades the inadequacies of applying a too mechanistic approach to the problem of enculturation, and personality formation, has been brought home to anthropologists by social psychologists, other social scientists and by critics within their own field. Applications of Rorschach tests, Murray's thematic apperception tests, and other devices for determining personality characteristics have forced most social scientists to abandon the notion of common personality structure and to admit that individual variation within societies, and the overlapping of personality characteristics between societies, are too great to justify any but the most general descriptions of personality type. (See Anthony F. C. Wallace, "Individual Differences and Cultural Uniformities," *American Sociological Review,* 17 [1952], 747–50, and Ralph Linton, *The Cultural Background of Personality* [New York: Appleton-Century-Croft, 1945] especially p. 128).

At the same time, many social scientists have accepted the view that what is similar about individuals within a given social system, and particularly about members of the same subgrouping within that system, is not that they share common nuclear characters, or even common motives, but rather that they share a common set of broad themes, values, perspectives which shape how they understand the world, and which influences, without determining, how they act in it. Thus, Anthony Wallace, one of the severest critics of what he has termed the "microcosmic metaphor" approach to personality in culture admits that "an impressive consequence" of age patterning studies, particularly those done by John Whiting's group at Harvard and by Margaret Mead and her associates, "is the demonstration of the fact of multiple imprinting of a relatively small number of broad themes or values, each with its special phrasing for various age, sex, and other conditions, by the immensely complex sequential pattern of experiences to which the growing person in subjected in any organized society." (Anthony F. C. Wallace, *Culture and Personality,* Second Edition [New York: Random House, 1970], p. 157.)

The importance of determining and analyzing these "broad themes" is twofold. First, by determining the themes of a given social system at a particular time in its history the social scientist has isolated a part of that system's culture which, if studied over time, can provide meaningful insights into the nature of the cultural change process. As Pitirim Sorokin has pointed out, "We know that any group retains its identity and the continuity of its existence as long as its component of meanings, values, or norms remains essentially the same." (Pitirim A. Sorokin, *Society, Culture, and Personality: Their Structure and Dynamics* [New York: Harper and Brothers, 1947], p. 381). Second, a knowledge of a given social system's basic themes allows an understanding of some of the forces that will influence the actions of the individuals within that system. While not allowing predictions of the response of any particular individual to a given stimulus, it does allow the prediction of the response of a significant number of individuals in the system to a stimulus which affects the system as a whole. Thus, Thomas and Znaniecki argue in their classic study, *The Polish Peasant,* that these general attitudes find "an indirect manifestation in more or less explicit and formal *rules* of behavior by which the group tends to maintain, to regulate, and to make more frequent the corresponding type of action among its members." (William I. Thomas and Florian Znaniecki, *The Polish Peasant in Europe and America* [New York: Dover Publications, 1958], p. 31.)

8. Opler, "Themes as Dynamic Forces in Culture," p. 198.

9. *Ibid.,* p. 199.

10. *Ibid.,* p. 200.

11. *Ibid.*

12. Opler, "The Themal Approach in Cultural Anthropology and its Application to North Indian Data," p. 218.

13. Opler, "Themes as Dynamic Forces in Culture," p. 200.

14. Ibid., p. 201.

15. Opler, "An Application . . . ," p. 138.

16. Opler, "The Themal Approach . . . ," p. 219.

Throughout the process of applying Opler's methodology, the study was cognizant of the four most frequently expressed criticisms of the thematic approach to cultural data: that it neglects the most fundamental biological determinants of human action and understanding and thus does not make possible the formulation of theoretical generalizations applicable to all cultures; that it separates the themes of a social system from the broader political, economic, social, and historical context within which that system grew and must now function; that while focusing on a certain set of themes, it may, by neglecting the nature of the institutions and social relationships by which the system is organized, leave much of that system's culture a nonthematic mess; and that it obscures or ignores the whole range of way in which human individuals reject, subvert, change, and transcend the basic themes of their cultural conditioning. (For some critique of Opler's concept of themes see Albert K. Cohen, "An Evaluation of 'Themes' and Kindred Concepts," *American Journal of Sociology,* 52 (1946), 41–42. See also the letter of A. L. Kroeber in Opler, "An Application . . ." . . . p. 162.

Rather than indicating fallacies in the model itself, these criticisms seem to make clear some of the limitations, as well as the central concerns of the thematic approach. The present study, in particular, does not seek to explore the similarities between all cultures, but rather to examine the fundamental values, attitudes, and beliefs of the quarter community and to compare them with those values and attitudes taught by whites. It does not claim, or attempt, to analyze the growth of the historic, economic, political, social determinants of either the plantation or the quarters except as these determinants are expressed in the plantation world created by whites and described in Part I. Nor does the study seek to determine either the basic slave personalities, or personality, on the one hand, or the overall culture of slaves as a group on the other. Quite simply, it is a study of what the members of the quarter community learned and of the educational agencies and relationships which helped them learn it. By describing and analyzing the educational instruments of the quarter community in Part III the study directly relates the themes of the quarter community to the quarter institutions which gave rise to them.

17. Marion Starling, "The Slave Narrative: Its Place in American Literary History" (unpublished doctoral dissertation, New York University, 1946).

18. James M. Williams, contained in Benjamin Drew, ed., *A North-Side View of Slavery. The Refugee: or the Narratives of Fugitive Slaves in Canada.* Related by Themselves (Boston: John P. Jewett, 1856), p. 43.

19. John Dollard, *Criteria for the Life History: With Analyses of Six Notable Documents* (New Haven: Yale University Press, 1935), p. 13. See, also, Gordon W. Allport, *The Use of Personal Documents in Psychological Science* (New York: Social Science Research Council, 1942).

20. Theodore Abel makes the point that Dollard's criteria are more applicable to the individual life study than to a cultural understanding of a group or society. He writes that Dollard's criteria are touchstones "for the kind of life-story material of particular interest to the psychologist. Actually they are guides for Allport's 'specially trained investigator,' who in his opinion, should write the life history rather than the person investigated." Theodore Abel, "The Nature and Use of Biograms," *American Journal of Sociology,* 53 (July, 1947) No. 1, p. 114.

21. Sterling Stucky, "Through the Prism of Folklore: The Black Ethos in Slavery," *The Massachusetts Review,* 9 (1968) p. 419. On the subject of folklore as a source for understanding the education of a group or people, Kluckhohn and Leighton write: "Folklore must be presumed to originate in the dreams and phantasies of individuals. But when the product of one person's imagination (as mingled with and modified by the phantasy of other persons over a long period) is taken over as a part of the mythology of a whole group, the themes may confidently be assumed to correspond to a widely current psychological situation." Clyde Kluckhohn and Dorthea Leighton, *The Navaho* (Cambridge, Mass: Harvard University Press, 1948), p. 136.

22. Clyde Kluckhohn, "The Personal Document in Anthropological Science," *The Use of Personal Documents in History, Anthropology, and Sociology,* eds. Louis Gottschalk, Clyde Kluckhohn, and Robert Angell (New York: Social Science Research Council), pp. 134–36.

23. The number of full-length narratives written by women is small, as is the number of well developed accounts of quarter life in the deep South.

24. George P. Rawick, ed., *The American Slave: A Composite Autobiography,* Vol. 1 (Westport, Conn.: Greenwood Publishing Company, 1972), p. xviii.

25. B. A. Botkin, ed., *Lay My Burden Down: A Folk History of Slavery* (Chicago: University of Chicago Press, 1945), pp. xi–xii.

26. Gilbert Osofsky, ed., *Puttin' on Ole Massa: The Slave Narratives of Henry Bibb, William Wells Brown, and Solomon Northup* (New York: Harper and Row, 1969), pp. 10–11.

27. In addition to the material gathered by interviewers there was also a steady

stream of autobiographies in the four decades following the Civil War. "These often were written by black ministers as fund-raising devices for themselves and their churches; consequently, they tend to be very moderate in their views of the slave experience, reflecting the required ideological posture blacks had to assume in order to get money out of whites." Rawick, ed., Vol. I, p. xv.

28. Although this vast amount of material has been used to achieve a better understanding of plantation life as a whole, and particularly of the thoughts, values, and actions of whites, it is the study's general position that white sources cannot be relied upon to achieve an understanding of the thoughts and actions of quarter slaves. Most large plantation owners had day-to-day dealings only with house servants and were usually uninformed as to what went on in the quarters. Even those who took an active interest in discovering what quarter slaves were thinking and doing were forced to rely for their information upon the testimony of other blacks, who, as we have seen, had a multitude of reasons for hiding the truth. The traveler accounts, which are often more questioning and critical of the institution of slavery, rely, in the main, upon plantation whites for their understanding of life in the quarters. Increasingly, as both northern and foreign criticism grew in the thirty years directly preceding the Civil War, plantation whites became extremely guarded about what they told visitors and about what they allowed visitors to observe. Rarely were visitors able to talk with slaves without the presence of a plantation white, and, in any case, it is doubtful whether any slave, left alone with a visitor, would have risked revealing himself to an unknown white person. Furthermore, the assumptions which most whites at this time had concerning the biological, psychological, and moral make-up of black people makes them highly suspect informants concerning matters of black values, understandings, and attitudes. In addition to providing an understanding of how whites thought and acted this material was used primarily to provide statistical information and descriptive material.

INDEX

Aaron, 143
Abel, Theodore, 329–30n
abolitionists, 31, 32, 45, 105
Abrams, M. E., 236
Abromson, Laura, 140
Adams, Isaac, 234
Adams, James, 162
Adams, John Quincy, 140
Adams, Louisa, 169
Adams, Williams, 145–46
address, terms of, 34–35
Affleck, Thomas, 44
Africa, 31
  absence of thematic reference to, 150
  God's reasons for bringing blacks from, 49–50
  stories of, 163, 170, 175, 176, 218–19
African burial customs, 312–13n
African dances, 35
African languages, 35
African songs, 35
Alabama Baptist Association, 46
Aleckson, Sam, 15–16, 19, 175, 188
Alexander, Archer, 112, 144, 171, 308n
Alexander, Lucretia, 51, 171, 195, 202
American Indian Reservations, 251–58, 322–24n
Ammond, Molly, 168
Anderson, Josephine, 121
Anderson, Mary, 33, 145, 241
Anderson, Robert, 13–14, 73, 95, 178, 198, 235, 240, 246–47
Anderson, Silva, 178
anger towards whites, 78–79
animal stories, 220, 316n
animals, 121
anthropology, 263, 326n
antiliteracy laws, 29
antipathy towards whites, theme of, 71–79, 151, 152
  anger, 78–79
  hypocrisy of whites, 78
  masters, 74–76
  overseers, 74, 79
  poor whites, 73–74
  topics avoided in conversations with whites, 72
  trustworthiness of whites, 71–72
Armstrong, Cora, 165
Armstrong, Orland, 66, 119
ashcake, 161–62
Atkinson, Henry, 84, 115
attitudes:
  songs and stories as transmitters of, 219–21
  white failure to instill their, 246–50
  see also cultural themes
aunts, 178
autobiographies as source material, 266–71, 330n
Avery, Celeste, 6

Bacchus, Josephine, 91, 226
Backus, Emma M., 216–17
Bailey, Jeff, 11
Bailyn, Bernard, 263
Baker, Georgia, 5, 174, 306n
Baker, Tom, 22
Ball, Charles, 35, 101, 109, 158, 166, 168, 170, 176, 215, 236, 239, 305n, 306n

family ties of, 113, 115
  on religious and moral views of slaves, 86–88
  on superstition, 118–19
ball games, 181
banjos, 315n
Banks, Henry, 36, 83–84, 105
Banks, Mary, 183, 301n
baptism, 46, 47, 82, 200
Bass, William, 283n
bathing children, 16
Beanland, Ephraim, 30
beatings, *see* physical abuse; punishment; whipping
Beckett, Harrison, 167
beds, 6, 18
Belt, Robert, 69
Berger, Peter L., 324n, 326n
Bibb, Henry, 38, 69, 82, 88, 103–5, 109, 115, 116, 119, 151, 292n, 295–96n, 298n, 308n
Bible:
  censored version of, 54, 82–83
  distrust for master's, 81–82
Biblical characters in spirituals, 217–18
Biddle, Mary, 168
Blassingame, John, 51–52
Black, Leonard, 134
Blue, Henry, 140
Body, Rias, 150
Bolton, James, 234–35
Bontemps, Arna, 220
Boone, Andrew, 32
Bost, W. L., 205
Botkin, Benjamin, 269
Bowen, Charles J., 312n
Boyd, Eli, 175–76
Branch, Jacob, 22
Brant, Henry, 78
Brantley, Mack, 178
breast feeding, 11
Broaddus, Susan, 228–29
Brown, Ben, ix, 8, 115
Brown, Easter, 234
Brown, Henry Box, 46, 49, 86, 103, 123, 143, 144, 200
Brown, John, 9, 64, 77, 81, 95
  on cruelty of slavery, 102–3, 105
  on moods of master, 110
  on mother, 163–64
  on separation of families, 114
Brown, Julia, 226–27, 237
Brown, William Wells, 21, 77, 106, 118, 127, 151, 172
Bruce, H. C., 21, 94, 105, 120, 136, 146, 163, 185, 227–28, 241, 245–46
Bruner, Edward, 252, 254–57, 260, 323n
Bruner, Peter, 73, 166, 232
Buckner, George, 69
Buh Rabbit (folkloric character), 220
burial customs, 312–13n
  see also funerals
burial grounds, 35
Burke, Sarah, 227
Burns, Anthony, 82
Buster, Garret, 171
Byrd, Sarah, 235
Byrnes, Titus, 134

Index

Index

Index

Index

Index

Index

Index

Stone, Kate, 8
stories, 17, 215–23
  of Africa, 163, 170, 175, 176, 218–19
  animal, 220, 316n
  communality and kinship transmitted by, 222–23
  father's role in transmitting, 170–71
  of legendary figures, 221
  of outwitting whites, 100
  values, attitudes, and sentiments transmitted by, 219–21
storytelling, 215–17, 221–22
Street, William, 75
Stroyer, Jacob, 6, 33, 85, 89, 118, 120–21, 171, 238, 293n
Stuckey, Sterling, 207, 267
style, superiority of black, 93–94
submission, religious instruction and, 49, 51
subservience, 35
suckling babies, 11
suffering, as redemptive, 86
suicide as sin, 51
Sumler, James, 132
Sundays:
  activities on, 18–19, 47, 235
  work on, 39
superiority of blacks, theme of, 91–101, 150, 205
  artful use of language, 99–100
  ineptness and laziness of whites, 91–92
  outwitting whites, 94–101
  stylistic superiority, 93–94
superiority of whites, belief in, 32–35
surnames, 34
Sutherland, Joe, 228
syphilis, 92

Talley, Thomas W., 314n
task system, 39
teachers, nursery, 15
teaching:
  definition of, xi
  reading and writing, forbidden, 29
  religious, see religious instruction
  by whites, see white teaching
teas, herbal, 13, 175, 226
teeth, extraction of, 121
themes in culture, see cultural themes
thieves:
  detection of, 120–21
  see also stealing
Thomas, Acie, 184, 188
Thomas, Shack, 170
Thomas, William I., 328n
Thompson, Ellen, 176
Thompson, John, 83, 86, 112, 132, 134, 140, 144, 171, 232–33
Tidwell, Emma, 51
Tims, J. T., 166
tobacco plantations, 23
total institution theory, 251, 321–22n
Towns, Phil, 176
Towns, William Henry, 182
travel, slaves forbidden to, 28
Trickster John, 220–21, 316n
Troy, William, 137
truck patches, 8, 236
true Christianity, 192, 248
  communality and, 150
  conversion of masters to, 84–85
  slaveholding priestcraft vs., as cultural theme, 80–90, 152
trust:
  among slaves, 64–65
  for whites, 71–72
  see also loyalty
Tubman, Harriet, 103, 285–86n, 314n

Turner, Nat, 45
Turner, Wes, 168, 229

uncles, 178

values:
  internalization of quarter community's, 258–61
  songs and stories as transmitters of, 219–21
  white failure to instill their, 246–50
  see also cultural themes; enculturation
Van Buren, Nettie, 129
Vaughn, Adelaide J., 219
Veney, Bethany, 48, 295n
Vinson, Addie, 6
Vinson, Peter, 6
voodoo, 119
voodoo bags, 121

Waldon, Henry, 23
Walker, Irella, 172
Wallace, Anthony, 328n
Warren, John, 116
washing clothes, 14, 160
Washington, Booker T., 22, 131, 137–38, 177
  on mother, 163, 167
  on slaves' knowledge of national issues, 241–42
"watchman," 55–56
water boys, 21–22
Watson, A. P., 123
Watson, Henry, 10, 36, 103, 187
Webb, William, 128, 142–44
weddings, 82, 116
West, David, 86
whipping(s), 20, 21, 41, 42, 64, 102–4, 285n
  of children, by mothers, 165–66
  children's game involving, 184
  for clandestine religious meetings, 195
  fear of, 103
  helplessness to prevent, 104
  resistance to, 106, 232–33
  see also punishment
White, Eliza, 175
White, Mingo, 14, 173–74, 205
white children, 20, 24, 29, 35, 247–48
  quarter members' view of, 93
  reading and writing taught by, 131–32
  suckled by black mammies, 92–93
white power, theme of, 102–10, 150–52, 246
  anxiety of slave parenthood, 103–4
  appearance of doing what masters wanted, 108–9
  fear of white power, 103, 105
  helplessness, feeling of, 104
  indirect ways of dealing with whites, 108–10
  resistance and defiance of white power, 106–8
whites:
  antipathy towards, see antipathy towards whites
  poor, see poor whites
  songs not sung in presence of, 221
  superiority of blacks to, see superiority of blacks, theme of
  see also masters; and specific topics
white teaching:
  failure of, 246–49
  successes of, 245
  see also missionaries; Sabbath schools; and specific topics
white women, 92–93
Williams, Charley, 4
Williams, George, 78
Williams, Isaac, 70, 122, 198, 200, 315n
Williams, Rev. J. G., 99
Williams, James M., 31, 140, 230, 266
Williams, Sally, 166–68
Williamson, Henry, 115
Wilson, Lulu, 164

338

Index

Wise, John, 241
witches, 118, 121, 299*n*
women:
  pregnant, 41, 121
  white, 92–93
  see also family; mother
Woods, Calvin, 194–95
woods, the, 184–85
Woods, Wes, 126
work:
  children's, 21–23
  over-, 236
  as privilege, 35
  religious instruction and, 44, 46

work incentives, 39
work songs, 211–12, 314*n*
Works Project Administration (WPA), 266, 268, 269
writing, *see* reading and writing
Wrong, Dennis H., 325*n*

Young, Clara, 192–93
Young, J. C., 40–41
Young, Joseph, 194
Young, Litt, 192

Znaniecki, Florian, 328*n*